Women in Popular Culture

Representation and Meaning

Political Communication
David L. Paletz, Editor

Women in Popular Culture

Representation and Meaning

edited by

Marian Meyers

Georgia State University

HAMPTON PRESS, INC.
CRESSKILL, NEW JERSEY

Printed in the United States of America

Library of Congress Cataloging-in-Publication Data

Women in popular culture : representation and meaning / edited by Marian Meyers.
     p. cm. -- (Political communication)
     Includes bibliographical references and indexes.
     ISBN 978-1-57273-827-0 (hardbound) -- 978-1-57273-828-7 (paperbound)
1. Women in popular culture. 2. Women in mass media. I. Meyers, Marian, 1954-
   HQ1233.W5964 2088
   302.23082.--dc22
                        2008017232

Hampton Press, Inc.
23 Broadway
Cresskill, NJ 07626

To Emma and Talia

Contents

Acknowledgments

This book is the culmination of the work and efforts of many people to whom I am most grateful. David Paletz, my editor, has been unflagging in his support and patience, as well as in his keen ability to see weaknesses in my arguments and writing. This book has benefited greatly from his guidance and editing. Barbara Bernstein, my publisher, likewise has been both supportive and patient in her work on this book. I am indebted to her, as well.

Thanks are due, also, to graduate students Nahed Tantawy, Sarah Halim, and Melissa Miller, who served as editorial assistants and proofreaders at various stages in the production of this manuscript. Their attention to detail, thoroughness and good humor greatly improved the book and made much of the work involved a pleasure.

I am indebted, as well, to Sujatha Sosale, whose conversations about work and the academy helped me with many of the routine obstacles one encounters in the writing or editing of a book. In addition, I am grateful to Lauren Rich, whose overall assistance, encouragement and support were invaluable in this process.

I am particularly indebted to the students in my "women and media" class, without whom this book would not have been written. Their comments, observations, and questions about the representation of women in popular culture, and the role of that representation in their lives, both challenged and inspired me—and convinced me of the need for a book that would look closely at the meaning behind those mediated images.

I owe considerable thanks, also, to the contributors to this anthology, for their work and patience during the long road to publication, as well as their belief that the representation of women does matter, that it affects all of us in multiple ways, and that this representation, at the least, is worthy of careful examination.

Finally, to my daughters, Talia and Emma, I am grateful for the love, laughter, and the joy they bring to my life and all that I do.

Part I

Introduction

1

Women in Popular Culture

All Sexed Up and Global to Go

Marian Meyers

The life-size poster of six attractive, naked women is plastered to the side of the bus shelter in Dresden, Germany. The women appear to be in their 20s or 30s, and they wear nothing but clear, vinyl stiletto heels and, for some, a necklace or earrings visible beneath perfectly coiffed hair that falls to or below bare shoulders. They are standing close to each other, their slender bodies touching as they gaze at the viewer. The blonde on the left has her arm around the Black woman next to her. At the other end of this line-up, a dark-haired woman stands, her body turned slightly away from the camera, her chest thrust forward so that her breasts are touching those of the woman next to her. A white, opaque, horizontal band runs across this image, obscuring but not completely hiding their bodies from mid-breast to the top of their thighs.

This sexualized image is part of a global promotional campaign for *The L Word*, the Showtime network's "on-demand" TV series about a group of lesbian and bisexual friends and their lovers living in the trendy Los Angeles neighborhood of West Hollywood. One of Showtime's most popular series, *The L Word* debuted in January 2004 and, according to Showtime's Web site, has generated "critical praise for its provocative, sexy storylines," as well as "dedicated fan Web sites and blogs, along with ancillary products such as THE L WORD®-branded perfume, jewelry and books" (http://www.sho.com/site/announcements/030807lword.do). Besides airing in the United States and Germany, *The L Word* can be seen in the United Kingdom, Canada, South Korea, and Israel.[1]

The L Word highlights two interconnected trends in the representation of women within mediated popular culture: the hypersexualization of women with its attendant mainstreaming of soft-core pornography, and the globalization of these images. In an era of media convergence, where "convergence" is understood to indicate the merging of new media technologies, globalization and the mainstreaming of pornography have similarly converged in the mediated representations of women shown around the world. This mainstreaming of pornographic images and their global marketing are not simply unrelated trends that have arbitrarily merged. Rather, the pornogrification of women in mainstream media—that is, their increasingly graphic portrayal as sex objects—is a result of calculated corporate decisions based on profit motives and economic imperatives within the context of global capital (Levy, 2005; Paul, 2005). As Lotz (2006) notes, "every programming shift in the U.S. system of commercial television can be understood as a marketing strategy to some extent, or as a ploy to enhance profits" (p. 175).

Of course, the mainstreaming of pornography and the distribution of those images worldwide are not new developments—they have been occurring in ever-escalating form for the past several decades. However, they now are more pronounced and irrevocably interconnected. Fueling this convergence are three social phenomenon:

1. The rapid adoption of ever-newer innovations in media technology, including the internet and satellite TV.
2. The explosive growth and increasingly hard-core nature of the pornography industries.

3. The seemingly unbridled transnational growth of corporate capitalism thanks to government deregulation—and, in some countries, privatization—of media industries worldwide.

Byerly and Ross (2006) similarly emphasize the link between the pornography industry, globalization, and the proliferation of pornographic images of women in mainstream media around the world:

> The underground nature of pornography industries has leached into the mainstream of many nations, with violent videos (featuring abuse and denigration of women) now available in the corner video store and numerous advertisements parading nude and near-nude figures of both women and men. Television programming in some nations—particularly in the late-night zone—features overtly sexual content, including graphic sexual assaults. Print and television news are similarly problematic, especially as they have shifted toward celebrity and lighter content. (p. 38)

Although *The L Word* is both symptomatic and reflective of the trends toward globalization and the mainstreaming of pornography, so, too, are other television shows, films, books, magazines, and other popular media and genres. Indeed, *The L Word* is not particularly groundbreaking in this regard—its significance is as the first mainstream television show to showcase the lives of lesbians. Some credit the U.S. cable television show *Sex and the City* with first breaching televisual taboos in its frank chronicling of the sexual exploits of four 30- and 40-something female friends in New York City—and thereby opening the door to similar and even more graphic sexual depictions. This HBO show, which premiered on June 6, 1998, and aired its last original episode February 22, 2004, is still in syndication in the United States, with the TBS, Fox, and CW networks showing edited reruns of the series. Additionally, it was and in many instances still can be seen around the world—sometimes edited into a "light version" that omits the more explicit sex talk and graphic sexual scenes to accommodate local sensibilities. For example, *Sex and the City* was banned in Singapore until July 2004, when the government then allowed a censored version to be shown. In Brazil, it was aired by Multishow and FOX channels, with Multishow offering both the standard and the light versions. And in Hungary, where it is shown on Viasat 3 and HBO, Viasat recut the episodes to remove scenes and dialogue that included, among other things, references to genitals, sexual conversations, some storylines and all non-heterosexual kisses so as to earn a rating equivalent to PG-13 in the United States.[2]

Sex and the City was able to breach sexual taboos by airing on cable, as opposed to the somewhat more staid broadcast networks. The award-winning series *Desperate Housewives—Sex and the City*'s hoped-for successor for fans mourning the end of that show (McCabe & Akass, 2006)—similarly upped the sexual ante for broadcast television with its soap opera-style tales of the secret lives of four affluent, suburban women as seen through the eyes of their dead neighbor on fictional Wisteria Lane. The ABC show was an instant hit, with 21 million viewers watching its pilot episode on October 3, 2004. Buena Vista Games even developed a Windows-based simulation game that lets the player become the newest housewife on Wisteria Lane. However, the show also generated protests about its sexual content and a backlash from Christian groups and parent associations, who targeted advertisers in their campaign to get the show off the air (McCabe & Akass, 2006). Despite right-wing objections, *Desperate Housewives* can be seen in 52 nations, in addition to the United States. Clearly, the sexualization of women within the media has a global as well as a domestic market.

MAINSTREAMING PORNOGRAPHY

This mainstreaming of soft-core pornography within popular culture owes much to the proliferation and global reach of hard-core pornography, which has pushed the limits on what previously was considered acceptable both in society and within mediated formats. Indeed, much has been written within recent years about the "pornogrification" of society (Paul, 2005) and the rise of "raunch culture" (Levy, 2005), with the Internet and new, interactive media technologies fingered as prime culprits in the spread of pornographic images of women around the world. So ubiquitous is pornography thanks to advances in communications technology that mobile phone services even deliver pornography to subscriber's cell phones. Pornography now is available not just anytime, but anywhere.

Paul (2005) notes that "with each iteration in technological advancement, pornography has become increasingly violent and nonconsensual" (p. 58) both as a way to "satisfy earlier, upgraded demand and to bring the viewer to the next level" (p. 59). Technology also ensures a global market for pornography:

> The internet has thoroughly internationalized the world of pornography so that to speak of international borders with regard to production and tastes is increasingly meaningless. Americans consume

Japanese manga (cartoon) pornography and gaze at nude photos of Dutch women. Russian women are virtually exported around the world, complicating the dimensions of international sex trafficking. Child pornography is pumped into Australia from across the globe. Men in Canada can visit the brothels of Bangkok from the comfort of their home offices. (Paul, 2005, p. 59)

Drawing on a variety of studies, Paul found that pornographic Web sites "are visited three times more often than Google, Yahoo, and MSN Search combined" (p. 60), and that the number of pornography Web sites has grown 17-fold in one URL database over the course of 4 years, from 88,000 in 2000 to nearly 1.6 million in 2004. Another measure of the phenomenal commercial success of online sex can be found in the record-breaking auction of the internet domain names *porn.com* and *sex.com*. The rights to *porn.com* brought in the second-highest payment for an internet address since the Web's creation, with MXN Ltd. paying $9.5 million in 2007. *Porn.com* previously sold for only $47,000 in 1997 (Menn, 2007). However, the record-setter remains *sex.com*, purchased in 2006 for $11 million in cash and stock by the Boston firm Escom (Menn, 2007).[3]

In 2003, *New York Times* writer Frank Rich, pointing to the recent proliferation of pornography on television—including *Skin*, the first prime-time network series about the adult entertainment industry— asked: "Is the mainstreaming of pornography the end of civilization as we know it?" His conclusion: Most people, including conservatives within the administration of President George W. Bush, just don't see pornography as a big deal anymore, other than when children are involved.

Indeed, pornography has become so ubiquitous, so commonplace, that sexual imagery and dialogue that once would have been off limits to all but the most hard-core and avid pornography users are now *de rigeur* in popular culture. The Oxygen network in 2002 introduced *Talk Sex with Sue Johanson*, a live, call-in show whose "sexpert" discusses such previously taboo topics as the pros and cons of specific sex toys. Romance novels—which have always traded in varying amounts of sexual innuendo and passion, depending on the target audience and imprint—have ramped up their sex appeal for a sex-saturated market. In steamy, porn-like novels, the newest imprints of major publishing houses are explicitly erotic, detailing X-rated activities that previously had been left largely to the imagination. These imprints include Harlequin's *Spice*, along with HarperCollins's Avon Red books, which include titles like *If This Bed Could Talk* and *Seduce Me*, and Kensington's new line of erotica, which includes the books *Pleasure Beach* and *Hot in Here*

(Oliviero, 2006). These books, like TV shows, magazines, films, and other popular media, are made for global distribution.

Publicly held telecommunications giants such as AT&T and Time Warner have substantial investments in pornography through their cable businesses (Paul, 2005), as do hotel chains such as Hilton and Marriott that reap significant profits providing guests with access to pornography in the privacy of their rooms. Pornography is estimated to bring in up to $20 billion in total annual revenues in America alone (Paul, 2005, p. 64). But it is not just U.S. media that have "gone porn"—it is a worldwide phenomenon. The British telecommunications company BT announced plans in 2006 to make soft-core pornographic movies available on its television service, BT Vision, as a way to generate more revenue (Parker, 2006), and telecommunications corporations in other countries are similarly seeking pornography profits.

So what's wrong with a little porn? Is this something we should be concerned about? Or should we view the mainstreaming of pornography in mediated popular culture—like most people do, according to Rich (2003)—as just no big deal? Considerable research indicates that even exposure to soft-core pornography can affect the viewer's perceptions about sexuality and violence against women, as well as disrupt relationships and families (Paul, 1995). A number of studies have focused on pornography's effects and whether sexually explicit materials can be linked to rape and other acts of violence against women. Although a causal link has not been established and these studies have been criticized for assuming that laboratory experiments reflect real-life behaviors (Boyle, 2003; Jensen, 2003), researchers have found that, at best, pornography leads to a sexual callousness about violence against women, in addition to, as Jensen (2003) points out, "a loss of respect for female sexual autonomy and the disinhibition of men's expression of aggression against women" (p. 418; see, e.g., Weaver, 1992; Zillmann & Bryant, 1982; Zillmann & Weaver, 1989). Jensen further argues that rather than assuming laboratory studies overstate the effects of pornography on men, "we should be at least as concerned that lab studies underestimate pornography's role in promoting misogynistic attitudes and behavior" (p. 418).

Levy (2005) argues that the rise of pornographic "raunch culture" reinscribes traditional power relationships between men and women, with women reduced to viewing themselves and other women as primarily sexual objects for the gratification of men. Paul (2005) also sees the mainstreaming of pornography in popular culture as detrimental to women, men, families, and relationships. She points out that pornography negatively affects intimacy between couples and male expectations concerning women, in terms of both their looks and sexual performance.

Radical feminists, according to van Zoonen (1994), consider pornography to be "the ultimate cultural expression of men's hatred against women; it is seen as a form of sexual violence against women, simultaneously a source and a product of a deeply misogynistic society" (p. 19). She states that pornography reflects and reinscribes social stereotypes and traditional understandings of women's roles and sexuality. It is "a social practice in which current beliefs and myths about women and sexuality are (re)constructed" (p. 21). The act of consuming pornographic images, she adds, "is more than a private pleasure, but also embedded in gendered social and cultural formations that have defined women's bodies as sexual objects" (p. 21).

Jensen (1998) similarly claims that a systemic examination of the production, content, and use of pornography provides convincing evidence of "pornography's role in the sexual and social subordination of women" (p. 1). He notes that a radical feminist anti-pornography critique:

> argues that the sexual ideology of patriarchy eroticizes domination and submission and that pornography is one of the key sites in which these values are mediated and normalized in contemporary culture. Domination and submission are made sexual, sometimes in explicit representations of rape and violence against women, but always in the objectification and commodification of women and their sexuality. (p. 2)

Researchers and psychologists also claim that pornography is particularly harmful to young children, providing them with unhealthy sexual role models and teaching them lessons about sexuality and sexual behavior before they even reach puberty (Paul, 2005). Additionally, the increasingly sexualized portrayal of young girls within popular media positions them as being appropriately desirable and available to men. The danger, of course, is not simply that 10-year-olds—and even younger girls—may be viewed as sexual prey, although that is certainly alarming enough. The other harm is that these girls will come to see themselves as such and view their primary worth and life goals in terms of their sexuality (Levy, 2005).

Lawrence Downes (2007), an editorial writer for *The New York Times*, blames well-meaning but misguided parents for allowing their little girls to be seduced by the media. During a middle school talent show, Downes reports, a dance routine featured girls in tiny skirts or tight shorts mimicking lap dancers and writhing on the floor to simulate sex while a Janet Jackson song urged them on: "Jerk it like you're making it choke. Ohh. I'm so stimulated. Feel so x-rated." Downes states that although suburban parents are overprotective of their children in many ways, they allow "the culture of boy-toy sexuality to bore unchecked into their little ones' ears and eyeballs, displacing their nimble and growing brains and impoverishing the sense of wider possibilities in life." The result, he adds, is a "cramped vision of girlhood that enshrines sexual allure as the best or only form of power and esteem"—creating a constricted horizon that boys would never tolerate (p. 5).

There is, of course, a marketing component to the sexualization of children. The toy industry and other merchandisers have a name for the "strategy of getting tweens to buy sexy stuff. It's called 'age compression,' pushing adult products and teen attitude on younger and younger kids" (CBC Marketplace, 2005). The age compression by which society psychologically pressures children to age prematurely, so that girls come to see themselves as sexual beings at younger and younger ages, both blurs the line between girlhood and womanhood and all but guarantees a steady market for a multitude of "sexy" products. These range from the Victoria's Secret "Pink" line of underwear and other clothing for tweens and teens, to Abercrombie and Fitch's thongs in children's sizes, to Bratz Babyz dolls, with their skimpy clothes, heavily made-up faces, and marketing slogan that assures young girls that these babies "know how to flaunt it." Perfumes, clothes, cosmetics, games, toys, food, and innumerable other products are marketed to juveniles and adolescents with the promise of enhanced sexiness. Indeed, Higonnet (1998) notes that the "sexualization of childhood is not a fringe phenomenon inflicted by perverts in a protesting society, but a fundamental change furthered by legitimate industries and millions of satisfied consumers" (p. 153).[4]

This commodification of sexual allure is an integral part of the "beauty ideal" for girls and women. Indeed, statistics from the American Society for Aesthetic Plastic Surgery (ASAPS) indicate that sexiness rivals thinness—long a requirement for attainment of the beauty ideal—as the most desirable attribute for females. The ASAPS reports that the top two surgical cosmetic procedures in 2005 were liposuction, with 455,489 procedures performed—down 5% from the previous year—followed by breast augmentation, with 364,610 procedures, up 9% from 2004.[5] This explosion in cosmetic surgeries involving breast implants reflects a growing demand for breasts that look like they belong to Playboy Bunny Pamela Anderson or pornography star Jenna Jameson, author of the best-selling memoir *How to Make Love Like a Porn Star*.

Indeed, the proscription for women to exude sex appeal has transcended professional barriers so that even television news reporters and anchors are pressured to sex up their wardrobes and to expose more skin. At one national TV news network—and very possibly at other networks and stations—female journalists were told to wear "V-neck" style clothing on-air and to avoid high necklines (confidential personal communication). The result is ever-deeper plunging necklines for women who are on-air personalities—a fashion trend increasingly seen on female TV reporters and anchors nationwide. Levy (2005) points out that when news anchor Katie Couric—the highest paid person in television news—guest-hosted the *Tonight Show* in 2003 for regular host Jay Leno—"she wore a low-cut dress and felt the need to emphasize her breasts by pointing at them and proclaiming 'these are actually real!'" Levy adds that Couric "had guys with power tools cut a hole in Leno's desk so that the program could be a more complete peep show—a Google search for 'Katie Couric legs' provides links to dozens of pornography sites with her calves in close-up" (p. 32). The overarching mandate of sexiness for female journalists undermines these women's credibility and their claim to professionalism by encouraging viewers to see them first as sex objects and then, perhaps, as journalists.[6]

GLOBALIZATION

Although the trend toward the mainstreaming of pornography, with its attendant hypersexualizing of women and young girls, is fairly obvious to even the most casual cultural observers—let along researchers and writers—the trend toward the globalization of women's mediated images for consumption on a world market is less apparent but no less significant. This globalization mirrors a surge in the transnational sale of their corporeal bodies (in the form of sexual slavery/prostitution and "mail-order brides") as well as an explosion in the number of Internet sex sites. As the mediated images of women change to appeal to a more global market, they exhibit both stereotypical characteristics as well as challenges to traditional understandings of women's roles and representations within different societies and cultures.

Of course, the fact that U.S. media products—from films and television programs to books, magazines, music, and Internet sites—are seen and heard around the world is nothing new. Hollywood's global media dominance has long been aided by the economics of production: It is cheaper for poorer countries to purchase syndicated U.S. television programs and movies than to make their own. But even wealthier, Western countries show U.S.-made media fare. Additionally, advances in media technology, including satellite TV, have extended the reach of Western media products not previously accessible in many corners of the world.

The global movement of capital, as well as the tendency toward consolidation and merger among transnational media conglomerates, has resulted in a handful of mega-corporations distributing media products internationally. The result, according to critics, is a lack of diversity within media ownership and content, with media consolidation and government deregulation decreasing the already paltry number of women and minorities who own television and radio stations (Byerly, 2006). This lack of diversity and alternative voices within media content helps ensure that the perspectives of a Western, White, male elite—always and already dominant—have become even more pervasive. The prevailing perspectives advanced within the media promote Western values and ideologies, including consumerism, materialism, and capitalism, throughout the world in a process of cultural imperialism. The result, critics say, is an undermining of local, regional, and national identity and culture.[7]

Postcolonial theorists emphasize the interdependence of colonizer and colonized, arguing that the purity of a culture is a false concept due to the hybridity of modern societies (Ashcroft, Griffiths, & Tiffin, 1999; Bhabha, 1999). They maintain that the mingling of different cultures creates hybrid identities that fuse elements from various traditions and societies in a destabilizing and blurring of cultural boundaries. Television shows such as the ABC hit *Ugly Betty* attest to the ubiquity and popularity of hybrid forms. The show, produced by Mexican actress Salma Hayek and featuring Latina actress America Ferrera in the lead role, showcases a working class Latina and her family, which includes a father who is an illegal immigrant, as honest and good-hearted Betty out-maneuvers her evil co-workers at a high fashion magazine in New York City.

The cultural flow on which hybridity depends is a two-way street—albeit one in which traffic disproportionately travels from Western nations to less-developed parts of the world. Still, this unequal relationship belies the complexity of hybridity's cultural fusion. For example, the hottest, new trend in Berlin nightclubs is "Bollywood chic,"[8] with Bhangra and Punjabi pop, Indipop, and remixed Hindi film music infused with hip-hop, reggae, and techno elements. DJs are often flown from India to Germany to play the latest Bollywood music from Indian films and Bhangra pop. The trend in Bollywood chic is spreading to the club scenes of London and Paris ("Come to the cabaret," 2003), as well as cities in America. In another example of hybridity, a popular Chinese reality show, *Lovely Cinderella*, provides contestants with extreme makeovers along the lines of the U.S. reality show after which it is modeled—Fox TV's *The Swan*. One contestant, 30-year-old Chen Jing, lost 40 pounds and underwent cosmetic surgery to slim her jaw, redefine her eyes and nose, and lift her breasts. Although *Lovely Cinderella* copies its American counterpart in the use of surgery and cosmetics to attain a feminine beauty ideal, that ideal is based on a traditional Chinese aesthetic rather than American standards. The surgeries "play up," rather than distort, Asian beauty, with contestants stating their desire to look like Asian actresses, celebrities, and beauty queens rather than Western models of female attractiveness (Olesen, 2007, p. C-3). Both of these examples attest to the hybridity of popular culture—that is, its ability to incorporate facets from multiple cultures into something new and distinctive.

Indeed, hybridity and globalization—as well as more ethnically diverse domestic markets—have changed the face and form of mediated images of women, increasing diversity in some instances but also reflecting traditional patriarchal understandings of women as sex objects or wives and mothers. Byerly and Ross (2006) emphasize that any positive changes, such as an increase in diversity, remain "severely compromised by their mediated construction within the boundaries of existing patriarchal relations" (p. 32). For example, they note that, with few exceptions, global fashion advertising continues to construct the feminine ideal as White and emaciatingly thin, so that girls and women around the world are presented with a form of bodily perfection that is White and in other ways largely unattainable by the overwhelming majority of the world's women.

Nevertheless, global marketing imperatives have, in many instances, created more diversity in the representation of women. Byerly and Ross (2006) observed that two film versions of the popular TV show *Charlie's Angels*—one film came out in 2000 (*Charlie's Angels*) and the other in 2003 (*Charlie's Angels: Full Throttle*)—reconfigured the three lead actors, who were all White in the original TV series that ran from 1976 to 1981, into the ethnically diverse trio of Lucy Liu, Cameron Diaz,[9] and Drew Barrymore. They emphasize that the change was part of a marketing strategy that "signals Hollywood's need to respond to a growing multicultural, global audience" (p. 26). Additionally, Levy (2005) underscores the connection between *Charlie's Angels* and pornography by pointing out that the stars in the 2000 movie "were dressed in alternating soft pornography styles—as massage parlor geishas, dominatrixes, yodeling Heidis in Alpine bustiers" (p. 2). It is worth noting that the geisha- and Heidi-inspired outfits in the movies also fuse Asian and European cultural aspects to reflect a hybrid pornographic aesthetic.

The increase in ethnic and racial diversity is particularly notable within television, according to Greg Braxton (2007), an entertainment writer for *The Los Angeles Times* whose home turf is the epicenter of the U.S. film and television industries. Braxton points to "a flurry of interracial and inter-ethnic relationships that quietly have developed in prime time (television) during the past few seasons," including "mixed couples" on "programs as disparate as *House, Lost, The L Word, Boston Legal,*

My Name is Earl, *Men in Trees*, and *Desperate Housewives* (p. K-3). Braxton also singles out the relationship between the characters played by Julia Louis-Dreyfus, who is White, and Blair Underwood, who is African-American, in *The New Adventures of Old Christine*, as well as three interracial relationships on *Heroes*, an engagement between an African-American male and an Asian-American female on *Grey's Anatomy*, and a host of other inter-racial and inter-ethnic TV pairings. Although some may view this surge in inter-racial and inter-ethnic relationships as a positive development in its depiction of diversity and harmonious coexistence, Braxton reports that these couplings have been criticized as colorblind oversimplifications that are devoid of cultural conflict and honest exploration of racial difference.

But it is not just the U.S. film and television industries that are adopting marketing strategies to appeal to more diverse domestic and international audiences. Hollywood's primary international competitor in terms of reach and box office receipts—Bollywood—has successfully expanded its scope beyond a domestic market in India by recasting traditional Indian movie themes and representations of women to appeal to ethnic Indians living abroad as well as non-Indians in other countries. The effect of this, according to Venkatram (2002), is a new, "global stereotype" for Indian women that articulates Western notions of femininity and beauty that serve the interests of advertisers. This global stereotype requires that the ideal Indian woman be "Beautiful and sexy, in a world of her own where nothing matters except good clothes and make-up, five-star food and exercises in the gym" (p. 62). Malhotra and Rogers (2000) similarly found that the rapid adoption of private satellite television in India has resulted in representations of Indian women outside the traditional roles of mother and housewife, allowing them to be viewed as sexual beings with Western lifestyles and work outside the home.

SIGNIFYING DIFFERENCE

Although the mandate to be sexy may appear to be universal for women within Western cultures and those cultures most open to Western media,[10] it is not unaffected by considerations of race, class, sexual orientation, ethnicity, and other signifiers of domination and exclusion. As Valdivia (1995) points out, "issues of gender, race, class, sexual orientation, global origin, and ethnicity affect the coverage, portrayal and media production of everyone" (pp. 10-11).

The impact of race on societal standards of beauty was illustrated by a 16-year-old high school girl in New York, Kiri Davis, who filmed an award-winning short documentary[11] that explored how Black high school girls and young children are affected by society's light-skinned ideal. She found old stereotypes of gender and race very much in place. Davis, whose film, *A Girl Like Me*, has received extensive Internet exposure through Youtube.com and other Web sites, explained: "I wanted to make a film that explored the standards of beauty imposed on today's black girls. How do these standards affect her self-esteem or self-image?" (http://www.uthtv.com/umedia/show/2052/). In the documentary, Davis recreates the famous 1950's doll study conducted by psychologist Kenneth B. Clark in which African-American children are asked to choose between a White doll and a Black doll. Overwhelmingly, Clark found, the children preferred the White doll. More than 60 years later, Davis found essentially the same thing—15 out of 21 Black 4- and 5-year-olds thought the White doll was better.[12]

The stereotypes and cultural beliefs surrounding race and gender, internalized by even preschoolers, contribute ideological support for what hooks (1994) calls a "white supremacist, capitalist, patriarchal society" (p. 5). Stereotypes of African-American women include the hypersexual and promiscuous "oversexed-black-Jezebel," the "mammie," and the welfare cheat (Painter, 1992, p. 210), as well as the overachieving "Black lady" who emasculates the Black males in her life (Lubiano, 1992).

Flores and Holling (1999) state that Latin American women and men similarly are portrayed within the media as one-dimensional—as being "lecherous, thieving, dirty, violent and cowardly" (p. 340). For Latinas, they add, the emphasis is on their sexuality, with their most common depiction being a whore, although motherhood is also a central theme, "with Latina mothers often falling into the category of good mother, defined as the self-sacrificing and/or virginal mother" or the evil mother "who abandons or mistreats her children and often is sexually promiscuous" (p. 341).

Sexual orientation and social class also are reflected within the stereotypes accorded mediated women. Herman (2003) argues that "there is no such thing as sexuality uninflected by, for example, race and class" (p. 144). With few exceptions, she notes, the representation of lesbians within mediated popular culture is classed, linked to consumerism and commodification so that a universal lesbian lifestyle appears to be one of affluence and privatization, "where having babies and getting married are all that matter" (p. 156). The representation of lesbians within popular media also is linked to male fantasies of "girl-on-girl" sex, common in pornography, so that the monolithically portrayed affluent lesbian lifestyle is eroticized and seemingly consumed with sexual activity and desire (when not consumed with the desire for babies and marriage).

Indeed, gender, race, class, sexual orientation, ethnicity, and other signifiers of dominance and subordination are inextricably bound to one another in representation to shape meaning in distinct and specific ways. For example, the representation of a White, *middle-class* woman signifies differently and carries a different meaning than that of a White, *working-class* woman, just as we have different understandings of what it means to be a poor African-American *male* as opposed to a poor African-American *female*. The stereotypes and cultural expectations of gender, race, class, sexual orientation, and ethnicity add layer upon layer to representation so that meaning is always complex and reflects this multiplicity of intersecting signifiers. Thus, it is necessary to look at the intersectionality of gender, race, class, sexual orientation, and ethnicity—at the ways they interact with each other in unique and predictable ways—to understand the meaning behind the mediated representation of women in popular culture. For example, a study of news coverage of violence against African-American women during a college spring break weekend concluded that the convergence of gender, race, and class oppressions minimized the seriousness of the violence, portraying most of its victims as stereotypic Jezebels whose "lewd" behavior provoked assault (Meyers, 2004).

Social understandings of gender, class, race, ethnicity, and sexual orientation are, at base, ideological. Critical cultural studies scholars have long noted the media's support for the values, beliefs and norms of a ruling elite that wields social, economic, and political power within a hierarchy of social formations (Hall, 1982, 1997; Hall, Connell, & Curti, 1977; Hartley, 1982). The media are seen as primary agents in the maintenance and reinforcement of a dominant ideology whose goal is to sustain the status quo and those in positions of authority and power. According to Patricia Hill Collins (1991), when African-American women are defined as "stereotypical mammies, matriarchs, welfare recipients, and hot mammas" (p. 67), the status quo is upheld because these stereotypes naturalize and normalize racism, sexism, and poverty. These characterizations do the ideological work of blaming individual deviance or lack of initiative for the failure of Black people to achieve economic, social, and political equality, thereby diverting attention from the systemic social inequalities they face. Additionally, Collins (2004) points out that American movies, music, sports, dance, and fashion that feature African-Americans and Black culture "help shape contemporary ideologies of race, gender, sexuality and class in a global context" (p. 42). She notes that a new type of racism has evolved and is framed by new forms of global capitalism in which capital is increasingly concentrated in the hands of fewer and fewer transnational corporations that wield sufficient economic power to influence public policy at local, regional, and national levels. This new racism, Collins states, is "characterized by a changing political structure that disenfranchises people, even if they appear to be included" (p. 34).

Cultural critic bell hooks (1992) similarly emphasizes that male supremacist and White supremacist ideologies are institutionalized in the media, producing "specific images, representations of race, of blackness that support and maintain the oppression, exploitation and overall domination of all black people" (p. 2). Thus, popular media constitute an important ideological battleground over which meanings, definitions and identities are contested. As van Zoonen (1994) notes, "representation has always been an important battleground for contemporary feminism," with the women's movement engaged in "a symbolic conflict about definitions of femininity (and by omission masculinity)" (p. 12).

THE BOOK

This anthology is the third to examine the representation of women in mediated popular culture across a wide range of media and genres. The first book, published in 1978, was *Hearth and Home: Images of Women in the Mass Media* (Tuchman, Daniels, & Benét, 1978). At that time, media sociologist Gaye Tuchman famously concluded that the media "symbolically annihilate" women through absenting them from mediated and public discourse, as well as through the condemnation and trivialization of women and their concerns.

Fast forward 20 years, and the second book to broadly examine the portrayal of women in the media, *Mediated Women: Representations in Popular Culture* (Meyers, 1999), revisited Tuchman's thesis and asked whether symbolic annihilation was still an accurate description of the media's portrayal of women. In *Mediated Women*—which I edited primarily because I wanted an updated text for my "women and media" class—I concluded that although the media often still do engage in the symbolic annihilation of women, that term is no longer sufficient to characterize their representation within popular media. I argued that as a result of inroads made by the women's movement and feminism, the representation of women was more complex and contradictory than what Tuchman previously had found. Indeed, the representation of women just prior to the 21st century:

> could more accurately be described as *fractured*, the images and messages inconsistent and contradictory, torn between traditional, misogynistic notions about women and their roles on the one hand,

and feminist ideals of equality for women on the other. Mediated
women appear both hypersexualized and asexual, passive and ruthlessly aggressive, nurturing and sadistic, independent and dependent, domestic and career-oriented, silent and shrill, conforming and
deviant, and stereotypically racist and a departure from formulaic
conventions of racial and ethnic representation . . . the contradictions
of race, ethnicity, class, age, sexual orientation, and gender are writ
large over the body of the mediated woman. (Meyers, 1999, p. 12)

This complexity is the result of an ideological tug of war between patriarchal and feminist understandings over what it means within contemporary society to be a woman. The struggle over meaning, reflected
discursively in the representations of women, leads to a fracturing or
fragmentation of mediated women that ultimately may be more confusing than liberatory.

   This is not to say that women in mediated popular culture are not
frequently "symbolically annihilated," as Tuchman argued. Indeed, the
hypersexualization of women and their pornogrification within mainstream media is consistent with her thesis and certainly attests to the
durability of the "symbolic annihilation" of women by the media.
Steeves's (2007) findings indicate that Tuchman's conclusions in many
instances are as relevant today as they were in the 1970s. She notes that
studies "continue to critique the absence from and oppression of
women in media content," with the "neglect and distortion of women's
and feminist issues in news" an ongoing problem (p. 195). She also
points out that advertising remains a concern for feminist scholars not
only "because of the power of multinational advertising agencies, which
emphasize Western values (including conventions of gender representations) and target women as consumers," but also because advertising
affects the content of entertainment and news, which similarly reflect
the values of wealthier Western countries in a global marketplace (p.
196). But although both Steeves and Tuchman agree that women are
absent from representation in many cases, and that women's concerns
are distorted and neglected by the media, Steeves places these concerns
within a global framework shaped by the workings of multinational
corporations:

   The increased power and concentration of multinational corporations require feminist analyses, as the absence and oppression of
   women in media content plus women's economic disadvantages can
   be linked to these conglomerates and associated values of global
   consumerism. (p. 202)

This book, then, builds on and continues the work begun by Tuchman and extended by me 20 years later within *Mediated Women*. It attempts to understand the meanings behind the representations of women in mediated popular culture as they appear at the beginning of the 21st century. Although *popular culture* refers to cultural artifacts that range from popular footwear to fast foods, *mediated* popular culture refers to mass produced commodities—television shows, movies, books, news, music videos, DVDs, and so on—created and disseminated by the media for wide consumption by various targeted segments of the population. The issues explored in the following chapters of this book, then, are the following: how women are represented within mediated popular culture, and what that representation says about their position in society; the factors that shape this representation; and the roles that gender, race, class, ethnicity, and sexual orientation play in the portrayal of women within a designated form of mediated popular culture.

Women today continue to be, as Tuchman concluded 30 years ago, symbolically annihilated by the media. But that is not the only way they are portrayed within popular culture. They appear in multiple, often contradictory roles, their representation fractured and framed by conflicting depictions indicative of the ideological struggle over who they are and what their futures can be. Additionally, this book argues, the portrayal of women within popular culture reflects the hypersexualization of those images within the context of a global market in which the mainstreaming of pornography is increasingly accepted as the norm.

The following chapters construct a continuum of the representation of women within popular culture, reflecting a progression ranging from stereotypical portrayals that underscore the pornogrification of women to more positive and hopeful depictions in the media. This continuum exists within the opposing ideological poles of patriarchy and feminism as it illustrates the struggle over the meaning of women in its variety of contexts and forms within a global market.

The sections in this book reflect this complexity of representation, with many chapters exhibiting a fluidity related to the multiplicity of meaning within representation as well as the theoretical focus and choices of the author and this editor. As a result, a number of chapters fit into multiple categories and could have appeared in a different section of the book than the one in which they were placed. For example, Susana Kaiser's chapter on the Latino reality show *La Cenicienta*, in which a Texas Latina chooses her prince among 20 contestants, is in *Part IV: Hybridity and the Global Market*. However, the TV show also reflects a type of limited resistance to the status quo in that, although fairly traditional in its emphasis on family and marriage, it breaks with stereotypes of the socially acceptable Latina by featuring a single mother who is

making her own choices. Thus, that chapter might also have appeared in
Part V: Limited Resistance but instead was placed in that section of the
book which emphasizes the show's construction as a hybrid commodity.
Similarly, although I have emphasized at the beginning of this chapter
the more stereotypical, eroticized nature of *The L Word* and that show's
place within a global market, Rebecca Kern's chapter about *The L Word*
more broadly looks at the program's role in increasing queer visibility in
the media while simultaneously muting the resistant possibilities of that
visibility due to market pressures and the need for a crossover audience
of both lesbian and straight viewers. Additionally, the show espouses a
politically conservative agenda that unproblematically showcases affluence and idealizes the nuclear family—albeit an updated, lesbian version of family. In this way, Kern's chapter, like others in this book,
reflects the complexities and contradictions inherent within representation that is further complicated by the mainstreaming of pornography
and globalization.

Indeed, even primarily progressive representations are compromised at least somewhat by global marketing imperatives and the concomitant hypersexualization of women's bodies. The need for market
share in the television industry and box office at movie theaters mitigate
against the inclusion of most—but not all—controversial issues or politically progressive voices. Because texts are polysemic, they carry within
them multiple meanings and interpretations that are dependent on the
decoding capabilities of individual readers. That said, texts still can prefer or privilege certain understandings, and when they do, more often
then not within mainstream media they will privilege those understandings and interpretations that favor the current power structure. So even
as the Powerpuff Girls champion "girl power," as noted in Rebecca
Hains's chapter in the final section of this book, they distort and ridicule
Second Wave feminism.[13] And even in TV shows like *Law and Order*, in
which female detectives are as competent and capable as any male, the
women must still adhere to traditional standards of feminine beauty.

The following section, *Part II: The Pornografication of Women*, contributes to our understanding of how pornographic images of women
and girls have become conventional within advertising and other popular media, and the detrimental effects of their mainstreaming on individuals and society. In "A (Bad) Habit of Thinking: Challenging and
Changing the Pornographic Worldview," Jane Caputi ties pornography
to traditional, moralistic notions of masculinity and femininity that create social inequality and eroticize violence against women. Debra
Merskin follows up with "Lolita Lives: An Examination of Sexual
Portrayals of Adolescent Girls in Fashion Advertising." She concludes
that the sexualization of preadolescent and adolescent girls within these

ads have implications for their psychological and physical well being, as well as society's view of them.

Part III: Bodies and Difference examines race, class, and ethnicity as markers that signify and reinforce the subordination of women of color and working-class women. In "Nipplemania: Black Feminism, Corporeal Fragmentation and the Politics of Public Consumption," Kimberly Wallace-Sanders and Brittany Cooper examine the public and media hysteria over singer Janet Jackson's "wardrobe malfunction" during the 2004 Super Bowl halftime show, during which her costume was ripped open to reveal her right breast. The authors situate that event within the historical context of White, male consumption of Black women's bodies in a misogynist, racist culture. Next, Rosa Soto, in "Maid to be the Maid?: An Examination of the Latina as Maid in Mainstream Film and Television," explores the ubiquitous presence of the Latina maid within popular media and how her presence works to "class" herself and the family for whom she works in ways that reinforce stereotypes of Latinas as hypersexual and undeserving of class mobility. The final chapter of this section, "The Multiply Transgressive Body of Anna Nicole Smith," looks at the media attention paid to the one-time Playboy model who infamously, according to her critics, reinvented herself as a golddigger millionaire and then as an inarticulate reality show diva prior to her drug-related death in 2007. Karen Pitcher interrogates the overlapping transgressions of femininity and social class that converged in the body of Anna Nicole, providing a case study into the ways in which society upholds hegemonic notions of what constitutes proper performances of femininity and social class.

Chapters in *Part IV: Hybridity and the Global Market* explore the complexities of culture within mediated representations of women. Jill Birnie Henke, in "Climbing the Great Wall of Feminism: Disney's *Mulan*," looks at how the "Disneyfication" of the film *Mulan* transposed 20th-century American feminist attitudes and actions onto the 2,000-year-old Chinese legend, thereby denying cultural significance and difference. In "Bollywood and Globalization: Reassembling Gender and Nation in *Kal Ho Na Ho*," Anjali Ram examines the Bollywood blockbuster film to understand how Indian cinema is being reconfigured in relation to a global, transnational context that views women in multiple ways but ultimately reinscribes the patriarchal universe common to Indian cinema. The film, Ram argues, simultaneously rejects and reaffirms patriarchy while pointing to Bollywood's attempt to chart a space between tradition and modernity, West and East, home and abroad, convention and innovation. The complexities and contradictions inherent in hybridity are further examined by Susana Kaiser in "'I am *Cenicienta* ('Cinderella') and I'm Choosing My Prince': Reality TV Adapts an Old

Fairy Tale for the New Millennium." The reality show about a Latina single mother selecting her Prince Charming depicted the heterogeneity of Latino cultures while also providing a vehicle for the discussion of controversial issues within the Latino community.

Chapters in *Part V: Limited Resistance* look at the ways in which the contradictions and complexities inherent within the intersectionality of gender, race, class, ethnicity, and sexual orientation work to both limit and support resistance to the dominant ideology. In *"The L Word* and Queer Female Acceptability," Rebecca Kern explores issues of femininity and lesbian sexuality in the TV series, arguing that although *The L Word* does increase visibility for queer women, their representation and the show's thematic presentation sustain dominant ideals of femininity and hetero-normativity in Western society while eroticizing lesbian sexuality. The resistant possibilities of the show, Kern states, are subsumed by the need to attract a large, crossover audience. S. Elizabeth Bird similarly argues that while many ethnic groups have had varied but definite success in transforming stereotypical media imagery, American Indian women generally continue to be represented in very limited and stereotypical ways. But in "The Burden of History: Representations of American Indian Women in Popular Media," Bird finds some hope for change as American Indians gain greater control over their own image-making.

The concluding section, *Part VI: Finding Progress*, examines positive representations of females within popular media although, as noted previously, even these portrayals contain within them complexities and contradictions that may undercut their progressive nature. Rebecca Hains looks at the Cartoon Network's *Powerpuff Girls* in "Power(puff) Feminism: '*The Powerpuff Girls*' as a Site of Strength and Collective Action in the Third Wave," and she concludes that the cartoon's discourse exposes the false dualities of "power" and "puff" by presenting girls who are feminine and cute, yet physically strong and ready to fight. Hains argues that *The Powerpuff Girls* subverts stereotypical norms in the superhero genre while negotiating Third Wave feminism and the concepts of "girl power" and "power feminism." In "Feminism and Daytime Soap Operas," Elayne Rapping views soap operas as a world where feminist values hold sway, where the domestic world is prized, and where the portrayal of women characters and their relationships reflect a deep love and respect for each other through the most difficult of conflicts and the most joyful of shared events. And, finally, Carolyn Byerly, in "The Dialectical Relationship of Women and Media," considers women's various responses to misogynist media—responses that represent feminists' struggles in an historical process taking place over several decades and in multiple nations. Byerly, while acknowledging a backlash against activist gains, also takes stock of some of the advances feminist media activism has made possible, particularly in the areas of news and public discourse.

Taken together, these chapters reflect the on-going struggle over the articulation of what it means to be a woman within the context of a global market. This ideological contest, informed by patriarchy, on the one hand, and feminism, on the other, also is shaped by the marketing imperatives of transnational media giants, along with the complexities inherent within the intersectionality of gender, race, class, sexual orientation, and ethnicity, and the hybridity of blurred cultural boundaries and identities. But the diversity within the representation of women presented in these pages reflects not only the hybridity of cultures, nor simply the ways in which multiple signifiers of domination and exclusion intersect within representation to create meaning. In a very real sense, the mediated representation of women in popular culture signifies how far women have come, and just how far they have yet to go.

NOTES

1. The show is distributed internationally by MGM International Television Distribution, Inc., and appears on Pro7 in Germany, Living TV in the United Kingdom, Showcase Television in Canada, Catchon in South Korea, and yes+ in Israel.

2. In addition to the countries mentioned, *Sex and the City* was or continues to be shown in Canada, Germany, Ireland, the United Kingdom, Poland, France, the Netherlands, Sweden, Italy, Belgium, Greece, Spain, Finland, Norway, the Czech Republic, South African, Russia, Israel, Romania, Bulgaria, Turkey, Australia, New Zealand, Indonesia, Serbia, Mexico, Chile, Japan, Korea, Malaysia, Thailand, Singapore, Hong Kong, India, Pakistan, the Philippines, Taiwan, Estonia, Lithuania, Latvia, and Denmark.

3. By way of contrast, *business.com* sold for $7.5 million in 1999, *cameras.com* went for $1.5 million, and *scores.com* brought in $1.2 million.

4. I am indebted to Dlorah Jenkins for introducing me to these examples of marketing to young girls, as well as the concept of "age compression" and the work of Anne Higonnet (1998).

5. Statistics available at: http://www.cosmeticplasticsurgerystatistics.com/statistics.html#2005-HIGHLIGHTS. In all, nearly 11.5 million surgical and non-surgical procedures were performed in the United States in 2005.

6. It is not just on-air personalities that are portraying more skin. A publicity photo of Debora Wilson, the president and chief executive officer of The Weather Channel, shows her seated in a dark business suit and what looks to be a silk shirt that is unbuttoned to mid-chest. The photo accompanied an article about The Weather Channel's plans to build news studios for high-definition programming (Leith, 2007).

7. Supporters of globalization, on the other hand, claim that it has the potential to increase understanding and cooperation among different nations as citizens inevitably get to know each other through global media. And, as Croteau and Hoynes (1997) and Williams (2003) noted, the cultural imperialism thesis is undermined by its inability to account for the multiple ways that audiences may interpret media messages or differences in types of media.

8. The term *Bollywood* itself reflects cultural hybridity in that it fuses Hollywood with Bombay, the city that is the center of India's film industry. Bombay is now known as Mumbai, although the term *Bollywood* remains.

9. Diaz, a successful model before she broke into acting, is not overtly ethnic in appearance. However, her father, Emilio Diaz, is a second-generation Cuban American.

10. Some countries, particularly fundamentalist Islamic states, publicly denounce the sexualization of women in Western media as a sign of immorality.

11. *A Girl Like Me* was winner of the Diversity Award sponsored by The Third Millennium Foundation.

12. The documentary was created by Davis while attending the Urban Academy, a public high school in New York City. It was produced by Reel Works Teen Filmmaking, a free, after-school program for high school students which pairs them with professional filmmaker-mentors and allows them to write, shoot and edit personal narrative videos on subjects they choose. The program is supported by HBO.

13. The Second Wave of the women's movement began in the mid- to late-1960s and is often linked to consciousness-raising groups and collective action to achieve equality for women. The First Wave is associated with the struggle for women's suffrage, which was granted in 1920, and the Third Wave involves young women, often in their teens and 20s, who have fashioned a more individualistic form of feminism in response to Second Wave feminism.

REFERENCES

Ashcroft, B., Griffiths, G., & Tiffin, H. (Eds.). (1999). *The post-colonial studies reader*. New York: Routledge.

Bhabha, H. (1999). Cultural diversity and cultural differences. In B. Ashcroft, G. Griffiths, & H. Tiffin (Eds.), *The post-colonial studies reader* (pp. 206-209). New York: Routledge.

Boyle, K. (2003). The pornography debates: Beyond cause and effect. In G. Dines & J.M. Humez (Eds.), *Gender, race, and class in media: A text-reader* (pp. 406-416). Thousand Oaks, CA: Sage.

Braxton, G. (2007, February 18). TV's interracial romances seem curiously colorless. *Atlanta Journal-Constitution*, p. K-3.

Byerly, C.M. (2006). *Questioning access*. Available at www.ssrc.org.

Byerly, C.M., & Ross, K. (2006). *Women and media: A critical introduction*. Malden, MA: Blackwell.

CBC Marketplace. (2005, January 9). *Sex sells: Marketing and "age compression."* [Broadcast].

Collins, P.H. (1991). *Black feminist thought: Knowledge, consciousness, and the politics of empowerment.* London: Routledge.

Collins, P.H. (2004). *Black sexual politics: African-Americans, gender, and the new racism.* New York: Routledge.

Come to the cabaret, with a Bollywood twist. (2003, June 18). *Atlanta Journal-Constitution.* p. F-3.

Croteau, D., & Hoynes, W. (1997). *Media/society: Industries, images and audiences.* London: Pine Forge Press.

Downes, L. (2007, January 1). Middle school girls gone wild. *International Herald Tribune,* p. 5.

Flores, L.A., & Holling, M.A. (1999). Las familias y las Latinas: Mediated representations of gender roles. In M. Meyers (Ed.), *Mediated women: Representations in popular culture* (pp. 321-337). Cresskill, NJ: Hampton Press.

Hall, S. (1982). The rediscovery of "ideology": Return of the repressed in media studies. In M. Gurevitch, T. Bennett, J. Curran, & J. Woollacott (Eds.), *Culture, society and the media* (pp. 56-90). London: Methuen.

Hall, S. (1997). The work of representation. In S. Hall (Ed.), *Representation: Cultural representations and signifying practices* (pp. 13-64). Thousand Oaks, CA: Sage.

Hall, S., Connell, L., & Curti. L. (1977). The "unity" of current affairs television. *Working Papers in Cultural Studies, 9,* 51-93.

Hartley, J. (1982). *Understanding news.* London: Methuen.

Herman, D. (2003). *"Bad girls* changed my life": Homonormativity in a women's prison drama. *Critical Studies in Media Communication, 20*(2), 141-159.

Higonnet, A. (1998). *Pictures of innocence: The history and crisis of ideal childhood.* London: Thames & Hudson.

hooks, b. (1994). *Outlaw culture: Resisting representations.* New York: Routledge.

hooks, b. (1992). *Black looks: Race and representation.* Boston: South End Press.

Jensen, R. (2003). Pornography and the limits of experimental research. In G. Dines & J.M. Humez (Eds.), *Gender, race, and class in media: A text-reader* (pp. 417-423). Thousand Oaks, CA: Sage.

Jensen, R. (1998). Introduction: Pornographic dodges and distortions. In G. Dines, R. Jensen, & A. Russo, *Pornography: The production and consumption of inequality.* New York: Routledge.

Leith, S. (2007, March 8). For Weather Channel, new HD era beckons. *Atlanta Journal-Constitution,* p. C-2.

Levy, A. (2005). *Female chauvinist pigs: Women and the rise of raunch culture.* New York: The Free Press.

Lotz, A. (2006). *Redesigning women: Television after the network era.* Urbana: University of Illinois.

Lubiano, W. (1992). Black ladies, welfare queens, and state minstrels: Ideological war by narrative means. In T. Morrison (Ed.), *Race-ing justice, en-gendering power: Essays on Anita Hill, Clarence Thomas, and the construction of social reality* (pp. 323-363). New York: Pantheon.

Malhotra, S., & Rogers, E. (2000). Satellite television and the new Indian woman. *Gazette, 62*(5), 401-429.

McCabe, J., & Akass, K. (2006). *Reading "Desperate Housewives": Beyond the white picket fence.* New York: Palgrave & Mcmillan.

Menn, J. (2007, May 20). Porn.com beats business, but can't top sex. *Atlanta Journal-Constitution,* p. C-2.

Meyers, M. (1999). *Mediated women: Representations in popular culture.* Cresskill, NJ: Hampton Press.

Meyers, M. (2004). African-American women and violence: Gender, race, and class in the news. *Critical Studies in Media Communication, 21*(2), 95-118.

Olesen, A. (2007, March 11). Modern China gets a new face. *Atlanta Journal-Constitution,* p. C-3.

Oliviero, H. (2006, June 7). Risqué reads aren't your mother's romance novels. *Atlanta Journal-Constitution,* pp. E-1, 4.

Painter, N.I. (1992). Hill, Thomas, and the use of racial stereotype. In T. Morrison (Ed.), *Race-ing justice, en-gendering power: Essays on Anita Hill, Clarence Thomas, and the construction of social reality* (pp. 200-214). New York: Pantheon.

Parker, A. (2006, January 24). BT turns to pornographic films in battle for broadband customers. *Weekend Financial Times for Europe,* p. 2.

Paul, P. (2005). *Pornified: How* pornography *is damaging our lives, our relationships and our families.* New York: Times Books.

Rich, F. (2003, July 27). Finally, pornography does prime time. *New York Times,* Section 2, pp. 1, 15.

Steeves, H.L. (2007). The global context of women in communication. In P.J. Creedon & J. Cramer (Eds.), *Women in mass communication.* Thousand Oaks, CA: Sage.

Tuchman, G., Daniels, A.K., & Benét, J. (1978). *Hearth and home: Images of women in the mass media.* New York: Oxford University Press.

Valdivia, A.N. (1995). Feminist media studies in a global setting: Beyond binary contradictions and into multicultural spectrums. In A. Valdivia (Ed.), *Feminism, multiculturalism and the media: Global diversities* (pp. 7-29). Thousand Oaks, CA: Sage.

van Zoonen, L. (1994). *Feminist media studies.* Thousand Oaks, CA: Sage.

Venkatram, S. (2002). *Women in print.* New Delhi: Unnati Features.

Weaver, J. (1992). The social science and psychological research evidence: Perceptual and behavioral consequences of exposure to pornography. In C. Itzin (Ed.), *Pornography: Women, violence and civil liberties* (pp. 284-309). Oxford, UK: Oxford University Press.

Williams, K. (2003). *Understanding media theory.* London: Arnold.

Zillmann, D., & Bryant, J. (1982). Pornography, sexual callousness, and the trivialization of rape. *Journal of Communication, 32*(4), 10-21.

Zillmann, D., & Weaver, J.B. (1989). Pornography and men's sexual callousness toward women. In D. Zillmann & J. Bryant (Eds.), *Pornography: Research advances and policy considerations* (pp. 95-125). Hillsdale, NJ: Erlbaum.

Part II

The Pornogrification
of Women

2

A (Bad) Habit of Thinking

Challenging and Changing the Pornographic Worldview

Jane Caputi

THE PORNOGRAPHIC WORLDVIEW[1]

A magazine advertisement for shoes (Fig. 2.1), curiously enough, doesn't show a shoe at all. Instead, it shows an apparently naked woman and man. She is cradling his foot in her hand and kissing it. There is nothing wrong with foot kissing, of course. But look closely at his hand on the back of her neck, holding her—maybe even forcing her—down. Is this simply an ad for footwear? Or is it also one for female subordination?

A music video, *P-Poppin* by Ludicris, is built around a strip club. It gets some pointed criticism from Marcus Flowers, a community educator at Atlanta's Men Stopping Violence: "The way that the women are paraded in front of fully clothed customers, their bodies for sale, reminds me of how half-naked slaves were exhibited to white buyers at auctions, as if they were animals" (Mendez Berry, 2005, p. 166).

It might not surprise anyone to learn that whole genres of pornography are devoted to what one Web site, www.sickestsites.com, approvingly describes as "women being totally degraded and turned into sperm ashtrays." "Sickest sites" applauds the pornography site "Meatholes" for showing one woman "reduced to tears with verbal abuse, forced ass-licking, toes forced into her mouth, and dirty sneakers pressed onto her tender pussy." These kinds of actions are understood by sociologists as "ceremonies of degradation," and such ritual demolitions of self-esteem are regularly done by abusers to victims in places like slave plantations, prisons, and torture chambers. References to these same types of ritual degradations show up not only in overt pornography, but also are coded into innumerable advertising images. Compare the Meatholes' enactment of dirty sneakers pressed into a woman's genitals with an image from a mainstream ad for sneakers, which shows a man's sneaker-shod foot pushed up against the mouth of a seemingly willing and aroused woman (Fig. 2.2).

As the title of this chapter indicates, it is not about X-rated pornography. Rather, the chapter is about a pornographic worldview, what Patricia Williams (1995, p. 123) called a "habit of thinking" based in the eroticization of domination and subordination as well as pervasive sexual objectification. Catharine MacKinnon and Andrea Dworkin (Dworkin, 1989, pp. 253-275) originally shifted the debate around pornography from questions of morality and chastity to those of power relations. They defined *pornography* as the "sexually explicit subordina-

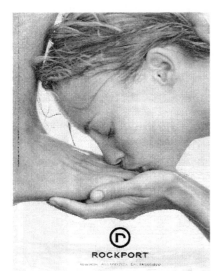

Fig. 2.1. Enforced submission   Fig. 2.2. Ritual degradation

tion of women" or those used in the place of women. Pornography, in this view, is not about the appreciation of women and the pleasures of sex but about the "denigration of women and a fear and hatred of the female body" (Kaplan, 1991, p. 322). Throughout this chapter, I explore the way these themes are ubiquitous in mainstream imagery. But first, I want to deal briefly with the charge that when feminists criticize pornography we play into the hands of right-wing forces.

Pornography's defenders argue that pornography radically challenges a moralistic and anti-sex worldview propagated by patriarchal religions. At first this seems to make some sense. Aren't those anti-feminist, family values types always railing against pornography? But let's think twice about this. The pornographic worldview is actually the secret twin of the puritanical one. Both worldviews rely on and uphold the *same* fundamentally sexist beliefs: that men are superior to women, and that women are in need of control and best suited for sexual and reproductive functions. Pornography as we know it is a direct result of patriarchal moralism's fear and hatred of women and of sex itself, which it also understands as something essentially taboo—"dirty," unintelligent, uncivilized, sinful, and shameful.

All of this counters millennia of human understanding that sexuality is a way of knowledge and pleasure and a force that—in its intimacy, creativity, potency, ecstasy, and dynamism—reflects and participates in the cosmic energy that powers the universe. In the ancient world, this understanding of sexuality as sacred and cosmic was represented by the figure of a Goddess, often naked, sometimes even with spread legs, a Goddess who is the origin of all life (Gadon, 1989).

But patriarchal religions, particularly in the Abrahamic traditions, depose that Goddess and then turn her into pornography (Caputi, 2004). In her place, they put an all-male, anti-sexual, or erotophobic God. This new religion tells us that women are in need of domination, and that male domination of women will be the basis of sex. This outrage is given divine endorsement in *Genesis* 3:16, when God curses Eve by telling her: "Your desire will be unto your husband and he will lord it over you." More recently, the popular Christian-oriented advice book, *The Surrendered Wife* (Doyle, 2000) presents this as a blessing. It promises that if women just "surrender" to their husbands in all ways—financially, sexually, psychologically, spiritually—they will have not only happier marriages, but also hotter sex. The same message is transmitted, albeit more graphically, in pornography where women are literally bound and gagged before being "fucked" (a word which, in our sexist culture, means both to have sex with and to do gross, violent injury to). In truth, the pornographic habit of thinking is not really deviant at all. Rather, it is part of a social network—which includes law, medicine, military, family, and religion—that long has worked together to subordinate women, primarily by defining, controlling, exploiting, and punishing female sexuality and by defining male sexuality in mechanistic and dominating ways.

A global feminist movement challenges that patriarchal network as it takes various forms in different traditions. By criticizing pornography I am by no means advocating censorship or some return to respectability and female "modesty"—a tried-and-true method of stifling women and controlling female sexuality. I support sexual freedom and sexual representations and simultaneously want the liberation of erotic imaginations from both pornographic and moralistic paradigms. Sometimes, however, it seems impossible for those of us enmeshed in it to imagine anything other than what we've learned from conventional morality/pornography. Everywhere we are told that without a certain measure of domination, submission, sin (Fig. 2.3), danger, possession, obsession, humiliation, objectification, and violence even unto death (Fig. 2.4), there wouldn't be any "sex" at all.

The paradigm of eroticized domination and objectification is not confined to interpersonal relationships but serves as a basis for all manner of exploitative and abusive practices. Scientific metaphors tradition-

Fig. 2.3. Active female
sexuality associated with sin

Fig. 2.4. Pornography of
murder

ally have turned on pornographic themes exalting masculine sexual aggression against what is conceptualized as feminine Nature and the planet we still colloquially understand as Mother Earth (Keller, 1985; Merchant, 1980). Many observers have found eroticized domination at the core of Nazism (Griffin, 1981; Sontag, 1980), torture (Brison, 2004; Caputi, 1987), the cult of nuclear weaponry (Caputi, 1993), militarism, imperial conquest (Smith, 2005), racism and slavery (Collins, 1998; Hernton, 1988). Pornographic thinking influences all of these larger social dominations, but it basically begins in our most everyday ideas about sex and gender.

GENDER PORNOGRAPHY

Pornography depends on very conventional and moralistic notions of masculinity and femininity. Although there are complex differences along class, ethnic, and race lines (see, e.g., Collins, 2004), men and women conventionally are defined as opposite and inherently unequal. At the same time, men and women—and, the moralists thunder, only men and women—are ineluctably attracted to each other. This system links inequality itself to the erotic dynamic. The man is supposed to be taller, stronger, richer, older, and colder—in short, more powerful. The woman is supposed to be shorter, weaker, better looking, vulnerable, younger, warmer—in short, socially powerless. This scenario is played, for example, in one ad for lingerie. A woman clothed only in red undergarments looks up tremulously, lips parted, as a fully clothed man towers over her, holding something hidden, possibly threatening, behind his back.

A similarly sexist brand of heterosexuality also is pushed by a 1999 ad for L'Oreal "straight up" hair products. It shows a young, "clean-cut" White couple. The woman—with long, straight hair—gazes up, sweetly and trustingly, at her stern-faced boyfriend. He towers over her and is literally "in her face." The ad commands them to "play it straight." Certainly, that dictate refers as much to conformity to sexist heterosexuality—the male-dominant/female-subordinate kind—as it does to chemically straightened locks.

Those who uphold patriarchal family values claim that homosexual relationships threaten the very bedrock of civilization. Of course, because sexual inequality is the very bedrock of patriarchal civilization, they might have a point. Much of the antagonism to lesbian and gay marriage—unions among social equals—is based in fear of the idea of egalitarian, nonpatriarchal relationships spreading to heterosexual marriage.

OBJECTIFICATION

Objectifying others mean treating them as if they had no innate self, sovereignty, purpose, agency, or soul and using them for your own purposes, including for sexual gratification and for ego enhancement. Numerous images support this kind of dehumanization by making it seem as if women are literal objects—vehicles (Fig. 2.5), blow-up dolls (Fig. 2.6), furniture, collectibles, and so on. As objects, women are denied autonomy and presented as perpetually accessible, something to toy with, something to possess, something to be consumed (Fig. 2.7; Adams, 2003).

Different ethnicities are marketed as specific types of objects in pornography. For example, Asian women are cast as submissive "Oriental Dolls," or dominant "Dragon Ladies," Black women as sexually loose "Jezebels" (Collins, 1998), and so on. In the oppressive class and race hierarchy, the most socially valuable women are young, light-skinned, slim, and usually blonde, representing the "gold standard."

As feminism has demanded sexual freedom for women, the pornographic culture responds by equating pornography with liberation. Everywhere, women and girls are encouraged to make themselves into sex objects, adopting the stripper or the pornography star as a role model. Black feminist theorist Patricia Hill Collins (2004) criticized the ways that Black popular culture characterizes men as thugs and women as "whores" and "bitches." Moreover, she suggested, the fixation on

Fig. 2.5. Woman fused with car

Fig. 2.6. Woman as sex doll

women's buttocks is reminiscent of the way 19th-century European men fetishized the buttocks and genitals of the South African woman they dubbed the Hottentot Venus, whom they stripped and displayed for profit.[2]

The age of the sex object keeps getting younger. Louise Kaplan (1991) argued that when women demand and express their intellectual, sexual and emotional freedom, society responds with both woman-hating pornography and the increased sexual

Fig. 2.7. Women as consumable objects

objectification of girls (Fig. 2.8). In pornographic videos, women are marked with clothing and hair styles to suggest that they are children or teenagers (Jensen & Dines, 1998). So too, in advertising, grown women are posed as sexually available little girls. (Fig. 2.9)

Fig. 2.8. Sexualization of girls

Fig. 2.9. Women presented as sexualized girls

SEX AND VIOLENCE

Objectification is a prerequisite not only for inequality but also for violence. Much overt pornography is explicitly devoted to rape and abuse, and everyday pornography also regularly shows women in situations that suggest that they are about to be raped, often facilitated by alcohol or drugs (Fig. 2.10).

Fig. 2.10. Scene suggesting gang rape, facilitated by alcohol

Rape and other forms of sexual abuse are intended to silence victims. This is equally a concern of patriarchal religion. Saint Paul thunders: "Let a woman learn in silence with all submissiveness. I permit no woman to teach or to have authority over men; she is to keep silent" (1 Tim. 2: 11-12). Silencing women, not surprisingly, also is a central preoccupation of pornography. In 1976, for one of its jokes, *Hustler* magazine published a doctored photograph that depicts a woman's face whose mouth has been replaced by a hairy vulva. The copy beneath openly suggests rape as a way of silencing women's subversive speech:

> There are those who say that illogic is the native tongue of anything with tits. . . . It comes natural to many broads; just like rolling in shit is natural for dogs. . . . They speak not from the heart but from the gash. . . . The one surefire way to stop those feminine lips from driving you crazy is to put something between them—like your cock, for instance.

Pornography regularly features the binding and gagging of women, something reflected in scores of similar images in mainstream advertising that call for female silence. In one ad for gum, a teenage girl wearing a man's shirt and tie has a manhole cover shoved into her mouth; she is apparently being punished not only for having a "dirty mouth," as the copy below the ad reads, but for cross-dressing. Another 2004 ad for voting rights asks women not to silence themselves by neglecting to vote, but it simultaneously shows Christina Aguilera with her mouth sewn shut. Presumably, this image is meant to convey irony. But such a horrific image actually works to communicate the threat that is meant to induce women to silence themselves before someone else does it to them

(Fig. 2.11). To understand more fully, it is necessary to recognize that this torturous image is not an isolated one. Similar ones are regularly reiterated in explicitly misogynist contexts. It is, for example, uncannily similar to one that advertised the 1998 horror film *Strangeland*. This ad showed the face of a teenage girl whose mouth was similarly sewn up; a killer does this to his victims prior to raping and murdering them, in effect, permanently silencing them. The ubiquity of such imagery speaks loudly. It reflects not only the reality of *gynocidal*[3] violence against women, but also the intent of that violence and its representations—to terrorize women and girls and destroy our capacity to resist.

Fig. 2.11. Silencing of women

In the "snuff" genre of pornography, someone actually is raped, tortured, and killed. A faked film with the title *Snuff* was released in the United States in 1976, claiming to have been made in South America where, as its poster says, "life is cheap." This claim endorses the ways that economic oppression, racism, drug trafficking, and corporate greed make poor and/or racially stigmatized women especially vulnerable to prostitution, pornography, rape, and murder. These realities are horribly mirrored in the Mexican city of Ciudad Juárez and also in Guatemala, where hundreds if not thousands of women and girls have been tortured, raped, and murdered since the early 1990s.

In North American popular culture, White, male, serial sex killers, beginning with Jack the Ripper, have become cult heroes (Caputi, 1987) and "snuff" imagery has become the stuff of everyday entertainment, not only in horror movies (from *Psycho* on), television, and video games (e.g., *Grand Theft Auto*), but also in fashion advertising. Everywhere, we encounter images of women being shot, stabbed, strung up, and decapitated (Fig. 2.12). These images constitute a kind of virtual lynching, where mass audiences can enjoy the spectacle of sexualized murder of the stigmatized group. In one fashion photo from 2003, a seemingly dead woman wearing a green jacket is dumped by a river. The scene instantly reminded me of the "Green River Killer," Gary L. Ridgeway, who was convicted around that same time for raping and murdering 49 girls and women. According to prosecutors, Ridgeway explained himself: "I'd much rather have white, but black was fine. It's just, just garbage. Just something [to have sex with and] kill her and dump her." Ridgeway, like other sex killers, uses the word "it" to refer to his victims. His point of view is reflected everywhere in popular culture where women are identified with objects—cars, motorcycles, dolls, tables, and household items. In one fashion series, the woman's presence is really an absence as she is represented only by a chopped up mannequin, her body parts used to make furniture. In the *Sky Mall* catalogue, available on any domestic flight, readers find a table whose "legs" seems to be a woman's in high-heeled shoes. The table is described as "playful and oh so much fun." Fun for whom? The serial killer Ed Gein actually used the body parts of his female victims to make furniture.

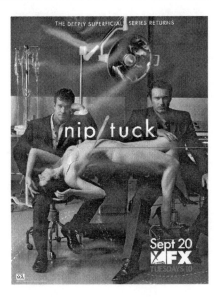

Fig. 2.12. Everyday snuff imagery

PORNOGRAPHIC MASCULINITY

James Gilligan (1996), who was the chief psychiatrist for the Massachusetts prison system, finds that men are more violent than women not because they are hormonally driven to aggression but because of the construction of patriarchal gender roles. These roles split the whole human psyche into two "opposite" and unequal sexes. These roles then ordain women to be sex objects and men to be violence objects. As such, men are mortified by any association with the feminine. The worst thing a man can be called is some variation of "girl," "wimp," or "pussy." Men are under enormous pressure to continually prove their "manhood" by showing dominance—militaristic, imperialistic, financial, intellectual, emotional, and physical. Gilligan also argues that poor and/or ethnically stigmatized men are kept from having access to social dominance, and so often resort to physical violence to prove manhood.

A seemingly innocuous ad for insurance stages a scene of high school humiliation around a trio of students. A young White man is mocked by a Black man and sneered at by a White woman for wearing a sweater identical to one the woman is wearing. This "wimp" temporarily loses not only his male privilege but also his White privilege. A similar threat to male voters' gender honor was mobilized by Republican supporters in the 2004 presidential election. As one bumper sticker warned: "Don't be a girlie man. Vote Republican."

One ad pitched to teenaged boys for Bitch skateboards handily pantomimes the basic process of becoming a man in patriarchal culture. Two figures—the universal signs for male and female—are represented; the male figure aims a gun at the female figure's head (Fig. 2.13). This, obviously, indicates hostility against girls and women. But another, hidden meaning may be that the teenage boy, in order to become a "real man," has to kill off his

Fig. 2.13. Bitch skateboards

feminine-identified traits. Much popular imagery sends a message that the real man must be hard and so self-absorbed that he actually becomes incapable of relationship and connection except, of course, with machines, like his weapons, his car, or his computer.

The pornographic worldview—reflected in Freudian psychoanalysis, military marching chants, and innumerable images in popular culture—openly identifies men as violence objects, often equating the penis with a weapon. A frankly pornographic film called *Mr. MX* (after the nuclear warhead), focused upon a White man with a supposed 16-and-one-half inch penis. An everyday variant on this theme informs an illustration for an article on male infertility that appeared in a 2007 edition of *Details* magazine. It shows a large and fully loaded handgun aiming directly at the viewer. The headline reads: "Why Isn't Your Wife Pregnant Yet? Alarming new infertility research says you may be shooting blanks." (Fig. 2.14) In these visual metaphors, the penis is a weapon and the most potent ejaculation is a bullet or a bomb blast. Implicitly, then, a woman's vagina is a target or a war zone.

Fig. 2.14. *Details* magazine

PORNOGRAPHIC FAMILY VALUES

Nawal El Saadawi (1980) suggested that it is male insecurity in the face of "the innate resilience and strength of the woman" that first led men to oppress and subjugate women, to try to "conquer the indomitable vitality and strength that lay within women" (p. 100). This took the form of men trying to control, punish, and exploit female sexuality, which is why "good girls," in the family values framework, must be virginal, chaste, and under the control of father or husband. Of course, because heterosexual men do not want to restrict themselves to chastity, they also consign some women to the "bad girl" status.

The friendly sound of the phrase "family values" masks its underlying strategy of dominating, exploiting, and controlling women—sometimes through forced reproduction brought about by denial of birth control and abortion, sometimes by forced sterilization, especially of women whom racists see as undesirable (Smith, 2005). Some patriarchal systems work by mandating that women be veiled and covered; others promote a central image of women as nearly naked sexual objects. But both strategies, however different, are ways to control female sexuality and destroy female self-definition.

Traditionally, patriarchal cultures foster paternalism, granting the father basic ownership over his wife, or wives, and children. The father is supposed to protect them in exchange for their absolute loyalty, but he also has the right to physically abuse and sometimes to sell or even murder them (Millett, 1970). Feminism challenges this model worldwide, but much family values rhetoric indicates a desire to return to a time when women and children were understood as men's property or valuables and the father was the ultimate authority in the home.

Radical feminist theologian Mary Daly (1973) boldly pointed to the political implications of religious representation: "The symbol of the Father God . . . [makes] the oppression of women appear right and fitting. If 'God' in 'his' heaven is a father ruling 'his' people, then it is in the 'nature' of things and according to divine plan and the order of the universe that society be male dominated" (p. 13). The iconic 1950's television show *Father Knows Best* packaged that divine plan in the form of a situation comedy, and that phrase still is approvingly cited by family values spokesmen like Florida mega-church Pastor Bob Coy (2005). Coy regularly prescribes male rule as the direct expression of "God's" plan, closing one of his weekly televised sessions with this prayer to gender difference and men's preeminence: "As the wife does her thing and the guy does his thing as a husband, Lord, we'll find our homes are those havens of rest, a place where weary souls can come and discover that Father knows best." Ironically, a similar reference shows up in an overtly incest-friendly feature in *Playboy*. It is titled "Father Knows Best" and showcases a father who photographs his own daughter naked as an adult. As an added treat, *Playboy* includes a naked picture of the daughter as a 3-year old child that the father snapped when he took her with him to his pornography shoots and where she mimicked the older models.

Obviously, family-values spokesmen like Pastor Coy would not, as *Playboy* seems to be doing here, endorse incest. But father–daughter incest and other forms of sexist abuse are the inevitable underside of paternalist systems. What those who advocate male authority in the home don't tell us is that the patriarchal home is not very safe at all for many women and children. Domestic violence is the most common cause of injury to women and, like incest, it then gets turned into a specialized type of pornography. One pornography Web site, "Brutal Family," assures its visitors that there is only one family law—"Man says, woman obeys"—as it shows naked women being beaten up by men. A three-part fashion spread in *Vibe* also promotes a domestic violence sequence. In the first image, a man appears to be yelling at a woman, who tries to cover her ears. In the second, he is grabbing her and appears to be slapping and shaking her (Fig. 2.15). In the third, he is outside the door to the home, which is half-way open. Scarily, he seems to be talking his way back in.

Fig. 2.15. Fashion imagery promoting domestic violence

THE PORNOGRAPHY OF WAR AND CONQUEST

The eroticized masculine domination over the feminine instituted in patriarchal family relationships and everyday gender roles is regularly marshaled to support war and colonization (Smith, 2005). Rena Swentzell (1993), a Native American scholar, pointed to the atrocious belief in "power as an integral part of sexuality," and added that this "is what the Inquisition was all about. That is what the whole conquest of the Southwest was about—power and control by males" (p. 167).

Historically, conquerors have conceptualized the land they sought as female and often naked, as in one visual depiction of the "Discovery of

America." This classic 1600 rendition depicts a conqueror standing erect and holding a flag on a pole. He is fully clothed and is associated with ships and gadgets. The land to be conquered is represented by a naked and reclining woman, who is associated with cannibals and animals.

The intimate connection between sex and conquest remains firmly established in American culture as revealed by events and images associated with the U.S.-led invasion of Iraq in 2003. Political cartoonist Ward Sutton shows the notoriously cocky Donald Rumsfeld, the first Secretary of Defense under President George W. Bush, masturbating to images of Baghdad being bombed. Whatever our political affiliation, everyone gets the joke.

In 2004, one pornography Web site, "Iraq Babes," devoted itself exclusively to images that purported to show American soldiers raping Iraqi women. Meanwhile, real harms were happening at Abu Ghraib prison in Iraq in 2003, where U.S. soldiers sexually abused and tortured Iraqi inmates, including by staging scenes of sexual humiliation (Danner, 2004) and photographing them. In May 2004, a number of these photos were released to the public.[4] The types of degrading abuses directed at the Iraqi prisoners are mirrored in the ordinary treatment of women in both pornography and mainstream imagery, where women routinely are put into shameful and vulnerable positions. In one of the photos from Abu Ghraib, naked men are made to pile on top of one another, with their buttocks in the air. Smiling and giving thumbs-up gestures are soldiers Charles Graner and Lynndie England, clearly enjoying this blatant demonstration of their power over the ritually abused Iraqis (Fig. 2.16). This torturous set-up is eerily mirrored in a photo in *Vibe* magazine, which appeared before the release of the Abu Ghraib photos (Fig. 2.17).

Fig. 2.16. Abu Ghraib   **Fig. 2.17. Commercial ritual humiliation**

Two men are seated at a bar. To their left, a woman in a very short skirt and stiletto heels bends over the bar, exposing her "panties" and baring part of her buttocks. In the top-left corner we read: "BOTTOMS UP: Tyrese and Bobbito enjoy the show." Clearly, the two men are enjoying not only the woman's sexual display, but also the show of their power. They, after all, are seated, fully clothed, and facing the viewer; one grins and the other gives a "thumbs-up" gesture. In one notorious photo from Abu Ghraib, the role of sexual dominator was taken by a woman, Lynndie England. In the pose of a dominatrix, England dragged a naked man on a leash (Fig. 2.18). The *New York Times* averred that Private England has come to symbolize the Abu Ghraib scandal. But we need to remember that the men in charge deliberately used a woman torturer because they knew that it would be far more humiliating for a man to be sexually tormented by a woman. Significantly, the ringleader at Abu Ghraib, Charles Graner, was England's lover, a former prison guard and allegedly abusive and adulterous husband, who sent off copies of this picture to friends saying, "Look what I made Lynndie do."

Everyday pornography regularly shows coded versions of the abusive dynamic so evident at Abu Ghraib—although usually with the man in the dominant role. One ad for Las Vegas has an uncanny resonance with the image of England dragging the man on the leash. In this image, there is no literal leash but one is suggested as a clothed man snaps his fingers and, in response, a lingerie-clad woman crawls across a bed on all fours to him. The accompanying copy, "Some Fantasies Just Don't Work Anywhere Else," suggests that Las Vegas is a special place, like a prison, where abusers can act out their desires (Fig. 2.19).

Fig. 2.18. Abu Ghraib   **Fig. 2.19. Las Vegas**

THE PORNOGRAPHY OF BONDAGE

In one publicity shot, Paris Hilton, naked save for high-heeled black boots, is elaborately bound in the cord from a microphone she is holding. Hilton at this time was involved with a man, Nick Carter, who allegedly was battering her, and some of her photos showed visible bruises. Carter claimed innocence and said that the injuries actually resulted from this photo shoot. Whatever the truth, this kind of image tacitly supports abuse, eroticizing female captivity, bondage and helplessness. Literally, this photo valorizes the point of view of a serial killer—someone like Dennis Rader, the self-named "BTK (Bind, Torture, Kill) Killer."

Bondage, literally, means a state of enslavement. Although pornography is supposedly about fantasy and sexual freedom, its imagery and practices are rooted in slavery. The eroticization of domination and the treatment of women as unpaid and forced domestic and sexual labor in the home began with the historical institution of slavery at the inception of patriarchal organization when elite men enslaved the women from conquered groups (Lerner, 1986). Later, men, too, were enslaved and even sometimes raped by masters and mistresses. But for women, "sexual exploitation marked the very definition of enslavement" (p. 89).

Patricia Hill Collins (1998) argued that contemporary pornography has strong ties to the treatment of Black women and men in U.S. slavery. Slavery eroticizes capture, bondage, punishment, whipping and rape; the master class justified itself by saying that slaves were like animals—and that it was acceptable to treat animals this way, which it also is not. These patterns continue in everyday imagery, such as one fashion ad, where a dark-skinned woman wears animal-print clothing and is posed with legs parted for accessibility. If you look closely, you can see that she is stapled to the fabric, looking like a doll, or a slave, for sale (Fig. 2.20).

Fig. 2.20. **Sexualized slavery**

Pornography, including everyday pornography, continually churns out fantasies sexualizing bondage, servitude, and submission, usually with women in the submissive position. In some contexts, both real and representational, privileged White women do play the master role—as in colonialism and

Fig. 2.21. White woman in sexualized "master" role

Fig. 2.22. Sexualized "slave" role

racism (Fig. 2.21). Concomitantly, the subordinated feminine role can be forced on men. One ad for sweatpants broadly suggests slavery and imprisonment (Fig. 2.22). Why is this heavily muscled, African-American man stripped from the waist up and then "emasculated," made to lower his head in submission? Ann duCille (1997) provided an answer, rooted in the historical institution of slavery: "Both male and female slaves were often exhibited and sold in the nude, their naked body fondled, and groped, and gazed upon by white men. . . . The dominant/submissive, master/slave power relation . . . was the perfect locus for playing out forbidden racial and sexual fantasies" (p. 308). Advertising then replays these sexual enslavement fantasies, albeit in coded forms.

THE PURE AND THE DIRTY

> . . . keep pornography. . . dirty.
> The way it should be.
> (Cromer, 2001, p. 28)

The religious historian Mircea Eliade (1969) wrote that sexuality's "primary and perhaps supreme valency is the cosmological function. . . . [E]xcept in the modern world, sexuality has everywhere and always been a hierophany [a manifestation of the sacred], and the sexual act an integral action (therefore also a means of knowledge)" (p. 14). In this view, sexual pleasure, rooted in our bodily nature, is something that can lead to wisdom and well as to spiritual understanding and connection with the divine. But all of this is reversed in many patriarchal religions that share a habit of associating sexuality, particularly female sexuality, with sin, "filth," and the forbidden. In this view, virginity and chastity are "clean," whereas sex is considered "dirty." This notion is the basis of the double standard, where women's sexuality is subjected to severe regulation and categorization, with women slotted as either "clean" virgins or "dirty" whores. The idea that sex can be something leading to wisdom is equally denied by pornography. Indeed, pornography *needs* sex to be "dirty," dumb, and forbidden, for without this taboo, sexuality and eroticism might be accepted and integrated into our culture in honest and open ways, and pornography as we know it would be obsolete.

A chilling ad from the 1970s is quite open about the abusive implications of making sex "dirty." The ad is for "Love's Baby Soft" fragrance. It depicts a heavily made-up child with an elaborate adult coiffeur (Fig. 2.23). A hand, one that looks far too big to be hers, reaches in front, holding a teddy bear, suggesting the presence of an adult abuser. The headline reads: "Love's Baby Soft. Because innocence is sexier than you think." This ad, while subtly endorsing child sexual abuse, also explains in part its thrill for those who practice it. When patriarchal religions make sexuality sinful and "forbidden," doing forbidden things actually can become more exciting, more compelling. And when sex is culturally understood not only as "power over"

Fig. 2.23. Sexualized childhood "innocence"

someone, but also as something that "dirties" or defiles, dirtying someone who is considered especially "powerless" and especially "innocent" or "pure" (e.g., a virgin or even a child) also can become especially compelling, especially for the most insecure and self-loathing men.[5]

Notions of purity and dirtiness also are manipulated to promote racism and genocide. One 1995 ad for soap shows an upright, young blonde woman in a white blouse, alongside the word *PURE*. It looks, on the one hand, like an ad for female chastity. On the other it might remind us of a neo-Nazi poster evoking racist notions of "purity" of blood. Those who claim to be the most civilized and "pure" regularly project all that they deny and fear in themselves on to people who are of other ethnic groups or races, whom they then castigate as "dirty" and "savage."

Alice Walker (1980) observed that although White women are represented as "objects" in pornography, Black women are represented as "shit." One cartoon in *Hustler* (1979) depicted a Black man wiping himself after defecating. Where he wipes, the underlying skin shows up as white. This utterly pornographic notion that dark skin is "shitty," whereas white skin is "clean" is reiterated in an ad for Diesel jeans from 1995. It shows a dark-skinned woman, prone on zebra-skin sheets and with jeans unzipped to signify that she is conquered, open to all. The small print says: "Right now, there are far too many dangerous animals running around, wasting space, wasting time, using the planet as a toilet! Take our advice. Don't be fooled by 'natural' beauty, stick em in practical, easy-to-clean metal cages." By associating this woman, and those like her, with waste, this ad basically presents a case justifying genocide, or what is euphemistically called "ethnic cleansing." Again, the makers of this ad might justify themselves by saying that their flagrant statements indicate they are being ironic. But, as with the supposedly anti-silencing image discussed earlier, this ad most effectively communicates fundamental racist and sexist symbolism. The ironic framing actually works to disarm some viewers, setting up a doublethink mechanism, and making the vicious messages even more potent.

Distorted notions of purity and dirtiness also are used to foment and justify homophobia. In March 2005, an extraordinary interfaith alliance of male religious leaders in Jerusalem formed to stop an international gay pride festival in Jerusalem. One Islamic leader stated the group's central concern: "We can't permit anybody to come and make the Holy City dirty." Once again, the scapegoating of another person or group as "dirty" is used as a way to exclude and demonize them, justifying oppression.

The idea that sex is "dirty" comes from an overall mind–body split in which the body and (female-identified) nature is seen as inferior and the (male-identified) mind and culture are seen as superior. This same split leads patriarchal cultures to disparage the Earth as mere matter, dirt, something for elite humans to exploit and use. In so doing humans forget that we are made of the Earth. The very word *human* is derived from the Latin *humus*, meaning earth or dirt. We are all equally dirty, equally human, and our body is inextricable from mind and spirit and is, moreover, "our most precious talisman," connecting us to the (Mother) Earth (Allen, 1990, p. 56). As we ponder the pornographic culture's body-hatred and concomitant notion of sexual "dirt," we can also consider the ways that violence against women and girls, as well as against peoples stigmatized as "savage," "shitty," "filthy," and "other," is part of an overall pattern of violence against the Earth and Nature.

GLOBAL SNUFF

What can be done, under patriarchy, to one female [or feminized] body can be done, under world patriarchy, to the entire body of

> earth. The pornographic images of women trussed up in chains and
> barbed wire, of female flesh bruised and bloodied and beaten raw,
> are really our species' maps of the mutilated earth. . . . The deadness
> of pornography is the deadness of the landscape created by patri-
> archy, in which nothing lives that is not hideously deformed, con-
> trolled, manipulated for the voyeur's eye, bound up for use. (Sjöö &
> Mor 1991, p. 411)

An illustration on the cover of a mid-1980s avant-garde rock compila-
tion album, "The Blasting Concept" shows a naked man strangling a
woman with a rope while raping her. Through a window, we see outside a corresponding blast—what seems to be a nuclear mushroom
cloud. How do we interpret such a horrific image?

One way is by recalling that in indigenous traditions throughout the
world, the Earth and Nature are recognized as a divine, feminine principle, although one including both female and male, and often represented by a female body. This perception is often expressed colloquially as
"Mother Earth" or "Mother Nature." In some traditions, this translates
into respect. In the pornographic worldview, the Earth and Nature are
still recognized as a feminine principle, but now this means that they
can be objectified, raped, exploited, silenced, and sexually murdered.

Patriarchal religion, philosophy and science have long conceptualized Nature as a pornographic object. Reflecting this tradition, one
sculpture, "Nature Revealed by Science" (Louis-Ernst Barrias) from just over a century ago represents Nature as a sexually available woman, stripped and with her "mysteries" revealed. Popular imagery continues to represent the Universe, the Earth and Nature as a passive and vulnerable sex object, one available for penetration, forced to yield up her secrets, and even implicitly murdered. An exceptionally violent ad for fax machines (Fig. 2.24) shows the face of a female figure symbolizing Nature being raped with objects through eyes, ears, and mouth. This image is meant to convey that this particular technology is so fast that it virtually breaks the laws of Nature.

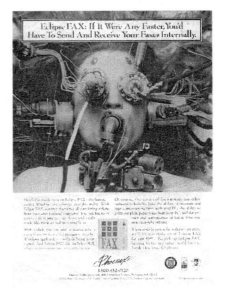

Fig. 2.24. Rape of Nature

One related ad for audio speakers shows a young woman, laid out as if dead, her naked body covered with maps: She is the Earth, explored, mapped, conquered. Correspondingly, images of the actual planet Earth are also shown as subject to White male domination. An ad for a multinational corporation shows the Earth as a toy, with four boy toddlers grouped around it. Three non-white boys sit on the floor, their eyes unfocused. But the little White boy stands right behind the toy Earth and raises his finger in a gesture of authority, signifying White male domination not only over men of other ethnicities and races, but also over women and the Earth itself. (Fig. 2.25) More explicitly

Fig. 2.25. White male domination

violent images of the Earth also are common; in many ads, the planet is carved up, objectified, targeted, and otherwise symbolically raped.

All of this abusive imagery culminates in the figure of a futuristic "fembot"—an artificial, thin, and slick sex object (Fig. 2.26). "She" at first might seem to prophesy elite men's coming total control not only over the female sex, but also over Nature. But this is an illusion. A global feminist movement openly resists patriarchy. And Nature is not completely passive, malleable, and manageable. As militaries and corporations systematically damage or poison the ecosystem, the Earth responds by withdrawing such vital services as production of food and purification of water.[6] These egregious polluters do not so much control Nature as they hasten our own and other species' demise as the outcome of nuclear war, catastrophic climate change, the enduring toxicity of nuclear waste, and the contamination of

Fig. 2.26. Fembot

the elements. The artificial sex object, the "fembot," does not really signify "mankind's" completed victory over Nature. What she does portend
is desensitization, alienation, and sterility.

REALITY CONTROL

The novelist and essayist Toni Cade Bambara (1993) tells us that the
experience of viewing racist and sexist popular culture fare for African-
American women is a kind of "mugging" (pp. 132-133). bell hooks (1992)
also argued, in even stronger terms, that such imagery can serve as a
"murder weapon" (p. 7). Similarly, in his study of the pornography post-
cards of Algerian women manufactured by French colonizers, Malek
Alloula (1986) argued that the postcard fully participates in the violence
of colonization and is "no less efficient for being symbolic" (p. 5).

Pornography's defenders frequently admonish its critics by averring
that pornography is simply a form of fantasy. Yet, hooks, Bambara, and
Alloula take a very different view, declaring that the misogynist, objectifying, racist, and environmentally destructive imagery of everyday life
not only endorses and normalizes violence but is itself a form of violence. Clearly, mass media representations, however heinous, are not
the equivalent of an actual instance of abuse. Nonetheless, it is useful to
draw out some of their correspondences.

Violence, including violence in intimate relationships, does not
always take the form of physical blows. Abuse also takes an emotion-
al/psychological form that is meant to destroy the self-esteem of the victim while enhancing that of the abuser. It appears as verbal assaults,
belittlement, cultivation of anxiety and despair, mockery, blaming, accu-
sation, humiliation, degradation, disrespect, and "reality control,"
which includes denying the harm of the abuse, creating an atmosphere
of threat, and *blocking awareness of alternative ways of living and being.*

Psychological battery by a lover or a family member is direct and
personalized and obviously will have much greater violent effect than
commercial representations. Still, repeated negative, mass-mediated
representation of a group is a public form of psychological violence and
degradation. It, too, serves as a form of psychological destruction meant
to squelch resistance and destroy self-esteem. It, too, feeds the sense of
omnipotence of the dominators. And it, too, serves as a form of *reality
control.* It tells us that this is the only world possible, that male domination is universal in time and space, and that the Earth is at the disposal
of elite men. At the same time—and this is key—such violence *blocks
awareness of alternative ways of living and being;* it stifles the development
of a worldview other than the pornographic one.

RECLAIMING THE EROTIC

> In order to perpetuate itself, every oppression must corrupt or dis-
> tort those various sources of power within the culture of the
> oppressed that can provide energy for change. (Lorde, 1984, p. 53)

On November 19, 1994, unknown vandals defaced bound volumes of
women, gay, and gender studies journals at the University of New
Mexico library. They took an issue of the journal *Lesbian Ethics*, crossed
out that title, and replaced it with "God's Ethics." Underneath, they
scrawled a swastika along with this pronouncement: "God made
women for men."

This "God" is that familiar patriarchal father who "knows best" and
who, allegedly, also made the Earth, animals and the elements "for
men" to use and abuse as they like. But for much of human history, this
was not the ruling view. Instead, there was respect for a "feminine principle" of nature—the intelligent, active, originating, and diverse life
force in which both women and men participate. The feminine principle,
often represented by a Sex Goddess, was understood and respected as
the source of energy, desire, life and growth as well as decline and
death, endings which became new beginnings in some form of rebirth.

In *Goddess: Myths of the Female Divine*, David Leeming and Jake Page
(1994) trace an ancient history of Goddess reverence and an accompanying worldview which included respect for women and for sexuality.
This was overturned with the advent of patriarchal civilizations, and
covered up by rewritings of myth, and system-
atic denigrations, taking Goddesses and turning them into pornography (Caputi, 2004).

One Sex Goddess is Inanna of ancient
Sumer (Fig. 2.27). Diane Wolkstein (Wolkstein
and Kramer, 1983, p. 169) describes Inanna as:
"the Goddess of Love. Formed from all of life,
the Goddess of Love gives forth desire that
generates the energy of the universe." Such a
cosmology recognizes the body as sacred and
perceives sexual desire not as "sin," but as a
manifestation of cosmic dynamism. It knows
the feminine principle as a unified and unifying force, as the source of life, and as something that must be respected. And that cosmology recognizes *power* as generative and
creative energy, *not* as the ability to dominate
everyone and everything.

Fig. 2.27. Inanna of
ancient Sumer

Some of the most vital resistance to the pornographic way of thinking can be found in an ongoing feminist reclamation and recasting of these ancient traditions honoring the feminine principle and sexuality, what poet Audre Lorde (1984) calls "the erotic." Lorde claims that the erotic, a power source within our bodies as within the universe, is our conduit to cosmic forces of generation, ecstasy and relationship. The erotic is the energy source that enables us not only to desire sexually, but also to love, create, connect, resist oppression, and transform ourselves and our world. Patricia Hill Collins (2004) argues for the necessity of respecting the erotic and articulates a goal of "honest bodies that are characterized by sexual autonomy and soul, expressiveness, spirituality, sensuality, sexuality, and an expanded notion of the erotic as a life force" (p. 287). A diverse contemporary movement of artists, writers, activists, mystics, and environmentalists challenges the pornographic worldview by reclaiming an honest and erotic one (e.g., Anzaldúa, 1987; Caputi, 2006; Cisneros, 1996; Conner, 1993; Daly, 1984; De la Huerta, 1999; Ensler, 1998; Gadon, 1989; Griffin, 1981; Schneemann, 2002).

Pornography is a (bad) habit of thinking. It is a worldview, not the world. The pornographic passes itself off as the erotic, but it actually works by appropriating and then distorting the erotic energy that could otherwise be directed to enabling awareness, resistance, and transformation. Breaking the habit of pornographic thinking and activating the erotic, we can, in ways both large and small, empower ourselves to make another world—one that respects female sexual autonomy, finds objectification unattractive, and domination unethical and uninteresting, recognizes sexuality as a way of pleasure and knowledge, nurtures voice and listening, and instills respect for ourselves, each other, animals, the elements, and the Earth.

NOTES

1. In 2006, I completed a film, *The Pornography of Everyday Life* that also incorporates much of this material. It is distributed by Berkeley Media, www.berkeley media.com. I would like to thank all those relatives, friends and students who brought some of these ads to my attention, including Mary Caputi, Dan Caputi, J.D. Checkit, Heather Stewart, Natalia Gago, Augusta Walden, and many others. I especially thank Ann Scales, Andria Chediak and Jeff Meyers for our many fruitful conversations on this topic.
2. Saarjite Baartman, a young Khosian woman who became known as the Hottentot Venus, was brought to Europe from Cape Town in 1810 by an English ship's surgeon who wanted to publicly exhibit the woman's enlarged buttocks. Her body was displayed in England and France, including an exhibition of her naked body in a cage at Piccadilly, England.

3. *Gynocide*, originally used by both Andrea Dworkin and Mary Daly, and *femicide* were coined by feminists to define murders of women as a direct outcome of sexism (e.g., murders committed by men for reasons of sexual gratification, sense of ownership and punishment).

4. Both Iraqi women and men were abused, although only photos of the men were released to the public.

5. Perhaps something like this informed the motivations of two separate gunmen who staged gynocidal assaults on schoolgirls in late September and early October 2006. In the first case, a drifter, Duane Morrison, 53, took six girls hostage in a Colorado high school and sexually abused all of them before letting four go. When police stormed the classroom, he killed 16-year-old Emily Keyes along with himself. A few days later, Charles C. Roberts IV, 32, invaded an Amish school in Pennsylvania. He, too, sent away the boys and a few adult women, while keeping 10 girls with him. Roberts had brought an assortment of weapons, hardware, ties, wood, bolts and sexual lubricant, indicating that he intended to bind, torture, rape, and kill the little girls. As the police stormed the building, he tied them, lined them up, and then shot each in the back of the head before killing himself. Much public commentary on these crimes expressed the usual bewilderment. Few bothered to point out that girls had been deliberately selected; if all the victims were members of an ethnic or racial group other than that of their killer, these murders would have been instantly recognized as hate crimes. Rapes and gynocides are ritual enactments of male supremacy, in these cases, taking the form of "virgin sacrifice." For further discussion of the ritual aspects of such crimes and their relation to lynching, see "The Gods We Worship," in Caputi (2004).

6. The Millennium Ecosystem Assessment, a report compiled by 1,300 leading scientists from 95 countries, documents that pollution and exploitative practices are damaging the planet at such a rapid rate that the "ability of the planet's ecosystems to sustain future generations can no longer be taken for granted" (Conner, 2005). The planet, in response to this abuse, will no longer be so readily providing such "services" as purification of air and water, protection from natural disasters, and the provision of foods and medicines.

REFERENCES

Adams, C. (2003). *The pornography of meat*. New York: Continuum.

Allen, P. G. (1990). The woman I love is a planet the planet I love is a tree. In I. Diamond & G. F. Orenstein (Ed.), *Reweaving the world: The emergence of ecofeminism* (pp. 52-57). San Francisco: Sierra Club Books.

Alloula, M. (1986). *The colonial harem* (M. Godzich & W. Godzich, Trans.). Minneapolis: University of Minnesota Press.

Anzaldúa, G. (1987). *Borderlands/ La Frontera*. San Francisco: Spinsters/ Aunt Lute Press.

Bambara, T. C. (1993). Reading the signs, empowering the eye: *Daughters of the Dust* and the black independent cinema movement. In M. Diawara (Ed.), *Black American cinema* (pp. 118-144). New York: Routledge.

Brison, S. J. (2004, June 4). Torture, or "good old American pornography." *The Chronicle Review/ The Chronicle of Higher Education*, pp. B10-B11.

Caputi, J. (1987). *The age of sex crime*. Bowling Green, OH: Bowling Green State University Press.

Caputi, J. (1993). *Gossips, gorgons, and crones: The fates of the earth*. Santa Fe: Bear.

Caputi, J. (2004). *Goddesses and monsters: Women, myth, power and popular culture*. Madison: University of Wisconsin Popular Press.

Caputi, J. (2006). Cunctipotence: Elemental female potency. *Trivia: Voices of Feminism*. Available at http://www.triviavoices.net/.

Cisneros, S. (1996). Guadalupe the sex goddess. In A. Castillo (Ed.), *Goddess of the Americas La Diosa De Las Americas: Writings on the Virgin of Guadalupe* (pp. 52-55). New York: Riverhead Books.

Collins, P. H. (1998). *Black feminist thought: Knowledge, consciousness, and the politics of empowerment*. New York: Routledge.

Collins, P. H. (2004). *Black sexual politics: African Americans, gender, and the new racism*. New York: Routledge.

Conner, R. P. (1993). *Blossom of bone: Reclaiming the connections between homoeroticism and the sacred*. San Francisco: Harper.

Connor, S. (2005). The state of the world? It is on the brink of disaster. *The Independent UK*. Available at http://www.commondreams.org/headlines05/0330-04.htm.

Coy, B. (2005, Oct. 9). *The Active Word* [Weekly television broadcast]. Calvary Chapel, Fort Lauderdale, FL.

Cromer, M. (2001, Feb. 26). Porn's compassionate conservatism. *The Nation*, pp. 25-28.

Daly, M. (1973). *Beyond God the father: Toward an ethic of women's liberation*. Boston: Beacon Press.

Daly, M. (1984). *Pure lust: Elemental feminist philosophy*. Boston: Beacon Press.

Danner, M. (2004). *Torture and truth: America, Abu Ghraib, and the war on terror*. New York: New York Review of Books.

De la Huerta, C. (1999). *Coming out spiritually: The next step*. New York: Jeremy P. Tarcher/Putnam.

Doyle, L. (2000). *The surrendered wife: A practical guide to finding intimacy, passion, and peace with a man*. New York: Simon & Schuster.

duCille, A. (1997). The unbearable darkness of being: 'Fresh' thoughts on race, sex, and the Simpsons. In T. Morrison & C. B. Lacour (Eds.), *Birth of a nation'hood: Gaze, script and spectacle in the O.J. Simpson Case* (pp. 293-338). New York: Pantheon.

Dworkin, A. (1989). *Letters from a war zone*. New York.: E. P. Dutton.

El Saadawi, N. (1980). *The hidden face of Eve*. New York: Zed Books.

Eliade, M. (1969). *Images and symbols: Studies in religious symbolism* (P. Mairet Trans.). New York: Sheed & Ward.

Ensler, E. (1998). *The vagina monologues*. New York: Villard.

Gaard, G. 2004. Toward a queer ecofeminism. In R. Stein (Ed.), *New perspectives on environmental justice: Gender, sexuality, and activism* (pp. 21-44). New Brunswick, NJ: Rutgers University Press.

Gadon, E. (1989). *The once and future goddess: A symbol for our time*. New York: Harper & Row.

Gilligan, J. (1996). *Violence: Reflections on a national epidemic*. New York: Random House.

Griffin, S. (1981). *Pornography and silence: Culture's revenge against nature*. New York: Harper Colophon.

Hernton, C. C. (1988), *Sex and racism in America*. New York: Anchor Books.

hooks, b. (1992). *Black looks: Race and representation*. Boston: South End Press.

Hurston, Z. N. (1983). *Tell my horse*. Berkeley, CA: Turtle Island.

Jensen, R., & Dines, G. (1998). The content of mass-marketed pornography. In G. Dines, R. Jensen, & A. Russo (Eds.), *Pornography: The production and consumption of inequality* (pp. 65-100). New York: Routledge.

Kaplan, L. J. (1991). *Female perversions: The temptations of Emma Bovary*. New York: Doubleday.

Keller, E. Fox. (1985). *Reflections on gender and science*. New Haven, CT: Yale University Press.

Leeming, D., & Page, J. (1994). *Goddess: Myths of the female divine*. New York: Oxford.

Lerner, G. (1986). *The creation of patriarchy*. New York: Oxford.

Lorde, A. (1984). Uses of the erotic: The erotic as power. In *Sister Outsider* (pp. 53-59). Trumansburg, NY: The Crossing Press.

Mendez Berry, E. (2005, March). Love hurts: Rap's "black eye". *Vibe*, pp. 163-168.

Merchant, C. (1980). *The death of nature: Women, ecology and the scientific revolution*. San Francisco: Harper & Row.

Millett, K. (1970). *Sexual politics*. Garden City, NY: Doubleday.

Schneemann, C. (2002). *Imaging her erotics: Essays, interviews, projects*. Cambridge, MA: MIT Press.

Sickest Sites. Retrieved 2005 from: http://www.sickestsites.com/sado-masochism.htm

Sjöö, M., & Mor, B. (1991). *The great cosmic mother: Rediscovering the religion of the earth*. San Francisco: HarperSanFrancisco.

Smith, A. (2005). *Conquest: Sexual violence and American Indian genocide*. Boston: South End Press.

Sontag, S. (1980). Fascinating Fascism. In *Under the Sign of Saturn* (pp. 73-108). New York: Farrar, Straus, & Giroux.

Swentzell, R. (1993). Commentaries on When Jesus came the Corn Mothers went away: Marriage, sex, and power in New Mexico, 1500-1846, by Ramón Gutiérrez, Compiled by Native American Studies at the University of New Mexico. *American Indian Culture and Research Journal, 17*(3), 141-177.

Walker, A. (1980). Coming apart. In L. Lederer (Ed.), *Take back the night: Women on pornography* (pp. 95-104). New York: Bantam Books.

Williams, P. J. (1995). *The rooster's egg: On the persistence of prejudice*. Cambridge, MA.: Harvard University Press.

Wolkstein, D., & S. N. Kramer. (1983). *Inanna: Queen of heaven and earth*. New York: Harper & Row.

3

Lolita Lives!

An Examination of Sexual Portrayals of Adolescent Girls in Fashion Advertising

Debra Merskin

Lolita, light of my life, fire of my loins. My sin, my soul. Lo-lee-ta.

—Nabokov (1958, p. 1)

First, there was the book. Then there was the 1962 film, followed by yet another filmic version in 1997 of Nabokov's (1958) infamous bestseller *Lolita*. This fictional account of the emotional and physical tensions surrounding an older man's lust for a teenage girl epitomizes the relationship between power and forbidden desire. Simultaneously repulsive and fascinating, mediated portrayals of young girls as inviting and willing participants in their own sexual exploitation have fueled many a male fantasy. Sexualized images of girls are not only found between the covers of books. Rather, "under-aged sexualized 'nymphets'" have provocatively posed in television programs, movies, magazine stories and, even more so, in advertising (Albright, 2002). The "Lolita look," although technically a misinterpretation of Nabokov's fiction, has become a dominant motif, not only of movies, books, and magazines, but also of advertising in general and fashion advertising in particular. Some consumer products are named after the literary vixen and celluloid coquette: Lolita Lempicka fragrance, Lolita leggings in a Nordstrom catalogue, or playing on words, Nolita hair care products with the subheading "no limits, no boundaries." Although not necessarily named after sexy stars, sexually alluring clothing has reached the prepubescent crowd as well. Abercrombie & Fitch, for example, faced criticism over marketing thong underwear, with the words "eye candy" and "wink wink," to the age 7- to 14-year-old crowd. A spokesperson for the company said, "The underwear for young girls was created with the intent to be lighthearted and cute" (Odell, 2002). Similarly, a Fetish perfume advertisement raised a stink with the image of a young-looking girl with blackened eyes and the copy "so he can smell it when you say no." The message from advertisers and the mass media to girls (as eventual women) is they should always be sexually available, always have sex on their minds, be willing to be dominated and even sexually abused, and to be seen—always and primarily—as sexual objects.

The increased sexualization of children, and more specifically girls, in fashion advertising is a disturbing phenomenon (Kilbourne, 1999a). To examine this inclination, I apply Galician's (2004) seven-step media literacy analysis framework to magazine fashion advertisements. My central concern is the fetishization of young girls' innocence and their vulnerability to physical and emotional violence as possible outcomes of sexualized representations in the media (Kincaid, 1998). For purposes of this chapter, the concept of fetishization draws upon the works of Freud and Marx, and is regarded as the sexualization of objects or persons that ordinarily would not or should not be thought of in this way, conflating "the dynamic unconscious and the dynamics of capitalist accumulation" (Weeks, 2005, p. 131). Importantly, this reciprocity "masks the underlying, painful reality" of sexualizing girls and young women in order to sell products. Conversely, just as "eroticized gazes at the child-woman" are everywhere (Walkerdine, 1997, p. 166), so too are sexualized portrayals of women as childlike. In the media in general and fashion advertising in particular, the "merchandising of children as sexual commodities is ubiquitous and big business" (Rich, 1997, p. 23).

The implications of this are addressed by accumulation theory (DeFleur & Dennis, 1994), which predicts that if media messages are seen and heard consistently across media forms, corroborated between those forms, and persistently presented, they will have long-term, powerful effects on audiences. Hence, the accumulation process normalizes looking at images of and thinking about preadolescent and adolescent girls and adult women as sexually available.

In the following sections, I briefly discuss the sociological and cultural context within which girls are sexualized, explore ideas about the
use of adolescent girls' bodies in fashion advertising, and reflect on
the potential consequences of sexual images of girls in illustrative
advertisements.

IDEOLOGY OF THE SEXUALIZED CHILD

In contemporary popular culture, the name Lolita has become synony-
mous with forbidden lust and love of preadolescent, and by extension,
adolescent girls. Looking at sexualized portrayals of girls appropriates
them for male consumption. Defined as "the voyeuristic way men look
at women" (Evans & Gamman, 1995, p. 13), the male gaze appeals to
the scopophilic desire of seeing what is prohibited in relation to the
female body and "projects its phantasy onto the female figure which is
styled accordingly" (Mulvey, 1992, p. 27). An image "orchestrates a
gaze and its pleasurable transgression. The woman's beauty, her very
desirability, becomes a function of certain practices of imagining—
framing, lighting, camera movement, angle " (Berger, 1972, p. 43). This
"fusion of sexual and ideological issues" supports men as "active,
thinking subjects and women as passive, receptive objects" (Caputi,
1994, p. 16). Specifically, Walkerdine (1997) posited, "There is a hidden
and covered-over eroticization of little girls in the everyday gaze at
them" (p. 162). The girl model's return of the gaze offers the simultane-
ous appeal of the vampish and virginal, the forbidden and accessible.
The "pornographication of the American girl" (Junod, 2001, p. 133) is
found in television programs, movies, video games, music videos,
magazines, and popular culture. A plethora of "erotically coded"
images of adolescent girls pervades American popular culture
(Walkerdine, 1997, p. 3). Mohr (1996) described society as saturated
with "pedophilic images" that are "surprisingly common" considering
how we "careen from hysteria to hysteria over the possible sexiness of
children" (p. 64).

Before directing Britney Spears's videos, Gregory Dark directed
pornographic films. Dark described the transition of pornographic pre-
sentations from traditional sources into mainstream popular culture as
"not so much anomalous as inevitable," with an appeal based, at least in
part, on what he referred to as "the lure of jail bait" (Junod, 2001, p. 133).
Hollywood had and has a bevy of beguiling underage beauties. Mary
Pickford, Deanna Durbin, Carroll Baker, Tuesday Weld, Hayley Mills,
and Sue Lyon, all teens when their careers began, became known for

portrayals of underage nymphets "who enjoyed the attentions of men but made a game of arousing them" (Sinclair, 1988, p. 92). Adding to the mystique, Tuesday Weld declared, "I didn't have to play Lolita, I was Lolita" (Sinclair, 1988, p. 108). In the 1970s, 20-something actor Pia Zadora looked like a child and played "jail bait" roles (Burchill, 1986, p. 122). In the 1980s, Brooke Shields was "sold as a fully fashioned grown up sex child" at age 12 in *Pretty Baby*, as was 12-year-old Jodie Foster in *Taxi Driver* (Burchill, 1986, p. 123). Both played characters that were not only sexualized preadolescents, but also prostitutes, adding a layer of invitation, accessibility and possibility to the gaze. In the 1990s, in *Interview with the Vampire*, 9-year-old Kirsten Dunst played a woman trapped in a child's body. Drew Barrymore is the eternal cinematic wild child described in *Esquire* (Hirschorn, 1994) as "thespian, pinup, recovering addict, teenager" and 10 years later in *Elle* as "28, which technically is pushing 30, but she looks 16" (Glock, 2004, p. 122). Sinclair (1988) called these portrayals the "nymphet syndrome" in movies. Magazines also have a version of the teenage tart that cultivates a climate of acceptability. In an extensive study of images of children, crime and violence in *Playboy, Penthouse,* and *Hustler* magazines from 1954 to 1984, Reisman (1990) found 6,004 images of children in cartoons and advertising. Specifically, 27% of *Playboy*, 33% of *Penthouse*, and 47% of *Hustler* comics and ads included children. Importantly, the depictions of child sexual abuse showed the child unharmed or even having benefited from the activity (Reisman, 1990).

In 2001, a Dark art-directed *Rolling Stone* cover featured Christina Aguilera with shorts unzipped and her "athletic tongue licking her lascivious lips " (Junod, 2001, p. 133). Other examples include the cover of the June 1997 issue of *Spy* magazine with Christina Ricci, Alicia Silverstone, and Liv Tyler dressed in their pajamas and the word jailbait. The feature, which declared the state of "the new Lolitocracy," also included other teen girl stars such as Anna Paquin, Neve Campbell, Natalie Portman, Claire Danes, and Brandi. The March 1996 issue of *Playboy* showed a "knock-kneed adolescent in a parochial school uniform depicted as the 'stripper next door'" (Smith, 1996, p. 11). Used in this manner, "pornography can be considered mainstream" (Kilbourne, 1999a, p. 271). Today, Britney Spears, Christina Aguilera, Destiny's Child, and Beyoncé are "just adult enough to be available, just young enough to be non-threatening" (Asher, 2002, p. 23). Throughout the 1980s and 1990s, advertising became the domain of sexual symbolism and seduction where adolescent girls were continually "marketed as highly sexualized beings, ready to cater to the whims of men" (Asher, 2002, p. 23). In the early 1990s, a *New York Times* magazine fashion spread, "Lolita is a Come Back Kid," showcased grown women as adolescent girls, infantilized and powerless, standing around in baby doll-style dresses that reached only to mid-thigh, and hair arranged in bows and barrettes (Kilbourne, 1999b, p. 141). The 14-year-old-and-under emporium Delia's sells thongs with slogans such as "feeling lucky?" and tiny T-shirts proclaiming their wearer a "porn star" (Pollet & Hurwitz, 2004). This " beauty pornography" artificially connects commodified beauty "directly and explicitly to sexuality" (Wolf, 1991, p. 11). Fashion advertising imagery is replete with photographs in which women are "dressed down" like little girls and conversely, young girls are "dressed up" as grown women, offering a veritable visual feast based on pedophiliac fantasy (Cortese, 1999).

In 1980, 14-year-old Brooke Shields informed us that nothing came between her and her Calvins. As the Calvin Klein label grew, so did opportunities for creating controversy. Were the models in the campaign older than 18? What about the little boys and girls bouncing on beds dressed only in their underwear? Calvin Klein representatives stated these advertisements were intended "to capture the same warmth and spontaneity that you find in a family snapshot" (Media Awareness Network, n.d.). In the March/April 2004 issue of *American Photo*, 10 young women are presented as the "faces and figures that define beauty now" (Sterling, 2004). One model is described as "barely 15," a 16-year-old as "the girl the industry wants with abiding passion," a 17-year-old as having "faunlike [sic] beauty and impossibly long limbs," and another lambent girl as a "feline Canadian" (Sterling, 2004, p. 64). The strategy behind these advertisements goes beyond the sexualization of adolescent girls and supports an ideology of lower regard and class status for women and children (Goffman, 1976). Ideology is defined as "those images, concepts and premises which provide the framework through which we represent, interpret, understand, and 'make sense' of some aspect of social existence" (Hall, 2003, p. 89). Althusser (1969) suggested ideology provides "a representation of the imaginary relation of individuals to the real condition of existence" (p. 233).

Responsible for the social construction of sexuality, society shapes sexual desire, and the appropriate or inappropriate targets of that desire, through the controlled production of cultural images (Henslen, 1993). Eventually, beliefs supporting certain behaviors and images become reified or, drawing on Hall (2003), they are articulated in ways that make them appear natural, normal, and hence, unremarkable. Thus, sexualized representations of girls in advertising fuel the "ideology of girl as sexual agent in the imaginary relations between men and girls provided by these images" (Albright, 2002). The willingness, passivity, and availability suggested by these representations have the potential of fueling pedophilic desires.

METHOD

A visual textual analysis of fashion advertisements demonstrates my concern about what appears to be the hypersexualization of underage girls. Galician's (2004) seven-step media analysis model is used to deconstruct the ads. The steps are identification, description, deconstruction, diagnosis, design, debriefing, and dissemination.

Step 1: Identification

The selected ads are for Louis Vuitton, Gadzooks, Baby Phat, and Dsquared, and they appeared in mainstream American print publications (*Vogue, Elle, Cosmopolitan,* and *Lucky*). Although all models are conceivably younger than 18 years of age, the advertisements present, pose, position and make them up to look older, or in the case of Dsquared, a somewhat older looking young woman made up to look Lolita-like.

Step 2: Description

The first advertisement is from Louis Vuitton (LV), a 150-year-old couture house. LV is a high-end, Paris-based, international fashion house with global retail affiliations. In *W* (November 2004), the company ran an advertisement featuring a young woman who appears to be a preteen girl. The photograph is an extreme close-up of the deathly pale body of a young girl, revealed inside an open, red, ethnic folk art smock. Her head is turned to the right, highly glossed pink-pursed lips are slightly parted, vacant eyes glazed over. Her raven tresses flow across a pillow and are held off her forehead by a bright blue velvet ribbon tied in a bow. These details package her in a way that calls upon fairy tale pictures of the apple-poisoned Sleeping Beauty. She's vulnerable and open. The model's flaccid hand is draped across her left breast, baring a diamond studded silver ring and necklace. The necklace's black, snake-like cord wraps around her torso. The only copy is in the large, black words "Louis Vuitton," the tag line "sold exclusively in Louis Vuitton stores," and the company Web address (www.louisvuitton.com).

The second advertisement is for gadzooks, a clothing, cosmetics and accessories company. This ad, which ran in the shopping fever focused magazine *Lucky*, features a big-eyed, auburn-haired, school girl type wearing a black-and-white vertical stripped skirt that barely covers her buttocks. A white, long-sleeved shirt (unbuttoned low) sticks out beneath a tight black vest. Her legs are bare except for the mid-thigh-reaching black hose or boots. She stares directly at the viewer, her heavily made-up eyes seem to dare the spectator to approach. Her plump, pursed ruby red lips reinforce the visual invitation. Her blood-red fingernails stick out from the V of her chest-level, folded arms.

Baby Phat, a clothing company owned, until recently, by rapper Russell Simmons and his wife, supermodel Kimora Lee, uses advertisements that appear to be peopled by young girls. But the models are posed, positioned, and prepared in ways that border on pornographic. On the company Web site (http://www.babyphat.com), celebrities who wear Baby Phat clothing are listed and range in age from Alicia Keys to Madonna. This third example is an advertisement from the Summer/Spring 2003 collection. It displays a doe-eyed white girl with red, pursed, bee-stung lips. She is standing, leaning slightly to her right, wearing a sheer beige wrap that reaches just outside her breasts, which are covered by her long blond, messy, just-been-fucked hairstyle. A lavender and gold sash wraps just around and under her breasts. Her gold patterned blue jeans are not only hung low, but are unzipped. The

top of the pants is folded down, revealing her black silk, bikini underpants, emblazoned with Baby Phat's signature pussycat logo. Despite her downcast eyes, there is still a sense of invitation to the spectator to take her in: "I know this is what you want. You can look at me. What are you waiting for?"

The fourth advertisement is for Marc Jacobs clothing in which the model, who is photographed from above, reclines on her left elbow, wears a tiny strapped cream colored tank top with bright orange short shorts that end at the thigh/hip crease. The shorts have a V-pattern, with the vortex leading to the 1 to 2-inch wide crotch of the shorts. Her legs are parted; one is straight and the other bent, forming a V shape between them. She has candy-type plastic baubles attached to one strap of her top and the MJ monogram on the other. She is very thin and boyish in appearance. Her blondish brown hair is cut very short in a boy-style reminiscent of early Mia Farrow. She gazes up to and directly at the viewer. Her plump peach colored lips are slightly parted.

Step 3: Deconstruction.

Sexuality is an essential component of adolescent curiosity and, based on media representations, a clear path to popularity with peers and, most importantly, with boys. It is a time of conflicting demands—she should appeal to boys, but not too much; appear vampish, but be virginal. While her "parts"—breasts, hips—are developing, she is also learning what those parts do, are expected to do, and what behaviors accompany becoming feminine in American society. She learns to fashion, adopt, and present a false self (Goffman, 1976). On the inside, she might be shy, innocent and insecure. However, as shown in the gadzooks advertisement, for example, the self she shows to the world might be seductively posed, use seductive language, and her appearance might be suggestive. Kate Moss (and all things Calvin) was frequently portrayed as childlike and exploitable—frolicking in her underpants or lying naked on a sofa. Lederer (1995) pointed out "use of the pseudo-child technique—adults dressing and acting like children—is standard fare in pornography" (p. 139).

In the Louis Vuitton and Baby Phat advertisements, the "serious facial expressions, the absence of clothing, the adult hairstyles and makeup, and body gestures and postures" all contribute to making the girl models appear older (Cortese, 1999, p. 65). Conversely, the Marc Jacobs advertisement reverses the younger-to-older-looking technique by applying childlike cosmetics and presentation methods to a model who is clearly not a child.

Step 4: Diagnosis

Myths are recurring stories "that determine a society's perspectives about the world, about themselves, about what behaviors and approaches have meaning or value beyond the real" (Galician, 2004, p. 34). They are the mainstay of media content and communicate a version of reality or truth. Using images of prepubescent and pubescent girls (or grown women made to look that way) in advertising activates and facilitates voyeuristic fantasies about what is appropriate, inappropriate, possessable and safe. Although there are some variations, taboos against sexual predation on children are nearly universal. Yet, there remains a level of curiosity about children as sexual beings, even if that thought is simultaneously expunged.

Step 5: Design

What would be a realistic reframing of these advertisements? I suggest using girls in ads targeted toward girls and portraying them in healthy and realistic ways that have relevance to their lives. If the advertised product or brand is an article of clothing or fashion line, then it logically follows to show that item in a realistic way on realistic-looking examples of the intended target of the advertisement. For example, if the product is a swimsuit, why not show the model swimming? How likely is this? Not very. Despite research that suggests otherwise, sex is still thought to sell, even if what is being sold is not the product per se but rather the idea of a sexual connection between consumer and product.

Step 6: Debriefing

An oppositional reading of these advertisements reveals that what is really for sale goes beyond the product (if the product is even shown in the advertisements). As a site of power, the body is "conceived in terms of being inscribed, constituted or rendered meaningful in representation and culture" (Lewis, 2002, p. 302). In the Louis Vuitton advertisement, for example, the model's body is displayed in ways that communicate availability and willingness. The body as text is decipherable through use of sexual referents. These referents are "message elements (visual or verbal) that serve to elicit or educe sexual thoughts" (Reichert, 2003, p. 23). According to Foucault (in Lewis, 2002), sex is discussed and presented by social institutions with the need to control it, which by extension can also "incite and facilitate modes of sexual experience" (p. 302). A symbolic reading of adolescent girl bodies in fashion advertisements reveals that what is being procured, offered, and sold is an ideology that sexualizes girls and infantilizes women to control them and to legitimize that control. The implications are serious and far-reaching. Three stand out: (a) soft porn portrayals encourage the sexual exploitation of girls; (b) sexual portrayals contribute to the fetishization of girls and women in the media; and (c) passive and eroticized images foster an overall climate that does not value girls' and women's voices or contributions to society.

Step 7: Dissemination

This approach to media analysis speaks to the need for knowledge followed by action. Fortunately, several media literacy groups challenge stereotypical portrayals of girls and women. The Internet provides fertile ground for planting the seeds of online activism. Activist Web sites, such as About-face.org and adiosbarbie.com, teach and use media literacy skills in analyses of images and offer suggestions for taking action, such as writing to companies, boycotting products, organizing local protests, and forming positive images.

CONCLUSION

I don't want to be part of someone's Lolita thing. (Britney Spears)

This brief study explores the portrayals of girls as women and women as girls in fashion advertising. The Lolita look is not only found in fashion advertisements; rather, it is a multimedia phenomenon, the negative effects of which (high teen pregnancy rates, sex slavery, sexually transmitted diseases among teens and preteens, eating disorders, and suicide) are predicted by accumulation theory (DeFleur & Dennis, 1994). Steed (1994) found, for example, that as adult sex offenders "got older, they found their predilections reinforced by mainstream culture, movies and rock videos that glorify violent males who dominate younger, weaker sex objects" (p. 138). Several questions need to be examined in future work. These include (a) What message(s) do images like these send to young girls about sex? (b) What message(s) do images like these send to young boys about sex? (c) What do images like these suggest to older men about girls? (d) In what ways might this be dangerous? (e) Are there connections between how young models are portrayed in fashion magazines and child pornography? and (f) What is the nature of the pornography business and market in terms of adolescent erotics?

As parents, siblings, aunts, uncles, citizens, and scholars, we should be concerned about these questions. In 1997, the dead body of 6-year-old beauty queen, JonBenet Ramsey, was found in the basement of her parents' Boulder, Colorado, home. She had been beaten, and most reports say she had been sexually assaulted (Cottle, 1997, p. 21). Although the perpetrator of the crime remains unknown, media coverage of the investigation featured repeated displays of beauty-contest and promotional photographs that came "from the deceased's pageant portfolio, professional glossies showing the petite 6-year-old dolled up to look twice her age" (Cottle, 1997, p. 21). Some speculate it was this glamorized, sexualized look that motivated her assault and murder. According to Cottle (1997), "despite JonBenet's youth, [she] embodied the dual nature of Woman as The Virgin and The Whore, that nebulous combination of innocence and sexuality that has long titillated Man" (p. 21). JonBenet "was turned into a fashion plate before she could even dress herself" (Cottle, 1997, p. 24).

Similar to content that is regarded as "kiddie porn," sexualized images of girls in advertisements have the potential to contribute to the ongoing and increasing problem of child sexual abuse. These kinds of representations indirectly condone use of children in inappropriate sexual contexts and "not only focus and allow desire but also erase various social and political complications" (Kincaid, 1998, p. 20). The display of children as sexual objects, as sites of spectacle where "pleasure, desire, and commodification intersect" (Giroux, 1996, p. 16), works to desensitize and sets new standards for what is acceptable. The ubiquity of sexual representations in advertising also communicates to children that this is something adults condone. Indeed, the glamorization of this sexual representation celebrates girls as sexual objects. Even more alarming is the persistence of the belief "that children want to be sexually used by adults—paralleling the age-old myth women want to be raped" and supporting the argument of pedophiles that children are asking for "it" (Davidson, 1997, p. 61). However, "girls packaged to sell products or ideas to an adult marketplace are not making active choices to be sexual" (Asher, 2002, p. 22). Similarly, the "double-dealing that dresses the erotic woman as a child" (Kincaid, 1998, p. 105) reinforces the powerlessness of women and children in American society. Has Lolita been revived? Some argue she never died; rather, that by continuously representing her in the media, "the sexualized girl-child 'Lolita' has become a cultural icon" (Albright, 2002, para. 1). Lolita does, indeed, live—not just in the ads, but in the lack of agency little girls have in the process of becoming desirable.

REFERENCES

Albright, J. M. (2002, February 17). *Smoking fetishization and the sexualization of under-aged females.* Retrieved February 27, 2004, from: rcf.usc.edu~albright/lolitashort.htm

Althusser, L. (1969). *For Marx.* London: New Left.

Asher, T. (2002, May/June). Girls, sexuality, and popular culture. *Off Our Backs,* pp. 22-26.

Berger, J. (1972). *Ways of seeing.* London: British Broadcasting Corporation.

Burchill, J. (1986). *Girls on film.* New York: Pantheon.

Caputi, M. (1994). *Voluptuous yearnings: A feminist theory of the obscene.* London: Rowman & Littlefield.

Cortese, A. J. (1999). *Provocateur.* New York: Rowman & Littlefield.

Cottle, M. (1997, November). You've come a long way, maybe. *The Washington Monthly, 29*(11), 20-24.

Davidson, M. (1997, September). Is the media to blame for child sex victims? *USA Today Magazine, 126,* 60-63.

DeFleur, M. L., & Dennis, E. E. (1994). *Understanding mass communication: A liberal arts perspective.* Boston: Houghton Mifflin.

Evans, C., & Gamman, L. (1995). The gaze revisited, or reviewing queer viewing. In P. Burston & C. Richardson (Eds.), *A queer romance: Lesbians, gay men and popular culture* (pp. 13-56). London: Routledge.

Galician, M. L. (2004). *Sex, love, and romance in the mass media.* Mahwah, NJ: Erlbaum.

Giroux, H. A. (1996, February). What comes between kids and their Calvins? *The New Art Examiner, 23,* 16-21.

Glock, A. (2004, January). Miss congeniality. *Elle, 19*(221), 118-126.

Goffman, E. (1976). *Gender advertisements.* Cambridge, MA: Harvard University Press.

Hall, S. (2003). The whites of their eyes: Racist ideologies and the media. In G. Dines & J. M. Humez (Eds.), *Gender, race, and class in media: A text-reader* (2nd ed., pp. 89-93). Thousand Oaks, CA: Sage.

Henslen, J. M. (1993). *Sociology: A down-to-earth approach* (6th ed.). Boston: Allyn & Bacon.

Hirschorn, M. (1994). Drew Barrymore is. *Esquire, 121,* 69.

Junod, T. (2001). The devil Greg Dark. *Esquire, 135*(2), 130-135.

Kilbourne, J. (1999a). *Can't buy my love: How advertising changes the way we think and feel.* New York: Simon & Schuster.

Kilbourne, J. (1999b). *Deadly persuasion: Why women and girls must fight the addictive power of advertising.* New York: The Free Press.

Kincaid, J. R. (1998). *Erotic innocence: The culture of child molesting.* Durham, NC: Duke University Press.

Lederer, L. J. (1995). The price we pay: The case against racist speech, hate propaganda, and pornography. In L. J. Lederer & R. Delgado (Eds.), *The price we pay: The case against racist speech, hate propaganda, and pornography* (pp. 131-140). New York: Hill & Wang.

Lewis, J. (2002). *Cultural studies: The basics.* London: Sage.

Media Awareness Network. (n.d.). *Calvin Klein: A case study.* Retrieved February 19, 2004, from ca/english/resources/educational/handouts/ethics/calvin_klein_case_study.cfm

Mohr, R. D. (1996). The pedophilia of everyday life. *Newsweek, 127*(26), 64-65.

Mulvey, L. (1992). Visual pleasure and narrative cinema. In M. Merck (Ed.), *The sexual subject: A screen reader in sexuality* (pp. 22-33). New York: Routledge.

Nabokov, V. (1958). *Lolita.* New York: Putnam.

Odell, P. (2002). Abercrombie markets children's thongs, riles critics. *Direct Marketing Business Intelligence.* Retrieved February 27, 2004, from http://www.directmag.com/ar/marketing_ abercrombie_markets_childrens/

Pollet, A., & Hurwitz, P. (2004, January 6). Strip till you drop. *The Nation.* Retrieved February 19, 2004, from: http://www.alternet.org

Reichert, T. (2003). What is sex in advertising? Perspectives from consumer behavior and social science research. In T. Reichert & J. Lambiase (Eds.), *Sex in advertising: Perspectives on the erotic appeal* (pp. 11-38). Mahwah, NJ: Erlbaum.

Reisman, J. A. (1990). *Images of children, crime and violence in* Playboy, Penthouse, *and* Hustler (Report supported by the Office of Juvenile Delinquency Prevention Program, U.S. Department of Justice). Lafayette, LA: Huntington House.

Rich, F. (1997, January 18). Let me entertain you. *The New York Times*, Sect. 1, p. 23.

Sinclair, M. (1988). *Hollywood Lolitas: The nymphet syndrome in the movies.* New York: Henry Holt.

Smith, L. (1996). *Playboy*: R & R for pedophiles. *Action Agenda: Challenging Sexist and Violent Media Through Education and Action, 2,* 11.

Steed, J. (1994). *Our little secret: Confronting child sexual abuse in Canada.* Toronto, Canada: Random House.

Sterling, W. (2004, March/April). The top ten models. *American Photo, XV*(2), 64-67.

Walkerdine, V. (1997). *Daddy's girl: Young girls and popular culture.* Cambridge, MA: Harvard University Press.

Weeks, J. (2005). Fetish. In T. Bennett, L. Grossberg, & M. Morris (Eds.), *New keywords: A revised vocabulary of culture and society.* (pp. 130-132). Malden, MA: Blackwell.

Wolf, N. (1991). *The beauty myth.* New York: William Morrow.

Part III

Bodies and Difference

4

NippleMania

Black Feminism, Corporeal Fragmentation, and the Politics of Public Consumption

Kimberly Wallace-Sanders

Brittany Cooper

> [The number of] seconds that Janet Jackson's breast was exposed during Super Bowl halftime show: 2
>
> The rank of "Janet Jackson boob" among most-searched words in internet history: 1
>
> The value of "personal injury" a Tennessee woman says she suffered from the incident: $75,000
>
> The cost of advertising during Super Bowl, per second: $75,000
>
> —*Facing South:*
> *A Progressive Southern News Report* (2004)

On February 1, 2004, during the Super Bowl halftime show, singer-actress Janet Jackson's costume was ripped open to reveal her right breast during her musical performance with Justin Timberlake. Seven months later, on September 22, 2004, the Federal Communications

Commission (FCC) fined Viacom and 20 CBS television affiliates a total of $550,000 for violating "broadcast indecency standards" (Ahrens & de Moraes, 2004). Janet Jackson was forced to apologize,[1] and she was subsequently banned from significant television and film appearances, including the 2004 Grammy Awards.

Jackson also lost her contract to play Lena Horne in a biographical film, a role given to her at Horne's request. Justin Timberlake, on the other hand, was not required to apologize for tearing her costume open, and there were no similar consequences to his career. In the uproar following the Super Bowl halftime incident, it was as if Janet Jackson's breast existed separately from the rest of her body—as if, in fact, it were a separate entity altogether.

We find this to be emblematic of a long history of sexist and racist representations of black women being reduced to their body parts. From uncontrollable hair or dramatic hairstyles to enormous "bootylicious" buttocks to breasts that are maternal and full of milk or sagging and pendulous National Geographic-style, the Black woman's body is fragmented and, as Deborah Willis and Carla Williams (2002) stated, "reduced to its exaggerated parts" (p. 101).

During this maelstrom of publicity, Janet Jackson was barraged with questions about whether the incident was an accident or a publicity stunt, and who was responsible for her "indecent exposure" during a program in which all of the female dancers wore tight-fitting costumes and gyrated while Justin Timberlake sang: "I'm gonna have you naked by the end of this song." We don't presume that Janet Jackson is a feminist or that the exposure of her breast at the Super Bowl halftime show, whether intentional or accidental, needs to be defended. We suggest what made Jackson's body so indecent, so intolerable, was that she was wearing something meant to give herself sexual pleasure while she performed publicly.[2] Did she intend to make her autoeroticism public as part of a publicity stunt? Perhaps she did. But if that remains the central question, we will miss the larger meaning of the racist and sexist responses to Jackson's exposure. Most Black feminists would agree that we must continue to both expand and to contemporize our discussions of the Black female body.

This chapter is our contribution to a tradition of progressive and collaborative Black feminist dialogue. We seek to add our Black feminist, cross-generational voices—we are nearly 20 years apart in age—and present an alternative reading of the popular media's emphasis on Jackson's breast.

Three days after the Super Bowl, an Emory University law school student named "Adam" created a Web site entitled "Janet Jackson Breast Cupcakes" (www.amateurgourmet.com/the_amateur_gourmet/

2004/02/janet_Jackson) and stated that his mission was simple: He wanted to turn a close-up photograph of Janet Jackson's breast "into a work of edible art" (see Fig. 4.1). Adam frets about "creating the perfect breast color" and enlists the help of a friend who e-mails him this message: "Janet is more latte than bitter-sweet, I'd say. You could fla-

Fig. 4.1. Janet Jackson Breast Cupcakes: February 4, 2004.

vor the icing with coffee actually, and that would be yummy." Adam completed his edible Janet Jackson breast by using a Hershey's kiss for the nipple and white icing to duplicate what he called: "the nipple shield that boggled the minds of so many viewers the night of the Super Bowl."[3]

The Janet Jackson cupcakes are a perversely perfect echo of Black feminist author bell hooks' (1992) anecdote at the beginning of her semi-nal essay "Selling Hot Pussy," where she reflects on her memory of walking into a restaurant with White colleagues who find a display of deserts shaped like "gigantic chocolate breasts with nipples—huge edi-ble tits," more entertaining than offensive (p. 61). For hooks, the choco-late breasts are a "sign of displaced longing for a racist past" and for the ubiquitous mammy figure so prevalent in American culture and con-sciousness: "I look at these dark breasts and think about the representa-tion of black female bodies in popular culture" (p. 62).

The updated chocolate breasts that Adam concocted may be the ulti-mate example of "anti-mammy" breasts because the nipple shield that "boggled the minds of so many" was actually a nipple piercing, and per-haps this is what was so shocking to the viewing audience: a breast that clearly announced itself as more sexual than maternal and undoubtedly unsuitable for nurturing, a nipple pierced and decorated perhaps solely for the erotic pleasure of the performer.

How should we respond to the fact that Adam does not try to repli-cate the entire halftime incident in an edible art scene? For example, not only does he decide against creating Jackson's entire body in cake form, but it never occurs to him to bake a vanilla Justin Timberlake at all. He does not even make a small, white chocolate Timberlake hand to display near his Janet Jackson breast cupcakes. Timberlake has disappeared so effectively that the incident, now being called "Nipplegate" (Tyre, 2004), rarely uses his name at all. It was Janet Jackson's breast that was so offensive. The Janet Jackson breast cupcakes and hooks' example of "gigantic chocolate breasts" help to create a critical framework linking Black feminist theory and corporeal fragmentation with the politics of consumption in popular culture. Again, our aim is to shift the focus from the simplistic and superficial conversations about whether or not this was a publicity stunt to a more nuanced consideration of corporeal fragmentation: the many ways that Black women's bodies appear in pieces, bite-sized and easily digestible, and the ways that this representation deters acknowledging and accepting black women's sexual agency and by extension their existence as whole human beings.

This corporeal fragmentation results in more than "tits and ass" in blackface: It constitutes a specific kind of violence against African-American women and their humanity. For more than a decade, Black and mainstream feminists have launched salient and stinging arguments against this overemphasis on Black female sexuality. Yet, the noise surrounding Jackson's breast exposure has largely interpreted this moment as if it were unusual or unique. In her most recent book, Black feminist Patricia Hill Collins (2004) pointed out that from "the display of Sarah Baartman as a sexual 'freak' of nature in the early 19th century[4] to Josephine Baker dancing bare-breasted for Parisian society to the animal skin bikinis worn by 'bootylicious' Destiny's Child to the fascination with Jennifer Lopez's buttocks, women of African descent have been associated with an animalistic, wild sexuality" (p. 27). Along with this wild sexuality, we see the fragmentation of Black women's bodies into commodities that sanction their corporeal dismemberment.

The following illustrations reveal a historic preoccupation with Black women's breasts, which are served up for public consumption in ways that simply did not occur for White women before the 1950s. Each illustration is a reminder that Black women have historically been devalued and dehumanized to such a degree that "Black nipples" became toys for White children to play with.

In 1861, the clerk's office of the District Court for the Eastern District of Pennsylvania produced a number of patriotic envelopes. Patriotic Cover 8944 shows an African-American woman with one breast fully exposed so that she can nurse the enormous White baby on her lap.[5] (Fig. 4.2) Her

Fig. 4.2. An Institution of the "CSA" decorative envelope Courtesy of the Boston Athenaeum, Boston, MA.

breast serves as the return address location for the envelope.

In the late 1980s, Italian photographer Olivero Toscani created an advertisement for Benetton, the clothing retailer, featuring a close-up of a White infant nursing at the breast of a headless, dark-skinned Black woman wearing only a red Shetland sweater. Her right breast, including the nipple, is completely exposed. The advertisement was criticized by African Americans, yet it won more advertising awards than any other image in Benetton's advertising history (Fig. 4.3).

Fig. 4.3. 1988 Benetton advertisement courtesy of Benetton Spa Group

Diminutive Black mammy "nipple dolls" from the 1920s were made from rubber bottle nipples painted black.[6] The dolls are posed with tiny White baby dolls cradled in their arms and are considered an excellent investment among collectors of southern Americana (Fig. 4.4).

There is no date on the box of this set of swizzle sticks for stirring drinks (Fig. 4.5). There were several versions of this once-popular product, and all displayed silhouettes of six naked African women of various ages on the box. The text describes "Zulu Lulu" in terms of her aging breasts: "Look what a few years have done to Lulu! Nifty at 15, spiffy at 20, sizzling at 25, perky at 30, declining at 35, droopy at 40." The box also depicts cartoonish images of an African woman hiding behind a palm tree and one of the swizzle sticks in a cocktail glass: Zulu Lulu on the rocks. Zulu Lulu is often auctioned

Fig. 4.4. Black nipple dolls from the 1920s, author's collection

Fig. 4.5. Zulu lulu swizzle sticks from eBay site. www.ebay.com

on E-bay's Web site as "Black humor swizzle sticks."[7] The starting bid for one such box was $9.95.

Willis and Williams' (2002) book, *The Black Female Body: A Photographic History*, chronicles a long and deeply troubling past in which Black women's bodies are a disruptive force in American culture. They observe that beginning with Saartjie (Sarah) Baartman, "some famous black female bodies became a bona fide part of the popular culture, their images etched on the public conscience" (p. 84). Whatever Janet Jackson's success amounted to before the moment her right breast was exposed, her breast and the accompanying nipple piercing have become a "bona fide part of the popular culture . . . etched on the public conscience" and essentially eclipsing the rest of her career.

Feminist Iris Young (1998) claimed that the exposed nipple is taboo "because (it is) quite literally, physically and functionally, undecidable in the split between motherhood and sexuality. One of the most subversive things feminism can do is affirm this undecidability of motherhood and sexuality" (p. 127). There is nothing "undecidable" about Jackson's pierced nipple; it was clearly sexualized—and sexualized for her pleasure. The pierced nipple may well be the most obvious, and also the most disturbing, example of a nonmaternal breast.

Is a Black breast that is not maternal more disturbing than a White one? Apparently so.

Young (1998) also argued that our "phallocentric culture tends to think of a woman's breasts as belonging to her husband, her lover, her baby; it's hard to image a woman's breasts as being her own" (p. 125). Young's observation was affirmed by African-American comedian Chris Rock in his 2004 HBO performance, "Never Scared." Early in his routine, Rock shouts: "Janet Jackson showed her titty on national television. And a 40-year-old titty at that! You're not supposed to show that! Twenty-year-old titty, that's community titty. Forty-year-old titty, that's your man's titty!" Rock's categories of breast possession emphasizes the line drawn between decent (topless 20-year-olds) and indecent (topless 40-year-olds) and, by extension, tolerable and intolerable bodies. His comments also resonate with the Zulu Lulu swizzle sticks that portray six naked, African women as being "nifty at 15" but "droopy at 40."

Rock's assertion that Jackson "showed her titty" isolates Jackson as the deviant perpetrator of indecent self-exposure. In his version of the Super Bowl halftime show, Justin Timberlake is rendered not just innocent, but invisible: Janet Jackson simply appeared on stage, opened her costume and intentionally bared her breast.

Rock's two categories of breast possession are age-sensitive—"20-year-old titty" is acceptable for public exposure because the nature of the entertainment industry demands that Jackson compete with "20-

something" performers like Beyonce and Ashanti. Certainly, Jackson's body still looks more like a 20-year-old than a 40-year-old body, and Rock's reminder of Jackson's age helped to make Jackson seem desperate for publicity, which further exonerated and displaced Timberlake's role in the "costume malfunction." Rock suggests that not only is this something "freaky Janet" would do but also something we should expect her to do—and thus not a stunt by Timberlake for his own publicity. Rock's second category of breast possession, "your man's titty," suggests Janet's breast is unacceptable because it belongs exclusively to her (presumably) male partner. Here, Rock completely dismisses Jackson's earlier comments that claim her breasts for her own pleasure.

In July 2000, Jackson appeared on the television show *Oprah* extolling the advantages of her pierced nipples. When Oprah asked if the piercing was painful, Jackson smiled and said coyly, "A little, but in a good way." She goes on to say that feeling her clothes rub against the piercing assures her of several hundred small orgasms throughout the day. With a nod to Spike Lee's film *She's Gotta Have It*, if we ask, "Whose breast is this?" Jackson's resounding response is "mine." Jackson's appearance on *Oprah* may well be one of the most public assertions of Black female sexual agency that we have witnessed.

Does Jackson's overt sexuality play into the stereotype of the oversexed, promiscuous Jezebel that has haunted Black women for generations? Do Black women who assert their own sexual agency reinforce the Jezebel stereotype or defy it? Historically, in terms of the representation of African-American women, the Jezebel is depicted as a having an insatiable appetite for sex. Nearly all of the most well-known African-American female pop singers are represented as being very sexual in terms of the clothes they wear, the lyrics they sing, and are always linked or connected to the Jezebel stereotype—the way that large Black women are too often linked to the mammy stereotype—making the Jezebel stereotype the defining bottom line preventing Black women from any kind of sexual self-expression and thus preventing them from expressing themselves as healthy human beings.

What happens to Black female sexual agency when we move from the female-dominated sphere of a daytime talk show like Oprah to the male-dominated sphere of professional football and the Super Bowl? The discussion that allowed a Black woman to describe her own sense of sexual agency to an applauding (largely female) audience shifts dramatically when the audience is largely male. More specifically, it pits Black womanhood against popular public misconceptions and stereotypes. Unfortunately, any progressive notions of healthy, black female sexuality—especially ones that includes autoeroticism—seem to get lost in the fallout. It is certainly true that the Super Bowl halftime show was filled with sexually suggestive performances, including earlier ones by Timberlake (without Janet) and rapper Nelly, whose misogynist videos were so offensive to a group of Spelman College women that they successfully banned him from a campus appearance. Increasingly, part of Jackson's development of a distinctive public persona, separate from her membership in the famous Jackson family, has been the portrayal of herself as a highly sexualized person, committed to autoeroticism as a form of sexual expression.

Jackson's very public celebration and discussion of the sexual pleasure that she derives from her nipple and genital piercings has provided her a way to control the manner in which her body is marketed and her image as a sexual object is commodified for other's sexual pleasure. The Super Bowl halftime show relies on commodified images like Jackson's to secure its success as a public spectacle, and Janet Jackson's ability to market herself in a particular way assumes that she has the power to determine the limits and boundaries of public access to her body.

Mediated sports events in the United States in general rely on the interlocking relationship between the production of commodity and desire of the public for mass consumption. Sut Jhally (1989) argued that "the cultural and ideological role of sport in advanced capitalism (especially in the United States) is impossible to understand without locating the centrality of commodity relations to the framework of which it is a part. If we follow through the political economy of professional and college sports, we will see that each stage is dominated by a concern with commodities" (p. 79). The Super Bowl is no exception.

The Super Bowl reinforces traditional notions of masculinity based on physical aggression and by serving as an entertainment space that included Janet Jackson as spectacle in a performance as hypersexual Black female entertainer. This space also re-inscribes historical race and gender meanings that are associated with consumer desires within what hooks (1994) referred to as "White supremacist, capitalist, patriarchal society" (p. 5). The exposure of Jackson's pierced nipple forced an overwhelmingly male, American audience to acknowledge her as being active in the process of erotically experiencing her own body and to some degree rendering her male audience unnecessary to her sexual pleasure. Although Timberlake is responsible for exposing Jackson's breast, it is her star-shaped nipple shield that made the performance all the more spectacular. Jackson resisted society's circumscription of Black, female sexual agency by daring to wear the nipple shield for her own autoeroticism. Whether the exposure of her breast was intentional or not, historical understandings of the relationship of White men to Black women's bodies suggest a profound discomfort with a Black woman attempting to own her own sexuality. The audience's sense of entitlement—although perhaps unwitting—to a sexualized performance from Jackson makes this a historical battle mapped onto a contemporary field.

Given the public's investment in the right to spectatorship at sporting events, audiences also are invested by implication in the production and consumption of spectacle—in this case, in the spectacle of performing bodies. Furthermore, the spectacle that was the Super Bowl halftime show was a particularly public form of spectacle broadcast on CBS, one of five major, non-cable, television networks. In a sexualized spectacle, such as the performance with Timberlake and Jackson, the antics are designed to titillate the audience without surpassing the bounds mandated as decent versus indecent outlined in federal regulations standards. Had the performance occurred successfully, Timberlake would have sung his line from the song "Rock Your Body": "I'm gonna have you naked by the end of this song," then ripped the black leather covering from Jackson's breast, leaving the thin, red, lacy, see-through bra in place as a covering. Timberlake's failure to keep the thin veil intact is reminiscent of what Beverly Guy-Sheftall (2002) argued characterizes Black women's sexuality: "the private being made public, which subverts conventional notions about the need to hide and render invisible women's sexuality and private parts" (p. 18).

In other words, Jackson entered the performance as a Black woman owning her own sexuality unapologetically. She left as a victim of an American gendered and racialized discourse that validates the right of White males to enjoy sexually suggestive performances by Black women but expects them to maintain the moral integrity of these performances. Ironically, hypersexual representations of Black women are successful only to the extent that Black women can be viewed as immoral agents. The FCC's judgment reinforced historical notions of Black women as being outside the discourse of "decency" because of their brazen and dangerous sexuality. Little attention was paid to the fact that Janet did not expose her own breast. The American public seems incapable of believing that she might have been a victim of a social embarrassment.

Black women and their bodies have always had a troubled relationship to the state, which has used its power to inscribe their sexual and expressive, not to mention reproductive, agency to promote its own economic gain. Even when Black women have managed to achieve a large degree of economic privilege, as in Jackson's case, their class status has not saved them from the policing and containment of their bodies when those bodies are deemed inappropriate, which they all too often are. The FCC's policing of Black women in the case of Jackson and also in the 2002 case of the singer/songwriter Sarah Jones suggests that the government has a particular investment in containing the possibilities of Black female liberation. Jones' rap song "Your Revolution Will Not Happen Between These Thighs" is a Black feminist denunciation of misogynist hip-hop and rock lyrics that uses those lyrics, which are regularly played on the radio, in order to critique them. An Oregon radio station was fined $7,000 for broadcasting Jones' song, claiming that the song's use of the term "six-foot, blow job machine" was in violation of federal standards—despite the use of similar wording in many rap songs.[8]

To argue that the 2003 halftime incident is a result of White capitalist patriarchy without acknowledging that the president of FCC was Michael Powell, who is an African American, would be irresponsible. But acknowledging his race does not undercut the ways in which Powell and his conservative politics are complicit in promoting patriarchal notions and values.

Within the scope of this chapter, it has been difficult to find space to trace the nuances and historical implications of the connections between Janet Jackson and Justin Timberlake. Timberlake has become virtually invisible in this act of public "indecency." What emerges is the sense that America's anxieties continually get played out on the embattled Black female body.

In the aftermath of the incident, Timberlake did not stand in solidarity with Jackson, a fact that cost him much of his African-American crossover fan base. Timberlake had enjoyed temporary status as an "honorary Black" performer since his videos routinely played on Black Entertainment Television (BET) and he performed at the 2003 BET Awards. Furthermore, he has been romantically linked to Jackson and has enjoyed pop status precisely because his dance and performance moves are reminiscent of Janet's brother, Michael. To what extent does the flimsy and malfunctioning breast covering reveal or serve as a metaphor for the flimsy separation between blackness and whiteness in the United States, particularly in regard to the "authentic" and the "performed" aspects of racial identity? How might this metaphor implicate Justin Timberlake's experiences as a White performer who is frequently granted "honorary blackness" by the popular media? These questions should be examined in the space of a larger work and dialogue that will certainly add another dimension to thinking about the public role of Black women's sexuality.

On December 27, 2006, almost 3 full years after the Super Bowl incident, Janet Jackson appeared on *Oprah* to discuss it for the "first and last time." When Oprah Winfrey asked: "Was it planned?" those three words needed no further explanation or detail—everyone knows what "it" referred to. Janet responded: "No. What people don't understand is, he was to rip the piece off that he did, but more came off than was supposed to. It was a very embarrassing moment." When asked if she felt

Timberlake "left her to take the blame alone," she replied: "Well, all the emphasis was put on me, not on Justin."

In a broader sense, "Nipplegate" was not just about Janet Jackson and the Super Bowl, just as Black nipple dolls are not about toys and "Zulu Lulu" is not about mixed drinks. It is really about Black women and all women whose body parts are being consumed by a misogynist, racist culture.

NOTES

1. Twenty-four hours after the Super Bowl, Janet issued an apology that she later said she regretted making: "Before I sat down to record the apology, I asked them, 'Why am I apologizing for an accident?'"
2. Jackson was wearing a nipple ring, described in most press accounts as a "shield."
3. Adam refers to Jackson's nipple decoration as a shield. We use the terms *nipple shield, nipple ring,* and *nipple decoration* interchangeably.
4. Baartman, a young Khosian woman from Southern Africa who became known as the Hottentot Venus, was exhibited in England and France, where her enlarged buttocks were a focus of popular fascination. After her death at the age of 26, her genitals were dissected and cast in wax for future public display. See also Fausto-Sterling (2002).
5. Courtesy of the Boston Athenaeum, Boston, Mass.
6. Lavitt (1982) noted that "rubber nipple dolls were popular in the 1920s and 1930s and were always Black. Many hold White babies" (pp. 40-42). See also Coleman (1971) and Lavitt (1983).
7. These items can easily be found for sale at E-bay. One seller attempted to distance himself from the racist product that he was auctioning: "Content of this auction does not reflect my values or opinions as they were probably mfg prior to my birth. Even though these may be in Poor Taste I am just selling as a vintage Humor Collectable item. Any other explanation/motive is simply incorrect. Stir sticks depict a woman between the age of 15 and 40 . . ."
8. See Hines (2004). For the full text of the song's lyrics, see http://www.fcc.gov/eb/Orders/2001/da011212.doc. In February 2003, the FCC reversed its initial ruling, declaring that the song was not patently offensive.

REFERENCES

Ahrens, F., & de Moraes, L. (2004, September 23). FCC throws flag at CBS's halftime play; commissioners propose $550,000 indecency fine. *The Washington Post*, final edition.

"Bowl Barings" in FACING SOUTH: A progressive Southern news report. www.southernstudies.org, Feb. 6, 2004, issue 71.

Coleman, E. (1971). *The collector's encyclopedia of dolls*. New York: Crown.

Collins, P. H. (2004). *Black sexual politics: African Americans, gender, and the new racism*. New York: Routledge.

Fausto-Sterling, A. (2002). Gender, race, and nation: The comparative anatomy of Hottentot women in Europe, 1815-1817. In K. Wallace-Sanders (Ed.), *Skin deep, spirit strong: The Black female body in American culture* (pp. 66-98). Ann Arbor: University of Michigan Press.

Hines, M. (2004), *The strange case of Sarah Jones*. Retrieved from http://www.fep-project.org/commentaries/sarahjones.html.

Gruneau, R. (1983). *Class, sports, and social development*. Amherst: University of Massachusetts Press.

Guy-Sheftall, B. (2002). The body politic: Black female sexuality and the nineteenth century. In K. Wallace-Sanders (Ed.), *Skin deep, spirit strong: The Black female body in American culture* (pp. 13-36). Ann Arbor: University of Michigan Press.

hooks, b. (1992). Selling hot pussy: Representations of Black female sexuality in the cultural marketplace. In b. hooks (Ed.), *Black looks: Race and representation* (pp. 61-78). Boston: South End Press.

hooks, b. (1994). *Outlaw culture: Resisting representations*. New York: Routledge.

Jhally, S. (1989). Cultural studies and the sports/media complex. In A. Wrenner (Ed.) *Media, sports and society* (pp. 70-96). Newbury Park, CA: Sage.

Lavitt, W. (1982). *American folk dolls*. New York: Knopf.

Lavitt, W. (1983). *Knopf collectors guide to American antiques: Dolls*. New York: Knopf.

Tyre, P. (2004, March 8). Shocking the jocks. *Newsweek*. Available at www.keep-media.com/pubs/Newsweek/2004/03/08/388321?extID=10037&oliID=229.

Willis, D., & Williams, C. (2002). *Black female body: A photographic history*. Philadelphia: Temple University Press.

Young, I. (1998). Breasted experience: The look and the feeling. In R. Weitz (Ed.), *The politics of women's bodies*. P. 127). New York: Oxford University Press.

5

"Made to be the Maid?"

An Examination of the Latina as Maid in Mainstream Film and Television

Rosa E. Soto

I was watching films one day when I noticed something similar throughout them that I never noticed before. I wondered how this similarity spoke to the way in which narratives are complicit in perpetuating a negative image of the Latina experience. Each of the films I was watching had a Latina maid. A few of these films, in just the last 20 years, include *Down and Out in Beverly Hills* (1986), *First Wives Club* (1996), and *Maid in Manhattan* (2002).[1] Just a few television shows include *Designing Women* (1986-1993), *Veronica's Closet* (1997-2000) and *Will & Grace* (1998-2006). Latina maids also appear in secondary roles in shows like *Who's the Boss, Sex and the City, CSI: Miami, Seinfeld, Bones, Nip/Tuck,* and a plethora of other TV shows and films.

Understanding just how the Latina maid functions in this popular discourse leads to an understanding of the politics of racial relationships and the politics of a Hollywood discourse. Thus, it is essential to explore the ways that the Latina maid or servant functions for mainstream Anglo—and sometimes Latino—audiences. My goal in taking a closer look at the significance of Latina representation is suggested in Krin Gabbard's (2004) *Black Magic: Anglo Hollywood and African-American Culture*, which examines the complicated politics of African Americans in films. Gabbard's book sheds light on the ways in which Angloness or Anglo people remain in "unquestioned centrality" in American films (p. 7). As Richard Dyer (1997) noted in his text *White*, "Research—into books, museums, the press, advertising, films, television . . . shows that in Western representation Anglos are overwhelmingly and disproportionately predominant, have the central and elaborated roles and above all else are placed as the norm, the ordinary, the standard" (p. 3).

UNDERSTAND HOW RACIAL "OTHERS" ARE CONSTRUCTED

It is in recognizing how Angloness is presented as a standard, and in analyzing it, that we can come to understand how racial "others" are constructed. Gabbard (2004) further argued that, "there is no better way of looking at how Angloness is constructed in movies than by examining how blackness makes these constructions work" (p. 8). Looking at the image of the Latina maid in film, television, and in culture in general allows us to understand the role of the marginalized Latina in Hollywood and the racial mythology about the nature of the Latina in general. And although the number of Latina maids in film and television may seem a coincidence, the overwhelming representation of them in that role suggests an ideological *need* for them by mainstream, Anglo audiences.

The image of the Latina servant or maid in film and television, from the beginning of the 1980s to today, performs a number of different narrative purposes, some of which have been fulfilled by different ethnic or racial groups in the past. Each, however, speaks to the ways in which the Latina maid is a necessary character for her Anglo counterparts. First, the Latina maid or servant clarifies the generally Anglo main protagonist, who most often is her employer, as a "classed" individual in that she signifies the class status that the Anglo protagonist has achieved. For example, in the 2002 film *The Banger Sisters*, the Latina maid serves to illustrate just how much Susan Sarandon's character, Lavinia Kingsley, has come up in the world. In the TV show *Veronica's Closet*, the Latina maid serves as an indicator of the wealth Veronica Chase has achieved through modeling.

Second, the Latina maid serves the function of allowing Anglo protagonists and characters to see themselves and to be represented as good and altruistic individuals worthy of care and devotion from their servants even in light of obvious character flaws. For example, in *First Wives Club*, Cynthia (an upper class woman played by Stockard Channing) gives Teresa, her Latina maid, an expensive pearl necklace as thanks for years of loyal service right before Cynthia jumps out of a window. The present indicates that Cynthia cares about her servant, even as she is preserved as a martyr for first wives everywhere. In *Maid in Manhattan*, the Latina maid, played by Jennifer Lopez, foregrounds the male Anglo character's dedication to the working class, helping to establish his worthiness as he struggles against an abusive political system. Lopez's character provides Chris Marshall (played by Ralph Fiennes) with an understanding of a class oppression that allows him to gain the trust of and help minority residents of a working-class neighborhood and thus become the film's hero.

Additionally, the function of the Latina maid serves to allow Anglo protagonists a sense of altruism as they help Latinas/os gain employment and provide for their own families. In *Down and Out in Beverly Hills*, the Anglo protagonists, David and Barbara Whiteman (played by Richard Dreyfuss and Bette Midler) proclaim themselves "good people" who have helped the underclass minority by employing them as maids and gardeners in their homes, as well as factory workers in David's hanger factory. On *Will & Grace*, Karen often forces Rosario, the Latina maid, to acknowledge all that she has done for her, from giving Rosario a job to getting her a green card.[2]

Third, the Latina maid serves as ethnic flavor for the Anglo protagonists. Ethnic "flavor" is how we understand that the Anglo characters are hip to the world, understanding culture and ethnicity in an ever-changing society. As such, having a Latina maid helps them achieve a perceived global perspective. In *Down and Out in Beverly Hills*, Barbara provides Carmen (played by Elizabeth Peña) with a job, and Carmen provides language and food lessons to Barbara, thus establishing Barbara's hipness in terms of a global sense of "culture." Thus, the Whitemans can present themselves as caring about the social welfare of Latinos/as while at the same time demonstrating that a personal relationship can exist that is mutually beneficial for both employee and employer.

Finally, Latina maids are often sexy servants (a throwback to the 1930s' Latina "spitfires") who threaten the status quo of the Anglo upper middle class and middle class. Their exuberant sexuality is both an ethnic threat to the assumed purity of sexuality within the Anglo household (specifically that of the Anglo woman), and also a threat if she uses that sexuality to break up the marriage and, hence, the value system of the Anglo household and Anglo society. In both the film *Big Trouble* and

Down and Out in Beverly Hills, the Latina maid threatens the seemingly secure and untouchable status of the Anglo marriage. These Latina maids are used by Anglo male protagonists as sexual relief from the hum-drum reality of their suburban lifestyles. Additionally, they are used by the Anglo female protagonists as the reason their marriages fail. These maids serve as scapegoats for the Anglo middle class, who would displace blame onto the Latina maid for their descent from privilege rather than fault political, economic, and social realities.

It is important, however, to explain that these roles are often conflated within one another. Therefore, a Latina maid like Carmen in *Down and Out in Beverly Hills* provides ethnic flavor in lieu of cultural lessons while simultaneously serving as a visual marker of the upper middle-class status of the Anglo family. At the same time, she is the sexy Latina temptress who threatens the Whitemans' marriage. When not threatening to break up a marriage, the Latina maid may function in film to affirm the power of love to resolve all manner of inequality. For example, as the ethnic "other" in *Maid in Manhattan*, Marisa confirms for an Anglo audience that ethnic and class differences will melt away in the light of love.

These characterizations of the Latina maid are used to complicate, problematize or situate Anglo middle-class or upper middle-class value systems as privileged and desirable, as well as to naturalize the social location of Latinos/as. I begin with an analysis of the film *The Banger Sisters*, which addresses the ideological process of denial that undergirds a classed sense of "Angloness," and then return to *Down and Out in Beverly Hills* to show how one character in one film can embody all of the functions and characterizations of the Latina maid that are described here.

MAID TO BE INVISIBLE

In the 2002 film *The Banger* Sisters, actress Goldie Hawn plays Suzette (no last name given), a bartender whose life has never measured up to her expectations in the 1960s, when she "banged" (slang for "having sex with") well-known rockers for a living. She seeks out her left-it-all-behind friend, Lavinia Kingsley (played by Susan Sarandon), an upper middle-class conservative who neither acknowledges her old life nor the reality that her current situation is stultifying. Suzette becomes frustrated by what she imagines is Lavinia's pretend existence, and she questions Lavinia's recollection of history, her position as a woman and her views about class oppression. One crucial scene establishes both

Suzette's superiority as a working-class woman who understands "true oppression" and explains the taken-for-granted system of exploitation in which the upper middle class depends on the work of invisible servants. Suzette lectures Lavinia's spoiled children, Hannah and Ginger, because they refuse to wash their own dishes. As they argue about the dishes, one of the young girls points out to Suzette that it is Rosa who normally does them. Suzette then asks the girls if they know Rosa's last name,[3] to which they reply, "No." Suzette then states, "You have people wiping your ass, and you don't even know their names." After this confrontation, she calls them spoiled brats, and they begin to clean the dishes.

Implicit in this scene is the moral of the film—that privileges must be earned, and without hard work, one is destined to become irrelevant, as Lavinia has become to her daughters and husband. This scene also elucidates how complicit Lavinia and her daughters are in a world that oppresses "workers," and begins the true focus of the narrative, Lavinia's awakening and self-discovery. Rosa, the maid, is spoken of but never seen, which says much about the invisibility of Latinos/as both within the film industry and society. The film's narrative had made Rosa, her history and her subjectivity invisible. However, *The Banger Sisters* uses the maid's invisibility to emphasize an Anglo, upper middle-class reality that refuses to see or acknowledge the ethnic "others" who make their privileged lives possible. Her subjectivity is displaced onto Suzette, whose work as a bartender through the years has been taken for granted by people like Sarandon's character. The invisible Latina maid was never significant to the narrative; she exists only to initially establish the Anglo family in the film as classed and clarifies how oblivious they are to the needs of ethnic "others."

Another film that includes remarkably similar dialogue and narrative purpose is *Clueless*, with Alicia Silverstone in the role of a clueless young girl named Cher Horowitz. In this film, Cher asks Latina maid Lucy (played by Aida Linares) to tell Jose the gardener to trim the bushes. Lucy replies that Cher should tell him herself, and Cher then says that she does not speak Mexican, to which Lucy replies, "I no a Mexican," and Cher is then admonished by her stepbrother, who clarifies for her that Lucy is from El Salvador. Similar to *The Banger Sisters* is the fact that Cher is initially oblivious to the lives and realities of the ethnic "others" that make her privileged life possible. And, as with *The Banger Sisters*, it is Cher's growth in the film that is significant and not the Latina maid's ethnicity, politics, or heritage. The Latina maid merely serves as a marker for Cher's "cluelessness." The narrative, which includes a scene with a background Latina maid, foregrounds the subtle politics of the film in establishing that the Anglo protagonist is both naïve and capable of change. The presence of the Latina maid, even an invisible one, provides evidence for the growth of an Anglo consciousness. As Richard Dyer (1997) argued in *Anglo*, "Anglo discourse implacably reduces the non-Anglo subject to being a function for the Anglo subject, not allowing her/him space or autonomy, permitting neither the recognition of similarities nor the acceptance of differences except as a means for knowing the Anglo self" (p. 13). It is also interesting to note that movie critics who reviewed *The Banger Sisters* and *Clueless* did not discuss the scenes with the Latina maids either, even though both scenes are positioned as critical junctures which foreground the politics of the film.

Therefore, the choice to position these maids as Latina reinforces the notion of Latinas/os as "background." Mary Romero (1990) stated that they are "shadow figures, walk-on props in films and TV programs celebrating family life among Texas oil barons or Wall Street executives"(p. 2). Additionally, the Latina/o worker is similarly effaced in Hollywood, where the assumption, with few exceptions, is that Latinas can only be seen in the role of the maid, not the role of the lead.[4] The film *Maid in Manhattan*, indicates a relatively new trend for the Latina maid in contemporary film in that she is clearly framed within the concept of upward mobility. The possibility of escaping the drudgery and subservience of manual labor, however, appears limited to the infrequent instances in which the maid is played by a star (Jennifer Lopez).

FICTIONAL SERVANTS:
HOW NECESSARY ARE LATINA MAIDS?

Mary Romero (1990) argued that Latinos/as are necessary because they fulfill a specific economic need in upper middle-class families: "Not only are they less expensive than employees hired by agencies who pay benefits, but they are easily exploited for additional work" (p. 6). Furthermore, Romero stated that the importance of the Latino/a worker to the upper-income family extends beyond that of the household maid. "Citizenship, race, ethnicity, class and gender continue to mark the boundaries of domestic service—an occupation that extends from the rare household staff that includes butler, driver, cook, maid, and nanny to the day worker who cleans 4 to 9 hours for a different employer each day" (p. 3). Romero's argument acknowledges a changing culture that threatens Anglo middle-class and upper middle-class security, for without servants, they face the threat of being positioned as part of the underclass themselves. Without servants, they would have to fulfill the obligations of child care and household now done by those they hire. Indeed, the hiring of a Latina maid is often represented as an altruistic act by the upper middle class, for they appear to be helping the under-class minority as well as their own financial bottom line and sense of security. In hiring ethnic help, upper middle-class individuals are able to assuage liberal guilt over their exclusion of Latinas/os as they perpetu-ate the myth that hiring ethnic labor is an altruistic act. As an example of this myth-making, Romero (1990) wrote about Linda Chavez, the former nominee for secretary of labor under President George W. Bush. As Romero explained, Chavez claimed that "the 2 years she provided shel-ter and cash to Marta Mercado, an undocumented Guatemalan, was not an employment arrangement, but rather an act of charity and compas-sion" (p. 14). Thus, Chavez, a politically conservative Latina, character-izes the relationship as a personal one unregulated by the law and not a public one that should be regulated.

The background Latina maid in real life and film is no new pattern. For years, servants, field hands, caretakers, and others have fulfilled the purpose of clarifying quickly the classed position of Anglos in mediated narrative and in real life. Furthermore, they serve to clarify and reaffirm hierarchal societal realities that are necessary for the upper middle class to feel good about their wealth and success. They also allow individuals to feel good about "helping" the ethnic "other." This is true for main-stream film and television productions and social reality. The wealthy individual today needs the ethnic servant. And the ethnic servant may feel he or she needs the Anglo patron for real-life economic realities and upward mobility. The film connection between Anglo employers and ethnic servants (played historically by Black characters) speaks to the real-life relationship between Anglos and people of color, which may appear today, in film and reality, to be built on altruism and mutual co-dependence, but elides a legacy of racism and gender inequalities.

THE HISTORICAL LEGACY
OF THE ETHNIC MAID IN FILM

The representation of the Latina maid exists within the context of other ethnic maids in films of the 20th century, often serving as a trope for the structuring of an Anglo, classed identity. In the early decades of film (1910–1930), the visible servant was often an Irish immigrant. According to Faye E. Dudden (1983), "When the famine immigration poured into the United States from Ireland in the late 1840s and early 1850s, it began to look as though every servant was Irish, at least in the major seaboard cities" (p. 60). This trend of hiring Irish women continued throughout the 19th century and found its way into the 20th century. Hiring Irish women was often convenient for Anglo women because the Irish spoke the same language, unlike Russian, German, or Scandinavian workers. As Dudden (1983) stated, "Facing no language barrier, they could find ready acceptance as servants, and entering service solved the problem of finding housing" (p. 60). The trend of hiring Irish servants made its way into early cinema, along with the stereotype of the female, Irish servant as the "Irish biddy" who was helpless and problematic:

> The Irish domestic, stereotypically referred to as "biddy," which dominated the labor market at mid-century and therefore drew the blame for servant problems, tended to make an unsatisfactory servant. She carried to extremes what were, in the eyes of the employers, the characteristic faults of domestics. Among "faithless strangers" the immigrant woman was most faithless, not just personally but culturally. (p. 65)

This reinforced for upper middle-class women, both in reality and in film, the belief that they were helping or rescuing immigrant women from their inability to take care of themselves. At the same time, by hiring these women, they were taking care of their families. The domestic servant allowed the Anglo, upper middle-class woman to "welcome the prospect of more elevated activities than constant domestic drudgery" (Dudden, 1983, p. 47).

However, Irish immigrant women became increasingly unwilling to work for low wages and often viewed domestic service as a temporary working condition before marriage, which David M. Katzman (1978) attributed to an assimilation of Anglo, cultural values in the next generation of Irish Americans, the first to be born in the United States. "Clearly," he stated, "for Irish immigrants, service had provided the vehicle for entry into American society and for upward mobility" (p. 70).

As Irish women began moving into the middle- and upper middle-class, Black servants, who had been commonplace in the South due to slavery, moved to large, northern cities in search of work, and Black women soon "comprised nearly a majority of servants and laundresses nationally" (Katzman, 1978, p. 72). Therefore, reflecting what was happening in real-life upper middle-class homes in the 1930s and throughout the 1950s, the servant in film was more often than not African American. This 1930s servant is most typified by actress Hattie McDaniel, the first Black woman to win an Oscar—for best supporting actress—for her role as Mammy in the 1939 film *Gone With the Wind*.[5]

The change in the ethnic makeup of maids in film and television, from African Americans to Latinas, came from the changing economic structure in African-American families. As Patricia A. Turner (1994) said:

Starting in the late 1950s and through the 1960s and 1970s, a window was broken in the kitchen to which African-American women had been confined. Suddenly they had increased opportunities to seek work outside their own and other people's homes. Educational opportunity grants afforded access to higher education, and employers were eager to display their liberal credentials by hiring African-American employees. (p. 56)

As African-American families began their upward mobility into the middle class, the opening for domestic servants in the home was again filled by new immigrants who, because of a lack of education, language barriers, and ethnic discrimination, often found themselves working as servants in Anglo households. It is important to note that this system of hiring is grounded in geographic realities reflected in film and television shows. For example, films like *Forrest Gump, Clara's Heart,* and *Corrina, Corrina* more often feature African-American servants because they are set in the South. Films or TV shows set in New York City, like *Will & Grace,* or Miami, like *Big Trouble,* often feature Latina or Central/South American workers. Films set in California, like *Hollywood Homicide* or *Big Fat Liar,* often feature Mexican maids. Additionally, films situated in a particular historical period, such as during the U.S. Civil War, tend to feature African-American servants, as in *Gone With the Wind.* Implicit, no matter what the decade or geographic setting, is that the hired hand will almost always be ethnic—the rare exception being, au pairs and cooks, who tend to be Anglo, more educated, and of unidentifiable European lineage, all of which suggest a division of labor according to ethnicity and skin color.

THE SEXY LATINA MAID
AS THE NEW LATINA SPITFIRE

The sexy Latina maid is a segue from the Latina spitfire roles of the 1930s through the 1950s. These roles, best exemplified in the work of actresses Lupe Velez, Dolores Del Rio, and Rita Hayworth, emphasized sensuality and frivolous behavior. The spitfire in early Western films functioned as a temptress who threatened the basic moral values of the Anglo, male protagonist. She is set in direct contrast to the morally upstanding, Anglo female heroine who ultimately saves the male protagonist from the Latina temptress. These spitfires are often superficial characters, generally not developed beyond their basic sexual desires and needs, whereas Anglo actresses in the film are generally fully developed characters with clear moral values and honest and correct ethics. Historically, the role of the early spitfire or Latina temptress has been in direct contrast to that of the morally upstanding, Anglo, female character, and in many films the male protagonist had to choose between them. The function of the spitfire was obvious; for the Anglo male protagonist, redemption was found in resisting those treacherous "spitfire" women.

Today, the Latina spitfire has been updated and transformed but is nonetheless still evident within the role of the Latina maid in many films and television shows—for example, in the 1986 film *Down and Out in Beverly Hills*, starring Richard Dreyfuss, Bette Midler and Nick Nolte, and 2002's *Big Trouble*, starring Tim Allen and Rene Russo, with Sofía Vergara as the Latina maid Nina. Evidence of how this ideology permeates television also includes an episode of the television show *Bones*, which reconfigures the historical spitfire as a Latina maid. In the episode entitled "The Woman in the Garden," the Latina maid is killed by the Latino manager of the household who feels that she had tempted the young, wealthy, Anglo man of the house with her sexuality. Upset that she has overstepped her bounds, he argues that he killed her to maintain the status quo in the relationship between employees—the Latino men and Latina women evident everywhere in the garden and inside the house—and their Anglo employers. Implicit is that the Latina maid has somehow corrupted the young Anglo male and by extension his upper middle-class values.

In *Down and Out in Beverly Hills*, Elizabeth Peña plays the Latina maid Carmen, who provides the most memorable role of the spitfire in contemporary films. As a temptress who threatens the stability and upper middle-class values of the Anglo family for whom she works, Carmen is a reconfigured Latina spitfire. Even film critics positioned her as such: Most discussed Carmen in terms of her representation as a sexy spitfire. For example, Pauline Kael (1986) from the *New Yorker* called her "the Whitemans's hot live-in maid" (p. 105) and discussed her physical attributes rather than any social significance she may have to the politics of the film. She stated, "Elizabeth Peña plays Carmen as tantalizing and sulky; she has a bedroom mouth, and when it says no to Dave, the rejection is brutal, because that mouth looks as if it were made to say nothing but yes" (p. 106).

Down and Out in Beverly Hills, directed by Paul Mazursky, is a remake of a 1932 French film by famed director Jean Renoir. In *Boudu sauvé des eaux*, translated in English as *Boudu Saved from Drowning*, Renoir follows the story of Boudu (played by Michel Simon), a tramp who jumps into the Seine River after he loses his dog and is rescued by Edouard Lestingois (played by Charles Granval), a bookseller who gives him shelter and hopes to redeem him through induction into a bourgeoisie life of work and family. The young maid, Anne-Marie (played by

Sévérine Lerczinska), has sex with Edouard Lestingois in exchange for the possibility of upward mobility. Later, she sleeps with Boudu and appears allied with the Lestingois family's goal of making Boudu a respectable member of the community. The fact that Boudu ultimately decides to forego an upper middle-class existence, as he throws his bourgeois hat in the Seine River and swims, both literally and metaphorically, away from the Lestingois and all they represent, situates this film as class criticism. In the end, the tramp wants nothing to do with the compromises associated with living for and up to society's expectation for the bourgeoisie.

The 1986 re-make by Mazursky of Renoir's film fails to maintain the class critique of its predecessor. Whereas the maid in the original attempts to change her class status by seducing Lestingois, the remake positions the Latina as less powerful, for she is seduced rather than being the seducer, and she is framed as being dependent on her employers for her green card. Being a mainstream Hollywood film, *Down and Out in Beverly Hills* backs down from any attempt to explore or negotiate complicated class politics, even though it sets itself up to do so. In this version, Jerry the bum ends up a class convert, adopting the Whiteman family's bourgeois value system and lifestyle. Thus, any satire of the prevailing upper middle-class values that might have been suggested is eliminated. As Janice Morgan (1990) argued in *From Clochards to Cappuccinos: Renoir's Boudu is 'Down and Out' in Beverly Hills*, "Though at first the rebel had promised liberation from the relentless cycle 'work produce consume work produce consume' we are led to the cynical conclusion that he has, in fact, only eliminated the first two terms of the above three" (pp. 8-9). Morgan continued her critique of the Mazursky film: "Properly defused, stripped of any revitalizing potential to change or to challenge the social order . . . the Outsider is more than welcome to be co-opted into the system. Whatever promise, threat, or possibility Jerry's presumed otherness might have represented has, for the price of a cappuccino, been overruled" (p. 11). The film, in true mainstream Hollywood style, never follows through on its potential to satirically explain Jerry's opposition to the Whitemans' way of life as an opposition to greed. When he joins the fold, he joins their ideology. As Andrew Kopkind (1986) stated, "Mazursky exploits the myth but never exposes it" (p. 252). The film fails in its promise to expose problems inherent in class systems. However, an analysis of the role of the Latina maid Carmen moves us towards an understanding of class and racialized politics in this film.

Initially, I must explain how it is that we know Carmen is Latina. First, she speaks Spanish and has a clear accent throughout the film.[6] Second, she is often in her room watching Hispanic television shows and news. Third, she is often positioned as ethnic by the Whitemans throughout the film, as Barbara Whiteman frequently asks Carmen to correct her Spanish and David Whiteman talks often about his helping the ethnic poor, exemplified by Carmen.[7] Carmen is first seen in the background of the film, cleaning and cooking. As she cooks, she helps Barbara with her Spanish and they talk about the upcoming Thanksgiving dinner, which Carmen is invited to and which quickly situates the family as caring and generous enough to invite the help.

However, the narrative becomes more complicated as she dines with the Whiteman family on Thanksgiving. Her function there, as the audience is reminded, is as the maid which is foregrounded as she serves the meal. In one scene, one of the guests—all of whom are affluent friends of the Whitemans—asks Carmen in a familiar tone how her family is doing. Although it may seem that the interest is genuine—which supports the idea that the Anglo, upper middle class is concerned about the real problems of poor Latinos/as—when she responds that her family is not doing well and that her brother, a sugar cane worker, is out of work, the guests laugh at his misfortune. The response from one of the diners— that "there's not much of a call for that in Los Angeles"—re-affirms the stereotype that Latinos do not want to work, for if the brother did, he would learn some other trade besides the useless one (at least, in Los Angeles) of cutting sugar cane. This moment in the film establishes the superiority of the Anglo, upper middle-class work ethic and related values. However, it quickly glosses over the struggle of ethnic help and we quickly forget that Carmen and her family are in difficult financial straits. As Bonnie Thornton Dill (1986) explained, "Racial ethnics were brought to this country to meet the need for a cheap and exploitable labor force. Little attention was given to their family and community life except as it related to their economic productivity" (p. 15).

What is important in the narrative of *Down and Out in Beverly Hills* is the problems of the Whiteman family, and it is clear that Carmen (like the spitfire of the 1930s) is one of those problems. The family's breakdown is hinted at in the initial scene, in which the married couple is positioned far from each other in their bed. Following are allusions to a sexually ambiguous son, an anorexic daughter, Barbara's obsession with shopping, and David's guilt about his success. As clear as the allusions are to the instability of the family, the reasons for this are more subtle. What is clear is that the situation isn't helped by the Latina maid, who is sleeping with David.

The plot of the film revolves around David Whiteman attempting to help Jerry, a homeless, hungry bum (played by Nick Nolte) who has just lost his dog and attempts to drown himself in the Whitemans' pool. As in the Renoir film, the narrative positions the Whitemans' upward mobility, prosperity and value system in direct contrast to that of the bum they are trying to "help." Although the problems of the Latina maid and her family are dismissed, the situation of this Anglo man is taken far more seriously, for it represents the upper middle-class fear of downward mobility. It is clear in the film that what scares the family most is the possibility that they could become this bum, that they can and still have the possibility of one day being in the same position. As David Whiteman states, "There by the grace of God go you and I." Carmen and her brother's obviously similar situation are negated by the more serious situation of the Anglo man out of work, for this threatens the status quo. In this way, the film reaffirms the idea that Latinos are where they should be and are there because of their own lack of motivation. David Whiteman becomes obsessed with finding out how Jerry became homeless and destitute. As Richard Dyer (1997) pointed out, ethnic concerns or issues are often displaced by Anglo concerns in films.

Furthermore, as the sexy maid, the Latina here reinforces the idea of the immorality of Latinos/as today. Their sexuality is problematic, and they therefore must be punished for it. Thus, Carmen is in the film to be used sexually by her employer and the bum. The fact that Carmen is an immigrant, dependent on David for a green card, positions her as a prostitute, for she is selling her body for the possibility of staying in the United States. The film positions the morality of the Anglo woman as superior to the degraded morality of the Latina woman, which is again a characteristic of past spitfire roles. Furthermore, Carmen's lack of morals and seeming promiscuity are reaffirmed when she sleeps with Jerry.

Nonetheless, the Latina maid in films seems to have no individual identity; her narrative function is to expose the problems of the Anglo, middle or upper middle-class family, thereby revealing that the seeming domestic bliss of the family is not blissful after all. For example, in *Down and Out in Beverly Hills*, the Whitemans' relationship has become dysfunctional as a result of Barbara's preoccupation with maintaining the image of wealth and David's sense of entitlement, which extends to the body of the maid. What is made evident in the film is that the Latina maid is incapable of bettering herself on her own, that she needs the guidance and direction of the Anglo world to escape poverty and develop a sense of self. This need for Anglo definition and guidance is evident when Carmen takes a Marxist stance in response to David's questioning her about having had sex with Jerry. Carmen tells him that she can see "the big picture" now, and that he is an "imperialist" who sees Carmen as "the Third World," ripe for exploitation. Furthermore, Carmen states: "Struggle is a great teacher. You see I am nothing. I am the worker and you are the capitalist. The only way we change this is revolution." When David Whiteman denies having oppressed her and tells her that he thought they were having fun, Carmen replies that fun is decadent. And when David points out that his father was a communist, Carmen calls him a traitor to his class. In this scene, Carmen is given agency and subjectivity. However, her newfound class consciousness is thanks to Jerry, who has introduced Carmen to Marxist class analysis and given her books about Marxist theory. Thus, it is an Anglo male who is responsible for Carmen's agency.

In past films, Anglo employers were often able to see themselves as altruistic and generous when they gave their maids time off, clothes, money or other support to facilitate their growth or individuality. Although it appears that Carmen has gained subjectivity and agency, it continues to be negated; she exists in the film primarily to underscore the goodness and honesty of the Anglo characters. At the end of the film, when we find out that Jerry is a scam artist who he has lied about his past, we understand Carmen's Marxist stance to be as contrived and insignificant as Jerry's bum impersonation. Ultimately, his lies and her misguided Marxist arguments are not as important as the allegiances Carmen, Jerry, and the Whitemans have created together. Carmen and the Whitemans continue to have a common purpose—to save Jerry from his misguided path and position him to reap the benefits of a bourgeois existence.

David Whiteman's claims to generosity toward poor, Mexican immigrants are undercut by his overarching concern for the welfare of the Anglo, male character, Jerry. This is clear from another scene in the film, when a black, homeless man who is Jerry's friend approaches them while they are dining. David is clearly upset by the man's intrusion into his private discussion with Jerry. Again, his concern is not with the struggles of the black man, whom he dismisses as seeming crazy. It is Jerry who is most in need of salvation because of the threat of Anglo, downward mobility. Interestingly, it is Jerry, who has sex with Barbara, who is regarded as worth saving—unlike Carmen, who has sex with David but is seen as potentially causing the moral breakdown of the family. She is vilified, while Jerry is idolized in the film. Her seeming lack of morality, which reaffirms the moral ambiguity of ethnic workers, is evident when she has sex with Jerry, further making her problematic because she has now become responsible for the moral degradation of two Anglo males.

What is important in this film is how the Latina maid functions for Angloness and not how she may function for herself. Her problems are never resolved. Carmen is offered no chance for upward mobility. If, in fact, she is allowed to escape her role (suggested but never fully realized), it is because the Anglo protagonist helped her to do so. In fact, Carmen becomes aligned with the Anglo, upper middle class when, in the film's final scenes, Carmen joins the Whiteman family (visually side by side in the scene) in asking Jerry to stay and help them out of the fallible, upper middle-class world in which they live. The Anglo homeless man is saved, and because of this, so is the Anglo family.

What we ultimately have to acknowledge about the Latina maid is that she is a necessary character in film and television today not simply because she positions the family that she works for as classed. Her figure also is necessary because she is intrinsic to structuring the economic and class privilege of "Angloness" in multiple ways. She exists in the narrative to allow Anglo people to see themselves as altruistic, as good moral individuals who care for their communities and are worthy of all the privileges that come with their race and class. In looking more closely at what media representations say about people of color, the underlying ideology is laid bare. In the United States, Mary Romero (1990) reminds us, maid's work "remains women of color's work, and it is never done" (p. 22).

NOTES

1. A more inclusive list is as follows: *The Incredible Shrinking Woman* (1981), *El Norte* (1983), *Goonies* (1986), *Troop Beverly Hills* (1989), *Regarding Henry* (1991), *Cape Fear* (1991), *Leap of Faith* (1992), *Universal Soldier* (1992), *Clueless* (1995), *Ransom* (1996), *As Good As it Gets* (1997), *Liar, Liar* (1997), *Enemy of the State* (1998), *Dr. T and the Women* (2000), *Don't Say a Word* (2001), *Storytelling* (2001), *Two Weeks Notice* (2002), *Big Trouble* (2002), *Mr. Deeds* (2002), *Big Fat Liar* (2002), *Mr. St. Nick* (2002), *Hollywood Homicide* (2003), *Man on Fire* (2004), *Dirty Sexy Money* (2007-.), *Noah's Ark* (2004-), *Gossip Girls* (2007-), *The Last Shot* (2004), *Win a Date with Tad Hamilton* (2004), *The Sisterhood of the Traveling Pants* (2005), *Spanglish (2005)*, *Crash* (2005), and *Materials Girls* (2006). Just a few television shows include *Charlie's Angels* (1976-1981), *I Married Dora* (1987-1988), *21 Jump Street* (1987-1991), *Designing Women* (1986-1993), *Dudley* (1993), *Veronica's Closet* (1997-2000), *Dharma & Greg* (1997-2002), *Pasadena* (2001), *Will & Grace* (1998-2006), *Curb Your Enthusiasm* (2000-), *Ed* (2000-2004), *Reba* (2001-2006), *24* (2001-), *O.C.* (2003-2007), *Whoopi* (2003-2004) and *Arrested Development* (2003-2006), as well as television shows on HBO and Showtime: *Entourage* (2004-), *Weeds* (2005-) and *Dexter* (2006-).
2. Admittedly, *Will & Grace* is a situation comedy that sets itself up as a satire of society. Rosario is often cheeky, and Karen often looks the fool for her outlandish behavior.
3. Suzette is given no last name, which positions her with the Latina maid, Rosa, who also is without a last name. Suzette, also like Rosa, is aligned with the working class because she is a bartender.
4. A small number of Latina stars, such as Jennifer Lopez and Salma Hayek, are among the few exceptions. However, it is worth noting that Lupe Ontiveros,

a Mexican actress, has played more than 150 maids in film. She narrated a 2005 documentary, *Maid in America,* which examines the experiences of maids in society.

5. In fact, McDaniel portrayed the mammy figure in more than 82 films. According to Carlton Jackson (1990), McDaniel refused to play mammy roles during the 1950s and as a result was boycotted by producers. Ironically, she subsequently became a real maid to make a living.

6. See Keller (1985) for further examination of early spitfire roles and their historical function within films.

7. It is probable that Carmen is Mexican as the film is set in Beverly Hills.

8. The name of the family appears to be a pun about how truly Anglo its value system is.

REFERENCES

Dill, B. T., (1986). *Our mothers grief: Racial ethnic women and the maintenance of families.* Memphis, TN: Memphis State University Press.

Dudden, F. E. (1983). *Serving women: Household service in nineteenth-century America.* Middletown, CT: Wesleyan University Press.

Dyer, R. (1997). *Anglo.* London: Routledge.

Gabbard, K. (2004). *Black magic: Anglo Hollywood and African-American culture.* New Brunswick, NJ & London: Rutgers University Press.

Jackson, C. (1990). *Hattie: The life of Hattie McDaniel.* Lanham, MD: Madison Books.

Kael, P. (1986). The current cinema: Anglo and gray. *The New Yorker, 61,* 105-110.

Katzman, D. (1978). *Seven days a week: Women and domestic service in industrializing America.* New York: Oxford University Press.

Kopkind, A. (1986). Films: *Down and out in Beverly Hills. The Nation,* 251-252.

Keller, G. D. (1985). *Chicano Cinema: Research, reviews, and resources.* New York: Bilingual Review/Press.

Morgan, J. (1990). From clochards to cappuccinos: Renoir's Boudu is "Down and out" in Beverly Hills. *Cinema Journal, 29,* 23-35.

Romero, M. (1990). *Maid in the U.S.A.* New York: Routledge.

Strum, P., & Tarantolo, D. (2003 September). *Women immigrants in the United States.* Proceedings of the Woodrow Wilson Center for Scholars and the Migration Policy Institute. Washington DC: Woodrow Wilson International Center.

Turner, P. A. (1994). *Ceramic uncles & celluloid mammies: Black images and their influence on culture.* New York: Anchor Books.

6

The Multiply Transgressive Body of Anna Nicole Smith

Karen C. Pitcher

On the evening of February 8, 2007, despite the ongoing war in Iraq, the criminal trial of the vice president's former chief of staff, and the emergence of presidential candidates all across the country, the American media were fixated instead on a shocking discovery in a Florida hotel room: the dead body of Anna Nicole Smith. The event was newsworthy not only because of Smith's untimely death by accidental drug overdose at age 39, but also because her 20-year-old son Daniel had died unexpectedly several months prior, within days of the birth of her daughter, Dannielynn, whose own paternity was under contention. It was a tragic death situated within already soap opera-esque circumstances. Yet for weeks throughout Spring 2007, Anna Nicole's death continued to dominate headlines—which was particularly intriguing given that, in the words of one Associated Press article, "many people were hard pressed to describe what exactly Anna Nicole Smith was" ("What made us care," 2007). However, the intense public and media fascination with the *death* of Anna Nicole Smith was really an extension of the already existing scrutiny that occurred throughout her *life*. In many ways, Anna Nicole Smith was the poster girl for transgressive behaviors on multiple fronts—specifically, her questionable performances of femininity, bodily discipline, and social class.

To probe the question as to why Anna Nicole's body has proven so fascinating—yet problematic—to the public, I reflect back to a different sort of media frenzy and the discourse that emerged after the August 4, 2002 debut of her reality show on the E! cable network. Television critics reviled *The Anna Nicole Show* throughout its inaugural season. The popular press had a field day bashing the newest "celebrity reality sitcom" (situation comedy) that followed the blonde, voluptuous Anna Nicole, a one-time Playboy and Guess! jeans model who is essentially famous for being famous. Her 1993 marriage to Texas oil billionaire J. Howard Marshall placed Anna Nicole in the spotlight even after her modeling career had faded, as their May–December marriage raised eyebrows and made headlines; at the time of their vows, he was 88, and she was 62 years his junior (King, 2002). Although the marriage was short-lived as a result of Marshall's death 14 months later, the ensuing inheritance battle between Anna Nicole and Marshall's family ensured that Smith was a constant presence in the tabloid media.

With the advent of the series that bore her name and exposed her life, *The Anna Nicole Show* pushed its star further into the media spotlight. Despite the criticism, the program was one of basic cable's most popular—and profitable—new launches. At the time, the debut made history as the second highest-rated premiere for any basic cable program, and ratings maintained enough vitality to prompt E! to command a second season (Umstead, 2002). The extraordinary popularity and attention garnered by the show kept audiences turning in each week and left popular critics bewildered. No one knew exactly what to make of *The Anna Nicole Show*. More specifically, no one knew what to make of Anna herself. Here's a sampling of critical opinion in magazines and newspapers around the time of the show's launch:

> *The Anna Nicole Show* . . . isn't really a TV show. It's a train wreck—with breasts. (Bianculli, 2002, p. 70)

Anna Nicole is a surgically altered, tabloid-ready sideshow act who has attracted exploitative hangers-on the way rotting meat attracts maggots. . . . As depicted here, the slurry, bloated and otherwise vacant caricature of Dogpatch's Daisy Mae, a cartoon character to start with, is nothing short of grotesque to observe. (Rosenthal, 2002)

Anna Nicole Smith is force-feeding me olives stuffed with jalapenos and garlic as we lie on her giant pink-satin bed watching Jerry Springer. After my eighth olive, my mouth on fire, she offers me a swig from her strawberry-yogurt chaser. "I've been in my jammies all day," she drawls in a Texas accent. Next we share a bowl of sliced pickles in lemon juice. She is not pregnant. (Stein, 2002)

The Anna Nicole Show put the media critics into a near tizzy—and not just because of its popularity, its strange hybrid genre of reality TV/sitcom/celebrity profile, or the banality of its content. Instead, popular critiques of the show center on one specific element beyond ratings, plot, or dialogue; in public forums, the *body* of Anna Nicole Smith gets all the attention.

A quick glance through the quotations above reveals a definite discomfort, and at times almost violent reaction, to Anna's corporeality. Clearly, Anna's body did not fit what is considered to be normal, appropriate, or worthy of an audience's time or gaze. To take a moment to compare her to her predecessor in the genre, some interesting discrepancies emerge. As depicted on his own MTV program of a similar nature, Ozzy Osbourne was regarded as foul-mouthed, physically out of shape, typically unintelligible, and generally mentally confused. Although nearly the same adjectives were used to describe Anna, public discourse generally considered Ozzy's unconventionality to be amusing and endearing (Pots, 2002); Anna, on the other hand, was typically crucified in the popular press for the same attributes. How were critics able to classify Anna's body "grotesque" or "disgusting"? Why, in particular, did television critics concentrate so intently on this specific body, its excesses and lacks, and its consumption? In other words, why was the body of Anna Nicole so troublesome?

In this chapter, I contend that the body of Anna Nicole Smith was more than just that of a notorious celebrity. It was a body that is multiply transgressive, in which dominant ideologies of femininity, bodily discipline, and social class converge and conflict. As the embodiment of both hyper- and subversive femininity, Anna Nicole served as a representation that both challenged and reinforced dominant ideologies of femininity. Additionally, her excessive physicality and tremendous appetites for food and sex further contributed to the discomfort evident in popular discourse. Finally, Anna Nicole's wealthy celebrity status was undercut by emphasizing her as the embodiment of "poor white trash," which in turn positioned her as a carnivalesque, low-class spectacle. To examine these issues, I analyze of two sets of texts. First, *The Anna Nicole Show* itself is considered. The guiding questions here are (a) How was the body of Anna Nicole constructed through the text of the program? and (b) How was Anna's body construed through the popular media discourse generated from and by that text? Engaging this material with the works of Susan Bordo (1993), Judith Butler (1993) and various other theorists of the body and social class reveals why Anna's body was so contradictory—and therefore so problematic to the public. I contend that the body of Anna Nicole Smith should be read as a site of cultural struggle, one that represents a clash of contradictory ideologies and that ultimately enforces hegemonic mandates of womanhood, body, and self.

SETTING THE STAGE: ANNA'S LIFE— AND LIFE ON CAMERA

There is no question that a large part of the public fascination with Anna Nicole's body was a byproduct of her professional and personal history. As described by one biographer, Anna "decided her anatomy would be her destiny" and managed to escape her working-class life as a Texas stripper via the pages of *Playboy* magazine, in which she was named the coveted "Playmate of the Month" in 1992 (Hollandsworth, 1993, p. 100). This lead to further modeling deals with the Guess! jeans line. By 1993, Anna was Hollywood's new "it" girl, turning heads with her 6-foot frame, blonde hair, gorgeous smile and, of course, "curves so big you could ride a motorcycle over them" (Hollandsworth, 1993, p. 97). In this period, Anna's style, looks, and curvaceous yet slender body often lead to comparisons to such feminine icons as Marilyn Monroe and Jean Harlow, as she embodied a new wave of Hollywood glamour and female voluptuousness. Anna's mainstream popularity, however, was short-lived, in large part because of her controversial marriage to billionaire octogenarian J. Howard Marshall in 1994, which put her in the tabloid limelight. The marriage was greatly criticized and lampooned in the media, and it further maintained the emphasis on her bodily assets and sexuality. In a televised interview, CNN's Larry King was insistent that Anna "explain the physical relationship" she had with the elderly Marshall (King, 2002). Although the tabloid frenzy initially damaged her career, according to a *Time* interview, the stress of Marshall's death and the subsequent inheritance trial led Anna Nicole to gain weight, further excluding her from the mainstream modeling world (Stein, 2002). Both through her early modeling days and infamous marriage, Anna Nicole was consistently reduced to her body in public discourse. As a result, her corporeality was central to discussion of her reality show.

If, as Chris Rojek (2001) claimed, celebrities' private lives are "part of the insistent cultural data that we use to comprehend ourselves and to navigate through the crashing waves of the cultural sphere" (p. 20), then the life of Anna Nicole Smith presented viewers with displays of sometimes odd, vulgar, and intriguing behavior. Basking in the windfall of the $88 million payout from her late husband's fortune, in her reality show Anna rode on the heels of her notoriety, with little to do other than spend money on herself and on a new home, make media appearances, and peruse the streets of Los Angeles with her lawyer, Howard K. Stern, personal assistant, Kim, and dog Sugarpie always in tow. The opening episodes of the first season centered on Anna's mundane yet privileged existence, with heightened moments of interest that occurred on her random outings to places such as a tattoo parlor, lingerie store, or strip club with friends.[1] The "action" of the show was interspersed with Anna's scripted monologues and calculated addresses to the camera.

Although the program's premise was to present a "day-in-the-life" view, it was clear from the get-go that the show's emphasis was on Anna's body. A combination of the cartoon opening sequence, careful editing, and Anna's self-presentation code her body in particular ways. Specifically, a textual analysis of the program reveals how it constructed Anna as the embodiment of an excessive femininity incapable of bodily discipline, and as a lower class spectacle. As a result, she is presented as an Other that defies current, normalized conceptions appropriate to her gender and social status.

As a model and sex symbol, Anna Nicole literally made a career out of her curves, and this aspect was underscored in the fast-paced cartoon montage that opened each show. In this moment, Anna is depicted as a colorful and exaggerated cartoon character with ample breasts, a protruding backside and a tiny, hourglass waist. Following the words of the theme song, audiences learn that Anna, in fact, "used what she got—and that was a lot" to achieve her celebrity status and wealth. The image is of a voluptuous Anna, prancing around in a tight pink dress, shaking her bosom and rear end, and winking at

the camera, as the jingle ends with the signature tagline that is repeated at every commercial break: "Anna, Anna, fabulous Anna, Anna Nicole— she's so outrageous!" Therefore, before the show even begins, viewers are presented with an in-your-face, unapologetic account as to how Anna effectively utilized her female bodily assets to obtain her wealthy celebrity status.

If Anna's past career and personal choices put her body in the lime- light, the actual content of the show enhanced this image. The on-camera persona was not far removed from the aforementioned caricature; she was typically featured wearing tight clothes that hugged her 200-pound frame and drew attention to her large, surgically enhanced breasts (Stein, 2002). Although Anna was clearly heavier than in her modeling days, her body maintained an hourglass figure, albeit in larger proportions. Additionally, she typically wore heavy makeup, and her bleached blond hair was stylishly coifed. In this sense, Anna embodied an extreme ver- sion of femininity that draws attention to her womanly figure and to the ritual upkeep of her hair and makeup—all of which are aspects that Bartky (1988) described as disciplinary ornamentation practices that pro- duce recognizably feminine bodies. Yet this sort of superficial, hyper- femininity becomes contradictory when coupled with Anna's behavior, which tended to subvert any notion of her body as under control.

Throughout the reality series, Anna frequently lacked corporeal dis- cipline. During the first season, her behavior provided evidence of over- stepped boundaries of corporeal propriety. Sometimes these transgres- sions seem intentional and self-referential, as Anna frequently referred to and grabbed her breasts while directly facing the camera. With clothes so tight and ill-fitting, there were moments in which her physical body literally exceeded its constraints. In the opening episode, as one reviewer noted, Anna was shown "tugging her sweater around her prodigious breasts, as she proclaimed, 'These babies keep wanting to pop out'" (Cox, 2002, p. 4). Anna was depicted as unable to properly contain her physicality in more mundane moments, as well. In one scene, she stumbles on the sidewalk while walking down the street; in another, she trips and falls over a beanbag chair. Anna's body appeared to have a life of its own, defying the dignified bodily comportment that Bartky (1988) explained as demonstrative of a disciplined femininity.

In addition to this excessive physicality, Anna also embodied what Bordo (1993) described as the archetypal image that runs counter to modern constructions of the normalized female: the voracious, hunger- ing, and all-wanting woman. Specifically, Anna appeared unable to con- trol her appetites for both sex and food; she always seemed to be long- ing for or indulging in one or the other. There were several scenes in which she simulated sexual actions (one recurring clip showed Anna gyrating, fully clothed, alone on a bed), or placed herself in sexually suggestive positions. In one episode, Anna sat in a limousine, faced the camera, and spread her legs in a provocative display. When not partaking in some sort of sexual performance, the show's attention to Anna and her food consumption constructed her as a compulsive eater. The central narratives of the show featured her either on a quest for food, or already happily indulging. In several car scenes, Anna demanded the driver pull up to the drive-through window for such items as cheeseburgers or ice cream cones, and at one point she threw a tantrum because she wanted a large, dill pickle. The next shot immediately cut to a close-up of her slurping away on the half-eaten pickle, seemingly unaware that juice was dribbling onto her fancy evening gown. As seen in the program, Anna demanded immediate satisfaction to her various cravings, and when she was shown eating, her consumption was messy and unrefined as she devoured every morsel of food in front of her. These instances helped construct Anna as a woman who lacked self-control, a veritable "id" whose behavior is dictated by primal desires—what Price (1997) describes as a characteristic of a "white trash" portrayal.

As the juxtaposition of "poor white trash" and wealthy celebrity, Anna Nicole's persona could be construed as one in which social class converges and conflicts. On one hand, despite her background, Anna was affluent and therefore privileged. With a hefty bank account, a life of leisure, and few career demands, she could afford to live luxuriously and enjoy her notoriety and celebrity status. However, from the beginning of the program it was clear to viewers that they were not to forget her lower class roots. The opening sequence explained that Anna was raised in a Texas trailer park, worked in a fried-chicken restaurant, married at 17 and had a child a year later.

Thus, the cartoon tableau emphasized Anna's poor, Southern upbringing and relied on stereotypical and iconic images that signify "poor white trash" to the popular consciousness (Bérubé & Bérubé, 1997). The jingle also made apparent that Anna's accomplishments were not the result of education or merit. Rather, she used her body to launch her career as a stripper, a relatively seedy profession that also connotes "trash" status (Kipnis, 1997; Penley, 1997). Even before the show began, the theme song and its images made clear that Anna hails from a Southern, uneducated, lower class background, reinforcing

the notion that once branded as "trash," the label can never be shaken (Goad, 1998).

While the inaugural array of cartoons established Anna's class background, the footage within the show reinforced it. Despite the fact that Anna's environment and income located her in the upper class, she embodied "poor white trash" through her fashion choices. Her wardrobe leaned toward a lower class style, with unflattering, ill-fitting clothes that could be articulated as trashy or too revealing by middle-class standards. Much like Birmingham's (2000) description of lower class women in talk shows, most of the time Anna could be considered a "freak of fashion [that defies] our middle-class articulations of taste with too much gold jewelry, tight jeans, big hair, 4-inch heels" (p. 136). While Anna's clothes were not necessarily out of date, their too-tight fit, coupled with her exaggerated makeup, situated her as defiant of the norms of her current position in the upper echelon of celebrity women who have access to a more refined, sophisticated wardrobe.

The emphasis on Anna's food consumption also helped reinforce her "classed" body. When not indulging in various fast-food fare, Anna was depicted as enjoying such brand-name items as Red Bull energy drinks, Doritos chips, or Yoo-Hoo chocolate drink. Despite the possible product placement in these cases, what's important to note is that Anna was constantly shown indulging herself with inexpensive, mass-produced junk food, although she clearly can afford healthier, more cosmopolitan fare. Anna defied the typical Hollywood diet culture for celebrity women by eating such "forbidden" and low-brow foods.

This discrepancy between Anna's background and status also was apparent through her speech, which further positioned her as lower class. Anna's speech was slow and laced with a Southern drawl. Her onscreen vocabulary was peppered with vulgarities that require frequent censoring, and when her voice wasn't shrouded by the bleep, it often emphasized her unrefined grammar. Such typical phrases included the misuse of the double negative ("I don't trust nobody," "I ain't goin' nowhere," or "She didn't have no teeth"), incorrect verb tense ("I don't have anywhere to stuck all of this stuff") and awkward syntax ("I bruised myself all up"). In their analysis of dialogue in prime-time television, Ellis and Armstrong (1989) contended that a character's language use is a key determinant in establishing class status for the viewer. Specifically, they claim that the use of "ain't" and the double negative are particularly socially diagnostic because it almost never occurs in middle-class speech (Ellis & Armstrong, 1989). Anna's constant in-articulations further reinforced her lower class status.

Through this examination of *The Anna Nicole Show*, it is apparent that the program emphasized Anna's body for viewers to interpret in particular ways. On one hand, Anna is the embodiment of both a hyper-

and transgressive femininity, as one that adheres to *some* of the demands of disciplined femininity but overall lacks corporeal control. At the same time, her body also serves as the site in which class converges and ultimately clashes; despite her celebrity and economic status, Anna's excesses and actions undermined her social environment. In other words, her body was one in which norms of both femininity and class conflict, creating a mediated "threat" that must be regulated.

"NOTHING SHORT OF GROTESQUE TO OBSERVE . . .": THE ANNA NICOLE SHOW AND PUBLIC DISCOMFORT

Although public commentary regarding *The Anna Nicole Show* reflects a definite annoyance with the program's banal subject manner, the reviews of the program primarily digress into diatribes about Anna's physical body. One harsh review proclaimed, "Anna's just a big waist of our time" (Williamson, 2002, p. B1), and the *New York Post* branded her with the title "Eating Machine" (2002). Even reports that praised the show's success employ bodily terms: *The Calgary Sun* ("Anna Nicole a smash hit," 2002) reported that "Anna-Nicole Smith's new reality-TV show is busting records," and one report informed readers of the show's second season renewal with "Anna Nicole Back for Second TV Helping" ("Anna Nicole back," 2002). And these are just the *headlines*.

As evident in the quotes at the beginning of this chapter, the popular press devoted a great deal of attention to critiquing Anna's appearance, behavior and food consumption in reviews of her reality show. Some commented more generally on the loss of her model figure: "her once Daisy Mae Playmate figure . . . has taken on a good deal more flesh than in the period she now calls her 'modeling' days" ("Of Anna Nicole," 2002, p. TV2). Others claimed she was "larger than life" (Schoeneman & Birnbaum, 2002), or referred to her as "the once zaftig and now simply Twinkie-fattened Smith" (Pots, 2002). More typically, references included callous remarks about Anna's backside—" the most appalling feature of *The Anna Nicole Show* is Anna Nicole's prodigious posterior, which could easily star in its own reality series" (Williamson, 2002) or "how did they ever squeeze the microphone transmitter inside the waist band of those pants?" ("Anna Nicole back," 2002); her breasts: "she's surgically enhanced" (Huden, 2002), and her eating. Several articles focused on her apparently constant consumption of dill pickles, olives, and chocolates ("Eating machine," 2002; Stein, 2002). Perhaps the following passage provides the best exemplar of a review of *The Anna Nicole Show* that ultimately transpires into a harsh critique of its star:

By pronouncing "cabana" "canabana," sneaking slices of watermelon from a fridge as she tours a house with a real estate agent, hump-
ing a bed, making eyes at the camera (or is it the cameraman?), talking baby talk to her teenage son and finally telling the shooting
crew, "Hold on, I gotta eat something," Smith is an embarrassment
of a human being. (Cox, 2002, p. 4)

Further adding to the embarrassment, as is hinted in Cox's quote, was
Anna's questionable mental state. She appeared to be constantly confused, often mumbling unintelligible words or awkward statements (i.e.,
she told her interior decorator, "I don't wanna have to pay for any more
money"). The assumption was that Anna was inebriated, high on
painkillers, or just plain stupid. Romano (2002) noted the public outcry:
"What viewers must have been talking about was her slurred speech,
unsteady gait and just plain space-cadetness" (p. 25). The following passage describes the quandary in detail:

No, what hits everyone about Anna Nicole Smith is her speech and
demeanor. She doesn't slur words, exactly, she speaks them in a ter-
minally spacey, fuzzy and whiny drawl . . . after a few minutes of
listening to Anna Nicole Smith, it might seem that a small vial of her
blood dropped into L.A.'s reservoir would count, in any world
court, as an act of all-out chemical warfare. ("Of Anna Nicole," 2002,
p. TV2)

Whether or not this was Anna's true state or the effect of (perhaps multiple) mind-altering chemicals is unknown. Representatives for the E! network insisted "she's far from dumb and is not on drugs" (Romano, 2002,
p. 25). Regardless, Anna is perceived to be a woman who is literally out
of her mind, lacking both physical and mental control.

ANNA NICOLE'S MULTIPLE TRANSGRESSIONS

Anna Nicole's body and behavior evinced such cultural nervousness
due to the complexity of its transgressions; it pushed boundaries on
multiple fronts. The body presented to viewers in *The Anna Nicole Show*
was one that challenged current conceptions of how female bodies
should look and behave. In other words, Anna was a body that strad-
dled boundary lines in terms of her femininity and social class. As a
result, it constructed a space outside of dominant ideologies that dictate
corporeal propriety for celebrity women. Anna's perceived lack of bodi-

ly and mental control undercut any means of positioning her as a resistant force inside the system. She was not a docile, disciplined body, as society demands. A major part of the problem is likely due to the dramatic bodily change that Anna underwent over the years. In her days as a cover girl in the early 1990s, Anna's body was considered a marker of the feminine ideal. Her heavier, changed body, emerging a decade later, violated that ideal, and the public took note. Although certainly heavier than she once was, at 6-feet tall and approximately 200 pounds, Anna was relatively proportional, and although fleshy, would not qualify as dangerously overweight. Yet the popular discourse considered Anna to be flat-out fat—one reviewer even claimed she was "obese" (Huden, 2002). Although her body was just inside the realm of "plus size" in a country where the average woman wears a size 14, the discrepancy between the old and new figures was reflected on with disgust.

As Bordo (1993) explains, the firm, muscle-toned body has become a symbol of "correct" attitude. It means that one cares about oneself and how one appears to others, suggesting willpower, energy, control over infantile impulse, the ability to "shape your life" (p. 195). Additionally, Bordo asserts that this taut body must be understood as a particularly classed body, one that is more likely obtained through the privilege of upper class opportunity. In a society that has learned to defy the materiality of the body and replaced it with what Bordo (1993) called "cultural plastic" that emphasizes a person's own abilities as master sculptor of her or his body (p. 246), this change in Anna's body would simply not do. For the public, the bottom line was that when Anna's show emerged to great success in 2002, she had let herself go—and viewers got to see firsthand that she had neither the willpower nor desire to change her fleshy body into one that was lean and therefore more reflective of her upward social mobility. Interestingly enough, however, one E! executive claimed that part of the draw to *The Anna Nicole Show* was that viewers were "rooting for her to get back in shape" (Orecklin, 2002, p. 113). Together, popular critics and audiences alike expressed a desire to chastise and regulate Anna's physicality, to simultaneously encourage a return to her previous model figure, as well as publicly reject her for the slippage into a body that falls outside cultural standards for upper class women.

The public's urge to repudiate Anna's body was not just a factor of her physical size and shape, but also due to her inappropriate performance of femininity. Drawing on Butler's (1993) conception of performativity, gender norms are constructed through a stylized repetition of acts, which is "always a reiteration of a norm or set of norms, and to the extent that it acquires an act-like status in the present, it conceals or dissimulates the conventions of which it is a repetition" (p. 12). In other words, these repetitive acts construct the materiality of sexual differences, how masculinity and femininity are read and regulated. Anna Nicole's excessive body and antics often demonstrated inappropriate feminine performances. She defied most of the norms our society has established for women in her position, and as a result, there was the intense need to regulate her actions and her body. At the same time, however, Anna's body hinted at the abject, which Butler (1993) described as the "necessary outside" that supports the bodies that materialize the norm and therefore "count" in society (p. 16). Thus, Anna's threatening position as one that violates gender performativity was urged to either be repudiated altogether, or viewed as a spectacle that served as a "constitutive outside," which ultimately serves to define society's boundaries and helps reinforce hegemonic norms.

If we accept Butler's (1993) notion of the abject body as what helps to constitute the culturally intelligible—or at least acceptable—one, then we must consider the spectacle of social class that Anna embodied. Specifically, Anna's performance of self engenders many of the stereotypes aligned with "poor white trash" that Newitz and Wray (1997) described: In mediated images she appears as highly sexual, possibly addicted to drugs or alcohol, and definitely portrayed as lazy and stupid. By positioning her as a spectacle of the lower class, she could be ridiculed with ease, and the show's narrative reinforces Anna's inability to shake her white trash status. As Goad (1998) explained, "there's no shortage of socio-illogical alibis for any other group's aberrant acts; with white trash, it's seen as some form of innate rottenness" (p. 23). As a scapegoat Other that could never fully mask her class status, the representation of Anna relieves insecurity for the desired and presumed middle-class audience. Birmingham (2000) concurred, "The spectacle of non-middle-class behavior is displayed so the middle class can define itself and its values" (p. 135). Thus, viewers were allowed to peer in and goggle at Anna Nicole's behaviors throughout her mediated life, yet remain assured that they are distanced from this irredeemable Other.

Along this same trajectory, the show's emphasis on bodily indulgence, portrayed through the concentration on Anna's physicality, sexually suggestive movements, and food consumption helped place her into the realm of the carnivalesque. Mikhail Bakhtin's (1968) carnival "celebrated temporary liberation from the prevailing truth and from the established order: it marked the suspension of all hierarchical rank, privileges, norms, and prohibitions" (p. 10). This theory of the carnival claims that this type of spectacle is characterized by "bodily pleasure in opposition to morality, discipline, and social control" (Fiske, 1987, p. 241). In their discussion of the emergence of the class divide via the carnival, Stallybrass and White (1993) indicated that:

> Historically, the bourgeois society constructed carnival as the cul-
> ture of the other. This act of disavowal on the part of the emergent
> bourgeois, with its sentimentalism and its disgust, made carnival
> into a festival of the Other. It encoded all that which the proper
> bourgeois *must strive not to be* in order to preserve a stable and "cor-
> rect" sense of self. (p. 290, italics added).

At its best, the carnival provided fleeting and temporary voyeuristic
glimpses of a promiscuous loss of status and decorum, which the bourgeois was forced to deny in order to emerge as a distinct and proper
class (Stallybrass & White, 1993, p. 292), a moment to indulge in the
pleasures of viewing those that were licensed to break social rules.
Because the program highlighted Anna's performance of femininity as
excessive and her behavior as outrageous and deviant, Anna was constructed as a lower class mockery, a modern-day one-woman freak show
exhibit in the "carnival" of reality television. Thanks to its tongue-in-
cheek opening sequence, strategic editing and banal story lines, viewers
of *The Anna Nicole Show* were encouraged to ridicule its star. However,
the harsh rhetoric in the popular press simultaneously served as a policing mechanism, reminding audiences of the social punishments for
those transgressions. In other words, the Anna Nicole as depicted on her
reality show provides the perfect model for the body that no one should
want to be.

CONCLUSION: CONTINUED FIXATIONS
ON A CONTROVERSIAL FIGURE

By the end of *The Anna Nicole Show*'s second season in 2003, Anna Nicole
essentially had been dismissed as little more than a ridiculous reality
show star not worth an audience's time or gaze, and she somewhat
retreated and maintained a low profile in the months leading up to a
debut of a new episode in February 2004. While filming and doing publicity for an upcoming special, Anna emerged once again in the media
spotlight with a dramatic, visible change—she had lost 69 pounds on the
weight-loss drug, TrimSpa, and was to be featured on the fashion run-
ways of New York City. The transformation was startling, as the "new"
Anna seemed to channel her former image as the sultry Playboy model.
What was perhaps most interesting was the rhetoric that surrounded
this return to the public eye. It featured a triumphant renewal of the
voluptuous-yet-svelte image to which most had been accustomed. In a
commercial for TrimSpa, Anna proclaimed, "I'm BACK!" In other
words, Anna and the ad campaign attempted to repudiate her image of

the previous 18 months. The message to the public was that they need not worry—Anna was sufficiently back to her "normal" self and, in the words of the TrimSpa campaign, once again had a "body to envy."

When examining interviews with the "new" Anna, it becomes apparent that she was very conscious of the public's ridicule of her size. In fact, she admitted to Larry King that this served as a major motivator to shed pounds:

> King: Now, what was the reason for all of this? Why did you lose weight, other than the obvious, you wanted to look better. But I mean, what got you motivated to do it?
>
> Smith: What got me motivated? To be honest, I really got tired of the—the fat jokes, you know? I mean, what really, really upset me the most was Howard Stern, when he got me on his show and then—you know, he got me there and then he's, like, "Okay, Anna Nicole, I know you weigh 300 pounds, and we got a scale here. We want to get you on the scale." And I was just, like, "Oh, my God. I can't believe he's doing this to me." And he had a bunch of callers call in and be really rude and say, "Oh, Anna, you know, get on the scale. I'll give you a bunch of jewelry. We know you weigh 300 pounds . . ."
>
> King: How soon after that did you get into the diet thing?
>
> Smith: But then I heard a lot more, a lot more, and all the fat jokes that everybody's saying, and then—you know, I really didn't care. And then, you know, I looked in the mirror, and I'm just, like, I am fat, you know? I am fat. So I just, you know, started losing weight. (King, 2004)

Yet the same public that was in an uproar over her heavy, unruly body also questioned the "authenticity" of Anna's thin figure. She reportedly posed nude for a fashion magazine just to prove she didn't undergo surgery to lose weight. The editor of the publication explained, "She thought it would be a good way to quash the rumors. I was there and can 100% vouch that she had no scars" ("Anna Nicole taking it off," 2004, p. 18). Ironically, amid the public's unease as to how Anna achieved such a drastic change were reports that she was becoming "dangerously thin" and obsessive about her weight loss—to the point that some said she was "wasting away" (Purves, Brooks, & Watts, 2004). These instances demonstrate the cultural unease *still* provoked by Anna's body, even after she managed to "take control" of her weight and figure. This discourse also reveals the ways the public relied on popular media as watchdogs to verify, classify, and evaluate this problematic persona.

However, what undercut any positive discourse about Anna's apparently disciplined, proper female body was the continual disdain with her transgressive and trashy behavior. A 2004 appearance at a computer game convention featured Anna "popping out all over" in what was viewed as a deliberate, "sad imitation of Janet Jackson's 'wardrobe malfunction'" at the Super Bowl earlier that year (Tilley, 2004). In another report about a Las Vegas outing, Anna "was, according to a partygoer, 'out of control—making out with men and women and groping any woman that came near her.' Smith—who didn't bother trying to hide the fact that she was not wearing underwear—even dubbed one piece of furniture a 'makeout' couch" ("Anna Nicole's kissing frenzy," 2004, p. S12). During a televised appearance on ABC's *The View*, Anna shocked both the program's co-hosts and viewing public by fondling her own breasts on morning TV—but only after host Star Jones proclaimed, "I gotta tell you—and I would never in a million years comment about another woman's breasts—you may have the biggest breasts I've ever sat next to in my life!" ("People in the news," 2004). What perhaps is most interesting about this statement is the unproblematic license Jones (herself having an increasingly controversial body after her dramatic weight loss in 2005) took to comment upon Anna's body. Even though Jones claimed to feel uncomfortable commenting on another's breasts, Anna's excessive physique begged for—and produced—public critique. A few months later, in November 2004, Anna sent tongues wagging again after her controversial appearance as a presenter on a nationally televised awards show. As best described by one newspaper account:

> People are still talking about Anna Nicole Smith's jaw-dropping (or should that be slack-jawed?) performance at Sunday's American Music Awards in Los Angeles. Poured into a black-and-red gown, the lass whose name is oft-linked with the phrase "bizarro behavior" appeared to have ingested something a tad stronger than TrimSpa, the weight-loss product she shills, before taking the stage to introduce hip-hop artist Kanye West. ("Bizarro behavior," 2004, p. B-1)

Additionally, she waved her arms over her head while asking a watching nation, "Like my body?" (Camilli, 2004). Thus, despite Anna's apparently successful weight loss that was indicative of a more disciplined body, the public still took aim at her undisciplined antics. Anna's uncontained body and rambunctious behavior continued to position her as a trashy spectacle post-weight loss.

Throughout the final months of her life and even in the weeks following her death, Anna Nicole's body continued to draw interest. With the June 2006 proclamation that that she was pregnant with her second child, even Anna herself invited attention to her expanding and changing body. As she mentioned on a video clip posted on her Web site, annanicole.com, "Let me stop all the rumors. Yes, I am pregnant. I'm happy, I'm very, very happy about it. Everything's goin' really, really good and I'll be checking in and out periodically on the Web and I'll let you see me as I'm growing" ("Anna's pregnant," 2006). With the promise to keep her pregnant physique in the public eye, once again Anna's out-of-bounds body drew further attention. Such public interest only intensified in the wake of Dannielynn's birth and questionable paternity[2] and son Daniel's subsequent and suspicious death, as this unbelievable sequence of birth and death engendered two more controversies from "bodies" physically linked to Anna Nicole. Although the complexities surrounding Anna's offspring fall outside the scope of this chapter, their respective controversies seem to ensure continued public intrigue, fascination, and criticism even though the body of their mother is no longer alive to push boundaries itself.

As a site at which multiple transgressions of femininity and social class converged, the body of Anna Nicole Smith—both in life, and perhaps, in time, in death as well—serves as an intriguing point of investigation into the "cultural grip" (Bordo, 1993) through which bodies are both produced and subjected. As a body that transgressed many cultural norms and therefore hinted at the abject, while simultaneously remaining "intelligible," Anna Nicole generated a fascinating, controversial figure that both defied and reinforced her socially prescribed positions. In turn, the public backlash remained focused on her transgressions in an attempt to repudiate it as a threat to gendered and classed norms of bodily appearance and actions. This investigation into the harsh reaction to this mediated representation of a female body serves as a case study into the ways in which society still works to uphold hegemonic notions of what constitutes proper performances of femininity and social class.

NOTES

1. These types of activities are representative of the first 13 episodes of the Fall 2002 season. The second season (which began airing on March 2, 2003) changed the focus of the program all together, as *The Anna Nicole Show* frequently parodies other reality programs or places Anna in obviously staged and scripted activities. By 2004, E! still ran the program as periodic specials rather than a weekly series.

2. On April 10, 2007, a court-ordered DNA test confirmed that Anna Nicole's former boyfriend Larry Birkhead was Dannielynn's biological father. The paternity of Dannielynn was questionable almost immediately following her birth, as Anna Nicole and her longtime companion/former attorney Howard K. Stern contended that Stern was in fact the biological father. The paternity battle had been underway at the time of Anna Nicole's passing, and intensified in light of the potential millions the baby stands to inherit.

REFERENCES

Anna Nicole a smash hit. (2002, August 7). *The Calgary Sun*, p. 35.

Anna Nicole back for second TV helping. (2002, October 25). *The Houston Chronicle*, p. A2.

Anna Nicole's kissing frenzy. (2004, September 19). *The Edmonton Sun*, p. SL2.

Anna's pregnant. (2006, June 2). *Newsday* (New York), p. A13.

Anna Nicole taking it off . . . to prove she took it off. (2004, July 31). *The Winnipeg Sun*, p. 18.

Bakhtin, M. (1968). *Rabelais and his world*. Cambridge, MA: MIT Press.

Bartky, S. (1988). Foucault, femininity, and the modernization of patriarchal power. In I. Diamond & L. Quimby (Eds), *Feminism and Foucault* (pp. 61-86). Boston: Northeastern University Press.

Bérubé, A., & Bérubé, F. (1997). Sunset trailer park. In M. Wray & A. Newitz (Eds.), *White trash: Race and class in America* (pp. 15-40). New York: Routledge.

Bianculli, D. (2002, August 6). E!'s cruel blond joke: Makes a sad spectacle of celeb's life. *Daily News* (New York), p. 70.

Birmingham, E. (2000). How talk TV articulates women and class. *Journal of Popular Film & Television, 28*(3), 133-140.

Bizarro behavior. (2004, November 16). *Pittsburgh Post-Gazette*, p. B-1.

Bordo, S. (1993). *Unbearable weight*. Berkeley: University of California Press.

Butler, J (1993). *Bodies that matter: On the discursive limits of "sex."* London & New York: Routledge.

Camilli, D. (2004, November 17). Bizarre behaviour of celebrity widow gets weirder: Smith asks audience if they like her body. And Britney Spears is going back to school; Web site says she's registered at Pepperdine College. *The Gazette* (Montreal), p. D7.

Cox, T. (2002, August 8). With "Anna Nicole," "Big Brother," the pathetic overwhelms the merely tedious. *Chicago Daily Herald*, p. 4.

Ellis, D., & Armstrong, G.B. (1989). Class, gender, and code on prime-time television. *Communication Quarterly, 37*(3), 157-169.

Eating machine. (2002, September 9). *New York Post*, p. 8.

Fiske, J. (1987). *Television culture*. London & New York: Routledge.

Goad, J. (1998). *The redneck manifesto: How hillbillies, hicks, and white trash became America's scapegoats*. New York: Simon & Schuster.

Hollandsworth, S. (1993, July). The making of a sex symbol. *Texas Monthly*, pp. 96-104.

Huden, J. (2002, August 10). TV so bad, it's unreal. *The New York Post*, p. 17.

King, L. (2002, May 29). Interview with Anna Nicole Smith. *CNN*. Retrieved October 3, 2004, from <http://www.cnn.com/TRANSCRIPTS/0205/29/lkl.00.html

King, L. (2004, February 9). Analysis of Scott Peterson case developments; Interview with Anna Nicole Smith. *CNN*. Retrieved October 3, 2004, from <http://transcripts.cnn.com/TRANSCRIPTS/0402/09/lkl.00.html>

Kipnis, L. (1997). White trash girl: The interview. In M. Wray & A. Newitz (Eds.), *White trash: Race and class in America* (pp. 113-130). New York: Routledge.

Newitz, A., & Wray, M. (1997). Introduction. In M. Wray & A. Newitz (Eds.), *White trash: Race and class in America*. (pp. 1-14). New York: Routledge.

Of Anna Nicole, Ozzy Osbourne and "reality" television. (2002, August 11). *The Buffalo News*, p. TV2.

Orecklin, M. (2002, November 4). Still more quality television. *Time*, p. 113.

Penley, C. (1997). Crackers and whackers: The white trashing of porn. In M. Wray & A. Newitz (Eds.), *White trash: Race and class in America* (pp. 89-112). New York: Routledge.

People in the news. (2004, September 9). *The Miami Herald*. Retrieved on Lexis-Nexis.

Price, A. (1997). White trash: The construction of an American scapegoat. Retrieved October 6, 2004, from http://xroads.virginia.edu/~MA97/price/open.htm

Pots, L. (2002, September 27). "Anna Nicole" too much reality even for TV. *Albuquerque Journal*, p. D1.

Purves, L, Brooks, N., & Watts, A. (2004, May 13). The Goss; Thin times for Anna. *Daily Star*, p. 13.

Rojek, C. (2001). *Celebrity*. London: Reakton Books.

Romano, A. (2002, August 12). E!'s great big blonde surprise; *Anna Nicole Show* debuts to large Nielsens and some rough critical response. *Broadcasting and Cable*, p. 25.

Rosenthal, P. (2002, August 9). Let's all laugh at the messed-up lady. *Chicago Sun-Times*, p. 43.

Schoeneman, D., & Birnbaum, D. (2002, August 6). She's come undone; something's wrong with reality TV star—but what? *The New York Post*, p. 37.

Stallybrass, P., & White, A. (1993). Bourgeois hysteria and the carnivalesque. In S. During (Ed.), *The cultural studies reader* (pp. 382-388). New York: Routledge.

Stein, J. (2002, July 22). Anna goes prime time. *Time*, pp. 48-50.

The Anna Nicole Show. (2004). *Eonline.com*. Retrieved May 26, 2004, from <http://www.eonline.com/On/AnnaNicole2/index.html>

Tilley, S. (2004, August 8). Really, as nerds we deserve better. *The Toronto Sun*, p. S25.

Umstead, R.T. (2002, August 12). E! ecstatic over panned "Anna." *Multichannel News*, p. 42.

What made us care about Anna Nicole? Combination of dysfunction and beauty made her perfect pop culture icon. (2007, February 8). *MSNBC.com*. Retrieved February 8, 2007, from <http://www.msnbc.msn.com/id/17054603/from/RS.1/>

Williamson, D. (2002, August 21). Anna's just a big waist of our time; Star of reality show is anything but for real. *Worcester Telegram & Gazette*, p. B1.

Part IV

Hybridity and the Global Market

7

Climbing the Great Wall of Feminism

Disney's Mulan

Jill Birnie Henke

Disney's 36th animated film, *Mulan*, was released in June 1998. It was the first Disney film with a female producer, Pam Coats; a female head screenwriter, Linda Woolverton, of the famed *Beauty and the Beast*; and a screenplay team led by a woman, Rita Hsiao. Also of note is that *Mulan* appeared to be a modern-day feminist tale derived from a story some 2,000 years old. Disney did not appear to have changed the story of Mulan in the same ways as it had "Disneyfied" its other stories, such as *Pocahontas* and *The Hunchback of Notre Dame*. Yet, questions remain concerning its representations of race, gender, and culture.

I examine whether, as Kim (1998) stated, Disney's Mulan "is a banana—yellow outside, white within. With her anglicized name, her perfect unaccented English and her wild gesticulations, it is easy to see she is not a Chinese woman warrior, but an Asian-American feminist" (p. 2). Are we Westerners reading the text from our point of view, or do Eastern cultures understand *Mulan* in the same way? Although Americans read Mulan as a strong protagonist who fights for her beliefs, who can do anything a man can, who rises among the ranks to become a general, and who is admired by all her people, a Chinese perspective may read the text as Mulan acting traditionally, being forced by conditions of her family to "become a man" to uphold familial honor.

What can we learn from examining *Mulan*? In this world of global diversity, we must learn to "look" at things from different perspectives. In America we can applaud Mulan for her strength of character, her bravery, her determination, her intelligence, her endurance under great adversity. But we need also applaud Mulan for her adherence to tradition, her sacrifice for her family, her intelligence and strength, and her love for family and commitment to honor.

What we learn from Disney is that, once again, smart marketing, now in this global arena, means big profits. Disney appears to climb the Great Wall of feminism with a strong female protagonist without a sexy figure or romantic storyline,[1] while at the same time honoring China's ancient heroine and adhering to China's basic traditions.

THE REAL MULAN

Fa Mulan is a folk poem that originated during the Northern and Southern Dynasties of China, from 420 to 589 *A.D.* The poem was recorded in court anthologies as early as the Tang Dynasty 618-907 *A.D,* but the version most often repeated for Chinese children is named *The Song of Mulan. Fa Mulan* is also mentioned in a book on military organization and strategy entitled *The Art of War*, written by Sun Tzu more than 2,300 years ago (San Souci,1998).

Fa Mulan joined the military disguised as a man, to prevent her elderly father from being conscripted into Khan's army. Fa Mulan's father had been a decorated general himself, and some of the stories recount him teaching her how to use a sword and the martial arts. Because Fa Mulan had no elder brothers to take her father's place in the army, she decided to disguise herself as a man and go in his stead, thus sparing her family dishonor and punishment because her father did not serve. Fa Mulan fought for 12 years and became a decorated general as a result of her bravery and adeptness at military strategy. At the end of the war, the emperor offered Fa Mulan a position as his highest counsel. Fa Mulan declined the position, asking only for a swift horse to return her to her family. As the legend goes, those who served with Fa Mulan did not realize "he" was really a "she" until a small honor guard of her companions saw her change into a "woman" after she removed her armor and dressed in traditional garb, once she arrived home.

By maintaining the Chinese tradition of strong filial ties, Fa Mulan acted to protect her family by serving her country in her father's stead. Many young Chinese girls have grown up hearing their mothers recount the tale of Fa Mulan. Some wondered if the brave, young woman warrior really existed at all. With the amount of renewed interest that Disney's *Mulan* created worldwide, the Chinese government confirmed that, indeed, Fa Mulan existed. Her tomb and a memorial temple stand today in Dazhou village in Yucheng County, in eastern Henan Province, where local villagers have opened a tourist attraction ("Mulan Mania," 1999).

Because the legend of Mulan is so prevalent, it is not surprising that several movies have preceded Disney's animated version, *Mulan*. The most noted among them are a 1939 black-and-white film entitled *Maiden in Armor (Mu Lan Cong Jin)*, directed by Bu Wan Cong, and the 1960 operatic version, *The Lady General Hua Mu Lan*, directed by Yue Fung (Kuo, 1998). However, feminists, like myself, who have been studying the Disney animated films, notably the princess films, were skeptical as to whether Disney would present a "true" version of Fa Mulan or a "Disneyfication" of the story as Disney had done with its version of *Pocahontas* (Henke & Umble, 1999). After viewing Disney's *Mulan* with my 9-year-old daughter, I turned to her and asked what she learned from the film. She replied, "Girls can do everything that boys can, and sometimes they can do it better!" Well, I thought, maybe Disney has redeemed itself and finally portrayed a historically correct feminist story.

As Disney's 36th animated feature, *Mulan* was released in June 1998 in the United States and took in more than $120 million at the box office (Fitzpatrick, 1998). Although *Pocahontas* (1995) grossed $142 million at the box office, *Mulan* fared better than both the *Hunchback of Notre Dame* (1996) and *Hercules* (1997), which made $101 million and $50.3 million, respectively (Lieberman, 1997). *Mulan*'s profits proved that "girl" films could succeed over "boy" films, even though *Mulan* had neither a romantic storyline nor did the lead character wear a sexy outfit like Pocahontas. *Mulan* also was the first of Disney's animated films to have a female producer, a screenplay team led by a woman, and a woman as head screenwriter. Woolverton, the screenwriter, was hailed as the first person to bring a strong female protagonist to the screen with Belle, even though in the end Belle settled for the traditional fairy tale ending of living happily ever after with her Prince Charming, formerly the Beast (Henke, Umble, & Smith, 1996).

With 1991's *Beauty and the Beast* and 1995's *Pocahontas*, Disney heroines continued to break ground with more feminist protagonists who act and speak for themselves. With *Pocahontas*, Disney appeared to even improve upon its formerly dismal showing of cultural stereotypes—such as its Native Americans in *Peter Pan* (1951), the Chinese in the form of evil Siamese cats in *Lady and the Tramp* (1953), African Americans and women in *The Jungle Book* (1967), Arab men and women in *Aladdin* (1992), and African-American and Latino stereotypes with their portrayals of evil hyenas in *The Lion King* (1994). However, *Pocahontas* continued Disney's sexist portrayal of females with its characterization of Pocahontas, who possessed a Barbie doll figure and a Playboy bunny-like costume. *Pocahontas* alá Disney also continued its portrayal of females without mothers, supportive female friends or relatives—regardless of the fact that the stories on which it and other Disney films were based often included such female characters. However, Disney did give Pocahontas a spiritual female willow tree and a spiritual mother wind who she could call on for advice. But in doing so, Disney perpetuated the cultural stereotype that all Native Americans are spirit-worshippers, or hallucinate and "see" spirits in nature all around them. Disney also veered away from the real, tragic story of Pocahontas, who likely was only 12 years old when she met Captain John Smith. The real Pocahontas would have been naked with a shaved head, according to historical accounts. She did not fall in love with John Smith, but later was captured by the English and imprisoned. Forced to deny her heritage, dress like an "English," and to marry an Englishman, she was taken to England, where she contracted smallpox and died (Henke & Umble, 1999).

But in 1998, with the U.S. release of *Mulan*, Disney seemed to have heeded the calls of feminists and people of color. Mulan appeared as a dignified person of color, a modern-day feminist carved from a Chinese heroine of some 2,000 years before. In Disney's *Mulan*, she has both parents, a grandmother, a demure outfit, a realistic physique, and no romantic storyline. Even as she frustrates the matchmaker, much to the chagrin of her parents and grandmother, she maintains her ideals. Is it possible that Disney became enlightened? Or did Disney find a tale that could appear feminist to its American audience while appearing traditional to its Chinese audience, thus satisfying both cultures in what appears to be a marketing coup. Because Fa Mulan is not of Euro-American ancestry, it is necessary for the rhetorical feminist critic to take into account both multiculturalism and feminism in analyzing the constructions of gender, race, class, sexual orientation, and culture in Disney's *Mulan*.

DISNEYFYING MULAN

In today's global society, Disney has extended its reach from its traditional North American audience to European audiences with its cultural icons. With *Mulan*, Disney captured the attention of China with its population of 1.2 billion, representing one of the largest potential movie markets in the world. According to Elaine Kurtenbach (1999), China "accepts only 10 American films a year. Hollywood studios, which can take about half their revenues from the foreign market, have been pushing Beijing to accept more American movies." After a run of anti-Chinese films such as *Seven Years in Tibet*, *Red Corner*, and Disney's own release, *Kundun*, the Chinese government accepted few American films into its borders. China initially refused in negotiations with Disney to import *Mulan* in 1998 but relented the following year. *Mulan* received nationwide release on February 23, 1999, just after the Lunar New Year holidays ended (Kurtenbach, 1999). The subject matter of *Mulan* no doubt helped the film's chances of being released in China because Fa Mulan has been revered for centuries by the Chinese.

However, it is important to note that *Mulan* is represented from Disney's cultural perspective. Because Disney's reach is so ubiquitous—marketing not only its films, but dolls, pajamas, lunchboxes, games, clothing, watches, books, theme parks, ice skating shows, and even packaging their film figure toys in children's fast food meals—audiences worldwide are invited to view her through Disney's lens. Thus, China's traditional folktale, intertwined with its own meanings and symbols, cultural definitions, religious, and philosophical backgrounds, is eclipsed.

The significance of Disney's influence is that if people do not know or bother to examine the historical and cultural stories of Fa Mulan through traditional means—reciting the *Song of Mulan*, retelling her tale in the oral tradition through poetry and literature—then Disney's version will be remembered, with its quirky additions of mythical dragon helpers and personified horses instead of the magnificent folktale that has stood for 2,000 years. Disney disregards traditional Confucian Chinese culture and instead provides the viewers with characters portraying 20th-century American values, complete with a mock dragon guardian ancestor in the form of a jive-talking Mushu, voiced by Eddie Murphy, who teaches Mulan "how to be a man." Providing its heroines with comic side-kicks is trademark Disney. Mulan also has a lucky cricket, Cri-Kee, given to her by her grandmother, and a heroic horse, Khan, who manages to save her neck more than once with his actions and personified nonverbal facial and body expressions.

DISNEY'S MULAN

At the outset of the film, the audience sees the Great Wall of China with its guards during the night. A large falcon cries as it flies overhead and lands on the wall. Next, thousands of oddly shaped hooks are thrown upon the upper reaches of the wall and suddenly, China is under siege by the Huns, led by one very large, yellow-eyed male villain named Shun Yu. Thus, we meet the first instance of "Disneyfication" to the traditional story of Fa Mulan. The Huns were not the invaders of China. Rather, Fa Mulan fought the Tartars, a nomadic band of barbarians from the North who often swept down into China to raid and pillage.

And even though Disney claims its film is based on the San Souci version of Fa Mulan, the Tartars are the marauders in San Souci's version, not the Huns. The historical discrepancy between the invaders is important from both a multicultural and historical standpoint. Both the Huns and the Tartars were of Asian descent and were considered roving bands of barbarians. However, Disney seems to confuse the two groups as Mulan's horse is named "Khan" (*Mulan*, 1999), a word used by the Tartars meaning "King." The Tartars comprised several nomadic tribes and clans, primarily of Mongolian, Slavish, and Turkish descent, who invaded China from the north over several centuries. In the *Song of Mulan*, the marauders streamed down form the north, which would be the most likely direction from which Mongolian tribes would arrive. While the Huns were also nomadic, warlike Asians, they devastated large parts of eastern and central Europe, but not China. Their greatest influence took place during the 5th century *A.D.* under Attila the Hun. Culturally, Disney is confusing the two cultural groups, changing history, and bombarding its audience with misinformation.

The following scene shows the emperor calling for the distribution of conscription rolls in every province throughout China, ordering its men to fight the invaders. The emperor remarks: "A single grain of rice can tip the scale; one man may be the difference between victory and defeat" (*Mulan*, 1999). The first glimpse of Mulan shows her digging into a rice bowl with her chopsticks while she repeats a memorized diatribe that she will have to repeat to the matchmaker later that day. In the folk tales of Fa Mulan and the Robert San Souci interpretation of the ancient legend, no such occurrence happens. In fact, Fa Mulan has a sister in the folk tale, but she does not appear in the Disney version. The sister in the traditional tale reprimands Fa Mulan for enacting an imaginary sword fight while on the way to the market and crying out, "I am a swordswoman like the Maiden of Yueh!" (San Souci, 1998, p. 1).[2] Fa Mulan's sister chides her and reminds her that women do not fight with swords. However, the Maiden of Yueh was another famous heroine in Chinese history who was revered for her bravery, like Fa Mulan some years later.

The next scene in *Mulan* depicts a rather inept Mulan who manages to ruin her chances with the matchmaker. Her family is distressed and scolds her for bringing them dishonor. Typical of Disney animated films of this genre, a song is used to foreshadow the coming action. Mulan sings:

> Look at me, I will never pass for a perfect bride or
> a perfect daughter.
> Can it be I'm not meant to play this part?
> Now I see that if I were truly to be myself, I would
> break my family's heart.
> Who is that girl I see staring straight back at me?
> Why is my reflection
> someone I don't know? Somehow I cannot hide
> who I am, though I've tried.
> When will my reflection show who I am inside?
>
> (Wilder & Zippel, 1998b, pp. 14-16)[3]

Mulan believes she is different but struggles with her identity and is not sure who she is just yet. Mulan carries the "traditional" thoughts of wanting to fit in, yet knows she does not. American audiences recognize the urge to break free of one's parents and convention. In American society, the ideal is to marry for love, not to honor family in an "arranged" marriage. Disney crosses multicultural boundaries by asserting its American view concerning matchmakers. However, in China at the time Mulan's story unfolds, matchmakers did not work out of an office nor did they give lessons on how to be a bride. Matchmakers came to the family home to discover the intentions of the family and acted to mediate between the families of the bride and groom (Mo & Shen, 2000).

In the next scene, Mulan sits on a garden bench under a magnolia tree with her father. She is upset because she brought dishonor to her family by being rejected by the matchmaker. Her father looks at a magnolia blossom that has not yet opened and remarks: "But look—this one's late, but when it blooms it will be the most beautiful of all" (*Mulan*, 1999). They then hear the war drums. As Mulan and her family hear her father's name called out on the conscription rolls, she runs forward to tell the man on horseback who has come for him that he is too infirm to serve. Her father steps up behind her as the man says, "You would do well to teach your daughter to hold her tongue in a man's presence." Mulan's father berates Mulan as he says, "Mulan, you dishonor me" (*Mulan*, 1999). That night, Mulan, determined to prove herself and restore her family's honor, cuts her hair, takes her father's sword and armor, saddles up the horse and leaves for battle without her parent's knowledge. They cry when they discover her gone the next morning. Her mother pleads with her father to go after Mulan because she might be killed. He replies, "If I reveal her, she will be" (*Mulan*, 1999).

Disney has once more strayed from the original story on which the film is based, as well as its cultural traditions. In the original tale, Mulan's parents are aware that she is taking the place of her ill father in battle, as she has no older brothers to do so. Chinese-born authors Weimin Mo and Wenju Shen (2000) pointed out that Confucian teachings allow children to replace their parents, and that Mulan is acting out of traditional Chinese values in joining the military in her father's stead. She is not, as Disney implies, acting on her own and disobedient to her parents. According to June Ock Yum (2000), social relationships and devotion to hierarchical family relations are the essence of Confucian doctrines. Whereas Americans applaud individualism, Chinese favor collectivism and tradition. These American values are illustrated in a female, Asian-American writer's interpretation of the scene:

> Too butch for the bride gig, Mulan is impulsive, disobedient and resolutely vocal in her defiance of the "seen and not heard" school of social conventions. She's a skilled martial artist and an intuitive strategist, a girl of action and intelligence who does the feet-sweeping, butt-kicking and outwitting. All at once. (Nguyen, 1998)

American feminist audiences interpret Mulan as a woman who finds her voice and challenges patriarchal conventions. Mulan defies the matchmaker, her parents, and society as she rides away from the family farm, determined to make it on her own in the military, disguised as a man. Although Mulan may look Chinese, she acts as though she is a modern American feminist.

Asian-American author Samuel Park (1998) wrote of the scene in which Mulan transforms herself into a male warrior: "the animators turn what is the equivalent of a girl dressing-up sequence into a deeply telling statement of a girl into woman, female into male, weak into powerful." From an American feminist standpoint, the audience views a disobedient girl-woman (ala *The Little Mermaid*'s Ariel), loved yet misunderstood by her parents and culture, who is weak as a girl yet becomes strong as a warrior. The scene "seems" to speak volumes about the status of women in Mulan's society, her powerlessness as a woman and power as a man. Yet, what it really offers is a scene that may be interpreted a multitude of ways, depending upon the culture and the values of the viewer. The larger problem with this scene is that Americans do not have the opportunity to understand or learn anything about Mulan's culture—including respect for it. Disney offers a distinctly ethnocentric viewpoint as we assume everyone shares American beliefs, traditions, and values.

Later in the film, Mulan is wounded while saving her unit from certain death at the hands of China's enemies. She is expelled from the army after her gender is discovered by the doctor who tends her injuries. Mulan chides herself for her motivations for joining the army, for dishonoring her family, and for her mistakes: "Maybe I didn't do it for my father. I wanted to prove I could do things right, when I'd look in the mirror I'd see someone worthwhile. But I was wrong. I see nothing" (*Mulan*, 1998). Mulan then hears the cry of the Hun leader's falcon, foreshadowing trouble ahead for the Chinese troops. When Mulan sees the falcon, she mounts her horse and rides into the Imperial City to warn her people that the Huns are about to capture their capital. Li Shun, her captain, ignores her warning. Mulan asks him why he doesn't believe her: "You trust Ping (Mulan's name as a soldier in disguise), why is Mulan any different?" Her ancestral dragon and comic sidekick, Mushu replies, "No one listens to a girl." Mulan then acts on her own to save the emperor from the Hun leader, Shan Yu.

American feminists may well read this scene as a protagonist who acts heroically through her intelligence and bravery. Chinese view a woman who acts out of honor, bravery and love for her country. As Mulan asks, "Who am I," she struggles against tradition, stereotypical gender roles and patriarchal dominance. Disney's Mulan is a postmodern American feminist, not a 5th-century A.D. Chinese woman warrior. From an American feminist perspective, Mulan is a strong, radical feminist who follows her inclinations, disregards her gender, becomes a "man," and proves she can "out-man" the men with her courage, intelligence, and bravery.

Yet, there are two more important points to be made about the sequence where Mulan's parents say she will be killed if the army discovers her gender. In the film, when the physician tends to her wounds, he tells her commanding officer that she is not who she appears to be. Her captain spares her life because she acted valiantly to save his earlier in the film. Another officer demands she be put to death, for disguising oneself as a man is a treasonable offense. Instead, she is ordered to go home in dishonor. Mo and Shen (2000) pointed out that "there has never been a law or tradition of banning girls from going to war" (p. 133).

In another filmic sequence, the audience meets Mulan's military comrades. Scene after scene parody the men and their American "manly" habits, such as patting one another on the buttocks, punching each other on the shoulder, expectorating, and fantasizing about their male prowess with females as evidenced by the song "A Girl Worth Fighting For" (Wilder & Zippel, 1998a). These scenes are more reminiscent of the American images we view on the newsreels and historical footage of our soldiers returning from World War II than that of 5th-century Chinese warriors. When Mulan interjects a line of her own into the song about a woman who has a brain and speaks her mind, similar to a line from Belle in *Beauty and the Beast*, the men boo her. It appears as though the characters on the screen are drawn with Chinese features, yet they speak in clear, American accents, and act the way in which patriarchal 20th-century American men are expected to behave. Has Disney created "banana" characters—yellow on the outside and white on the inside—as some critics profess? Katherine Kim (1998), an Asian American who reviewed *Mulan* for *Salonmagazine.com*, said Mulan is just that—"not a Chinese woman warrior, but an Asian-American feminist."

So although Disney would have us believe that *Mulan* is based on a real, historical Chinese woman warrior, she is really anything but true to the original tale. *Mulan* follows Disney's formulaic animated film genre that began in 1938 with *Snow White*. Although Disney has updated its characters and stories with time, it always follows a similar track, which includes comedic animal or inanimate pals that speak verbally or non-verbally to the female protagonist; moving the action along with songs and popular themes that reflect American culture during the time of the film's original release; and, true to Disney form, a happy ending.

Mulan is no exception to the rule. Themes that appear in *Mulan* are love of family, honor, bravery, intelligence, beauty, and self-sacrifice. Although *Mulan* tells an ancient tale of a brave, Chinese woman warrior, Disney adds embellishments of its own which stamp it with the Disney trademark. And, in doing so, it usurps the audience's ability to distinguish between the authentic story and that of Disney's writers. The subterfuge does not lie with the comedic sidekicks or even in the addition of a grandmother or deletion of a sister. The enculturation or "*re-culturation*" of what is Chinese and what is not is the real issue. For the audience, the children who view the film believe what they see. Instead of the ancient legend that was once passed from one generation to another in the form of oral poetry, the Disney version is what children around the world have come to know. Subtleties of the Chinese culture, respect for one's ancestors, action due to filial piety and honoring one's parents are all lost on this new audience. While Disney manages not to perpetuate negative stereotypes of Chinese people to its American audiences, it nonetheless fashions the Chinese as Americans.

In fact, *Mulan* did not do well in China until the marketers of Disney changed the film in some significant ways—to make it "more Chinese." Changes included special posters reflecting more of the "true" Mulan legend; dubbing of voice-overs by Chinese actors rather than the American actors used in the U.S. release; changing the musical score; and concentrating on different poster themes in Taiwan and Hong Kong, where the film was released prior to its 1998 release in China. Consumer interviews conducted by BuenaVista films, distributors of Walt Disney films, found that the marketing approach used in America did not work very well with young, Chinese families. As a result:

> Distributors launched posters specially tailored to the Taiwan market—a first for Disney—featuring the bright-eyed, plucky heroine

riding her horse before an expansive Chinese landscape. In Hong Kong, promoters launched their own poster series playing up Chinese culture by superimposing the calligraphy for intelligence, honor, inner grace, and courage against a mountain backdrop . . . Laura Folta, marketing manager for BuenaVista films in Taiwan said, "we tested this image, and it was overwhelming."

The strategy paid off in both markets. After only 11 days, *Mulan* broke Disney's Taiwan box office record of $49 million Hong Kong ($125,572,300) pulled in by its 1994 hit, *The Lion King*. In Hong Kong, *Mulan* took in $14.5 million Hong Kong ($35,877,800) in 3 weeks and closed in on the Hong Kong $16 million ($41,000,000) record of *The Lion King* (Flannery, 1998).

In mainland China, *Mulan* did not fare as well. A number of theories were floated to account for the difference in profits, but two stood out: (a) large numbers of pirated copies of *Mulan* were sold on the mainland prior to its release in movie houses; and (b) the Chinese government scheduled the release of the film on the last day of the Chinese lunar holidays, after which the children returned to school (Bezlova, 1999).

But a male Chinese film-goer named Li Hui may provide a better insight as to why *Mulan* was not as popular at the box office in China. Hui said the movie "was strange. Only foreigners could make this kind of film. It wasn't like watching the Chinese story of Mulan. It could have been any other foreign cartoon" (Bezlova, 1999, p. D-3). Although some Chinese film-goers were not excited by the film, the Chinese government was happy enough with Disney's *Mulan* that it agreed to negotiate with Michael Eisner, Disney chairman and Chief executive officer, to build two theme parks in China, one in Shanghai and the other in Hong Kong (Savadove, 1999). This move on the part of the Chinese government demonstrated a shift in its opinion of Disney. The government had been disinclined to release *Mulan* in 1998 because of Disney's previously unflattering view of China's handling of Tibet in the film *Kundun*. Disney continues to profit as it markets Mickey Mouse, Winnie the Pooh, and now, Disney Princess merchandise to Chinese girls from ages 2 to 10. The Disney Princess brand will include images of Snow White, Cinderella, Belle from *Beauty and the Beast*, Mermaid, Jasmine from *Aladdin*, and Sleeping Beauty ("*Disney Princess,*" 2003). Daniel Tso, vice president of the company's Asia Pacific Region, said Disney estimates "the brand value of Disney Princess will exceed US $4 billion by 2006 . . . all of them rooted deeply in little girls' fantasy and the idea of 'prince and princess living happily after' is what girls dream about" ("*Disney Princess,*" 2003). *Mulan* is not included among the Disney princesses, and all but one, Princess Jasmine of *Aladdin*, are White. However, Jasmine is modeled after White women's "ideal" bodies, not East Indian women's bodies, so although her skin is dark, her features and body elements are White.

What, then, will be the message and impact of these images on Chinese girls? Does it say that only White women deserve to be happy? Does it mean that only White women are beautiful? Will the messages diminish Chinese girls' own sense of worthiness? Feminists might also wonder why Disney sees fit to portray strong, American feminist protagonists only as females of color, as Pocahontas or Mulan. What message does this give to Euro-American females who may strive to claim their own selves and voices? Chinese children swim in a ubiquitous sea of Disney images of historical misinformation, stereotypic representations of gender, and myths of happiness that mesh multiple cultures through its profiteering and globalization efforts. Indeed, according to the *Shanghai Daily*, "more than 100 Chinese companies are producing products under the Disney brand, whose sales reached US $50 million last year on China's mainland" ("Shanghai eyes," 2003). Disney continues to profit, but the real cost is to Chinese culture and Chinese children.

CONCLUSION

At the end of the film, Mulan is rewarded by the Emperor for saving China. He offers her a post as his highest counsel. True to the original legend, Mulan refuses the Emperor's offer, asking only that she return home to her family. The Emperor gives her gifts to take with her as proof of her heroism. Mulan's captain is speechless as Mulan leaves. The Emperor tells Shang Li that "a flower who blooms in adversity is the most rare and beautiful of all." In other words, he says, in true Disney fashion, "you don't meet a girl like that every dynasty." As Mulan walks into the garden and bows as she presents her father with the Emperor's gifts, her father says, "The greatest gift and honor is having you for a daughter." Unfortunately, the film does not end there, as Captain Shang arrives looking for Mulan. Her grandmother tells Mulan's mother that she wants to sign up for the next war if you meet men like him there. This comment diminishes everything that Mulan earned in terms of being a strong, brave, female protagonist. So Disney, ever true to its animated female heroines, leaves the audience believing that Mulan will live "happily ever after" with her man—taking up the traditional role of wife and mother. While Mushu is reinstated as a legitimate spiritual dragon ancestor, he calls out for an order of egg rolls and Stevie Wonder plays the ending tune—once again, not adhering to Chinese tradition, as the order would consist of spring rolls, and the tune certainly would not be from Stevie Wonder (Mo & Shen, 2000).

Although Disney has the right to change things for dramatic license, and even to fit its filmic genre, there lies a danger when Disney changes historical stories. Through "Disneyfication," the cultural significance of the story is lost. New generations will remember the Disney version instead of the 2,000-year-old legend of Mulan. Mulan appears Chinese on the outside, but she exhibits 20th-century American feminist attitudes and actions. Disney audiences will have no appreciation or understanding of Confucian doctrine or what really motivated Mulan's actions. American audiences will come to believe that Chinese women and men differ only in physical appearance, for all other cultural differences have been made to disappear. Respect and appreciation of diversity is lost. Recreating other cultures from a Western standpoint, as Disney has done with *Mulan*, denies the legitimacy of other cultural traditions, stories, and values.

NOTES

1. Romance is not part of the storyline, but Mulan's captain pursues her in the end.
2. According to San Souci (1998), the Maiden of Yueh may have been a role model of Fa Mulan because her story preceded Fa Mulan's by several centuries. The Maiden of Yueh was well known and appears in Chinese poems, folk songs, and operas.
3. Ariel in *The Little Mermaid* (1989), Belle in *Beauty and the Beast* (1991), and Pocahontas in *Pocahontas* (1995) all sing similar songs about not fitting in with other girls or, for that matter, with society at large.

REFERENCES

Bezlova, A. (1999, February 24). Much-pirated "Mulan" plays to sparse Shanghai houses. *USA Today*, p. D-3.

Disney Princess coming to town Disney Princess coming to town. (2003, August 28). *China Daily*. Retrieved September 6, 2004, from http://www2.chinadaily.com.

Coats, P. (Producer), Woolverton, L. (Screenwriter), Cook, B. (Director), & Bancroft, T. (Director). (1999) *Mulan* [Motion Picture]. Glendale, CA: Buena Vista Home Entertainment.

Fitzpatrick, E. (1998, November 7). Mulan, Dalmatians, and Winnie-the-Pooh due in '99. *Billboard*, p. 92.

Flannery, R. (1998, July 31). Disney markets new animated film to tastes of Taiwan and Hong Kong. *The Wall Street Journal, Eastern Edition*, p. B-12.

Henke, J.B., & Umble, D.Z. (1999). And she lived happily ever after: The Disney myth in the video age. In M. Meyers (Ed.), *Mediated women: Representations in popular culture* (pp. 321-337). Cresskill, NJ: Hampton Press.

Henke, J.B., Umble, D.Z., & Smith, N.J. (1996). Construction of the female self: Feminist readings of the Disney heroine. *Women's Studies in Communication, 19*(2), 229-249.

Kim, K. (1998). The Disney peril. *Salon Magazine.* Retrieved February 8, 1999, from http://www.salonmagazine.com.

Kuo, A. (1998, December 6). Mulan FAQ. Retrieved February 8, 1999, from http://222.geocities.com/Hollywood5802/variations.html.

Kurtenbach, E. (1999, February 8). China allows disney film screening. *World Tibet News Index.* Retrieved July 24, 2000, from http"//www.tibet.ca/wtnarchive/1999/2/8_5.html.

Lieberman, D. (1997, July 7). Weak "Hercules" may sap Disney's strength. *USA Today*, p. B-1.

Mulan Mania. (1999, February 23). *USA Today*, p. D-1.

Mo, W., & Shen, W. (2000). A mean wink at authenticity: Chinese images in Disney's *Mulan*. *The New Advocate, 13*(2), 129-142.

Nguyen, M. (1998, July 5). Role models: Mulan. *San Jose Mercury News.* Retrieved July 24, 2000 from http://www.theory.org.nk/ctr-rol2.htm

Park, S. (1998, July 16). Mulan and Company. *Medianstrip.net.* Retrieved October 9, 2000 from http://www.medianstrip.net/arc/author/sp/071698.shtml.

San Souci, R. (1998). *Fa Mulan.* New York: Hyperion Books for Children.

Savadove, B. (1999, March 8). Two Disneys in China not too much? *Reuters News.* Retrieved July 24, 2000 from http://www.freerepublic.com/forum136e48c271c39htm.

Shanghai eyes 2nd Disney park for China. (2003, November 13). *China Daily.* Retrieved September 6, 2004.

Wilder, M., & Zippel, D. (1998a). A girl worth fighting for. In *Mulan Songs for piano, voice, guitar*. Milwaukee, WI: Hal Leonard Corp.

Wilder, M., & Zippel, D. (1998b). Reflection. In *Mulan Songs for piano, voice, guitar*. Milwaukee, WI: Hal Leonard Corporation.

Yum, J.O. (2000). Confucianism and interpersonal relationships and communication patterns in East Asia. In L. Samovar & R. Porter, (Eds.), *Intercultural communication: A reader* (9th ed., pp. 63-73). Belmont, CA: Wadsworth.

8

Bollywood and Globalization

Reassembling Gender and Nation in Kal Ho Na Ho

Anjali Ram

We live in a world where CNN simultaneously beams its news coverage to Baghdad, Beijing, Berlin, and Boston; where the Hong Kong-produced, Mandarin-speaking film *Crouching Tiger, Hidden Dragon* was a major blockbuster in the United States; where small towns all over Asia receive MTV and have witnessed J Lo's, gyrations; and where movie theaters in New York, Hong Kong, and Johannesburg alike exhibit the latest movies from India to packed houses. As Arjun Appadurai (1999) stated, we live in "a world of flows" (p. 230). Similarly, Morley and Robins (1995) explained that the globalization of media implies the creation of a global space, which is a "space of flows, an electronic space, a decentered space, a space in which frontiers and boundaries have become permeable" (p. 115).

Cinema has always been part of the global flow of media. Ever since the Lumiére brothers saw the potential of exhibiting their cinematic productions beyond Parisian cafés, and Nickelodeons in New York taught new immigrants English through talkies, cinema has been integral to the globalization of culture and capital. Most discussions of the globalization of cinema are centered on Hollywood and its large and pervasive presence in the world. In contrast, there has been less attention paid to ways in which Bollywood, the nickname for the Indian movie industry, travels around the globe. Like Hollywood, Bollywood is popular beyond its domestic market in India and is enthusiastically consumed in South Africa, Europe, the Middle East, Hong Kong, the Caribbean, the United Kingdom, and even Afghanistan. Bollywood surpasses Hollywood in the number of movies it produces every year, and as Power and Mazumdar (2000) asserted, "for hundreds of millions of fans around the world, it is Bollywood . . . not Hollywood, that spins their screen fantasies" (p. 52). Given its prolific production of media texts consumed by a global audience, questions about how Bollywood represents and constructs meaning are crucial.

Media texts are entangled in a complex arrangement of socioeconomic, cultural, and political associations and multiple layers of spectatorship. As Bollywood increasingly becomes a global media product, examining its texts for evolving ways of signifying gender becomes a crucial step in understanding the transnational circuit of media production and consumption. I telescope my analysis to reading the recent box office hit, *Kal Ho Na Ho* (*Tomorrow May Never Come*, 2003). Shot mostly in New Jersey and New York and released in 2003, *Kal Ho Na Ho* (*KHNH*) grossed over more than $4 million internationally when it opened and has been touted as one of the most popular movies in the international Bollywood circuit. Prompted by its enormous global success, I examine the ways in which gender is coded in *KHNH*. I argue that although the film offers multiple ways in which women are positively represented, it ultimately reinscribes the patriarchal universe common to Indian cinema. Simultaneously rejecting and reaffirming patriarchy points to Bollywood's attempt to chart out a space between tradition and modernity, West and East, home and abroad, and convention and innovation. Highlighting the ambivalent assembling of gender, *KHNH* provides us with an entry point to discuss how Indian cinema is being reconfigured in relation to the global, transnational context of its reception.

BOLLYWOOD AND ITS GLOBAL AUDIENCE

From *The New York Times* and *Newsweek* to ABC's *Nightline* and CBS's *60 Minutes*, news reports exclaiming and expounding on Bollywood as a global media phenomena have been increasing. Bollywood's global audience includes fans in the Middle East, Africa, and Asia. As Power and Mazumdar (2000), writing for *Newsweek*, claim, Romany Gypsies in eastern Europe and Swahili-speaking schoolgirls make up the diverse mosaic of the global Bollywood audience. Although non-Indian audiences make up a sizable proportion of the international reception, 55% of international ticket sales are accounted for by the Indian diaspora (Power & Mazumdar, 2000).

Not only do both men and women in the Indian diaspora[1] actively consume Bollywood, but as a genre Bollywood emerges in a range of cultural practices and products, from inspiring simulated, amateur performances at community gatherings, to being the main topic of discussion in Indian immigrant community television and radio shows. Chakravarty (1993) commented that Indian commercial cinema metoynomically references "India" for immigrants, and Das Dasgupta (1993) wrote that for Indian immigrants, Indian cinema plays an important role in maintaining a "continuity in their dislocation" (p. 56). Besides watching films, the Indian immigrant community often plays host to visiting film stars who perform at gala events in major cities in the United States. Frequently, the guest of honor for the celebration of national holidays and social/religious events in the Indian immigrant community is a prominent Hindi film star. On such occasions, young women in the community typically dress according to the latest Bombay cinema fashions and dance to songs from Hindi films (Dasgupta, 1993; Mukhi, 1998; Sen 2003).

Until recently, diasporic Indians figured primarily as spectators and consumers of Indian cinema. With the exception of a handful of movies such as *Purab aur Paschim* (*East and West*, 1970), Indian diasporic communities rarely appeared as central to the Hindi film narratives. However, since the 1990s, with the enormous success of *Dilwale Dhulhaniya Le Jeyenge* (*The Lover Wins the Bride*, 1995), where both the heroine and the hero were portrayed as British-born Indians, the Indian diaspora has become a primary subject in Indian cinema. Yash Chopra, the well-known director of *Dilwale*, commented that earlier "we used to go abroad because of the locations. Now we are basing our characters there" (cited in Jain & Chowdhary, 1997, p. 20). The director of another box office hit set in the United States, *Pardes* (*Foreign Land*, 1997), Subhash Ghai, commented bluntly: "My film is about American dreams and the Indian soul . . . every young person is dreamy [*sic*] about the place [America]. But only on reaching there does he realize that there are things about himself that he cannot change." Chopra echoed such sentiments and asserted that immigrants wish to rediscover their roots after seeing such films, stating "what they are looking for is . . . tradition" (cited in Jain & Chowdhary, 1997, p. 20). Dubbed as "pop patriotism," films such as *Dilwale* and *Pardes* interpellate the migrant viewer by presenting narratives of an eternal, idyllic India, and evoking nostalgic longings for the "homeland."

Scripting the nation into their narratives is frequent and pervasive in Indian cinema, and the movies located in the diaspora are no exception. Most of the movies that center on the diaspora, such as *Purab aur Paschim* and the more recent *Pardes*, present a series of polarizations that equate India with spirituality, tradition, culture and purity, as opposed to the West, which is associated with materialism, modernity, and depravity. Typically, this rhetoric of nationalism is organized through the female body, where the woman represents the nation. In the next section, I explain more fully how Bollywood cinema casts this gendered nation.

THE NATION/WOMAN QUESTION
IN INDIAN CINEMA

Ever since its inception, Indian cinema has contributed to the dialogue on Indian nationhood (Chakravarty, 1993; Ganti, 2004; Virdi, 2003) and drawn deeply on Hindu mythology for its thematic material. Consequently, Indian cinema's narration of the nation usually collapses "Hindu" with "Indian" and naturalizes mythic-religious representations of national identity. Entangled with such ideological configurations of the nation is the question of gender. Woven through many cinematic texts is the relationship between the purity/sanctity of women and the purity/sanctity of the nation (Thomas, 1989). In a pamphlet designed to introduce the film *Mother India* (1957) to Western audiences, the ideological framing of Indian womanhood is clearly stated. The Indian woman is described as "an altar in India." The same pamphlet points out that "Indians measure the virtue of their race by the chastity of their women," and that the Indian mother is "the nucleus around which revolves the tradition and the culture of ages" (Thomas, 1989, p. 21). Images of purity are maintained by representing chaste heroines, whose sexuality is confined within the bounds of heterosexual marriage. Moreover, the common narrative strategy in Indian cinema, where the villain threatens to violate the heroine and is foiled in his attempts by the hero, serves among other things to re-establish the moral order, which includes preserving the chastity of the woman.

The Hindu goddess *Sita* represents one such embodiment of purity, chastity, and the careful control of sexuality continuously circumscribed within the domain of heterosexual marriage, family, and the nation. Prescribed as the feminine ideal by the classic Hindu text the *Manu-Smriti*, stories about *Sita* are used to promote strong patriarchal ideologies primarily through the notion of *pati-vrata* or complete devotion to the husband (Courtright, 1995). *Sita* imagery can be seen in movies such as *Pati Parmeshwar* (*Husband/God*, 1988), *Naseeb Apna Apna* (*Different Destinies*, 1986), and *Daasi* (*Female Slave*, 1981) where, according to Saidullha, (1992), "the martyred traditional wife who wins her man from the bad, modern, ambitious woman is celebrated" (p. 38). Similarly, Vasudev (1983) referred to films such as *Thodisi Bewafaii* (*A Brief Betrayal*, 1980) and *Do Anjane* (*Two Strangers*, 1979) in commenting on how the woman who transgresses the role of the devoted, chaste wife is duly punished.

Often *Sita* images are interchanged with images of Ganga, similarly coding the feminine as the repository of purity and as a sign of nationhood. The river Ganga, which originates in the Himalayas and winds its vast way across the northern Indian plains to the Bay of Bengal, is considered immensely sacred in Hinduism. Personified as the goddess Ganga Ma (Mother Ganga), this river is believed to cleanse one of all impurities, blessing humankind and providing a link between corporeal and spiritual worlds (Kingsley, 1993). Given such luxurious, mythic reverberations, Ganga has been a popular name for Bombay film heroines, particularly when the epithets to be transferred symbolize purity and sacredness. Notable film examples using the iconography of Ganga are *Jis Desh Mein Ganga Beheti Hai* (*The Land Where the Ganga Flows*, 1960), *Ganga ke Saugand* (*Ganga as My Witness*, 1976), *Ram Teri Ganga Maili* (*Ram, Your Ganga is Polluted, 1986*), and the more recent film *Pardes* (1997). In contrast, adulterous women or stock characters such as the "vamp" or the gangster's moll are often given Western or Christian names (e.g., Mona, Dolly, and/or Lily), symbolically associating their "impurity" with Western culture, modernity, and materialism.

In the 1970 film *Purab aur Paschim*, the degeneration of the West is aggressively counterposed against the "purity and tradition" of Indian culture. Written, produced, and directed by Manoj Kumar, who is well known for making patriotic films in the 1970s and the 1980s, *Purab aur Paschim* was a box office success. The male protagonist, in Pygmalion fashion, transforms the heroine, a British-born Indian woman who acquired her wanton ways in the West, into the ideal Indian woman. This change is effected symbolically by the heroine abandoning her mini-skirts and coming to understand the meaning of *sharam* or shame. She emerges transformed at the end of the movie, demurely clad in a red and gold silk sari, her head appropriately covered to signify her compliance to traditional Indian precepts of femininity. Subsequent films set in the diaspora similarly transpose the construction of gender and nation onto each other in order to construct the Western-influenced diaspora as materialist, selfish, and "exhibitionist" versus the homeland as spiritual, "simple, and selfless" (Mishra, 2002, p. 268).

In the following section, I examine how *KHNH* repudiates some of the typical gendered tropes recruited in nation-building and the construction of the idealized homeland. By pointing out the ambiguities and contradictions in *KHNH*, I suggest that it represents Bollywood's effort to grapple with its role as an increasingly transnational cinema targeted at the evolving global spectator.

FROM NATIONALISM TO TRANSNATIONALISM

Although the nation/woman trope is used pervasively and persistently to organize the representation of gender in Indian cinema, its representation has not been static. Images that contest and contradict the stereotypical gendered formulation emerge periodically to subvert and transgress the patriarchal universe of Indian cinema. To document and comment on all the ways in which the representation of gender has shifted and changed in Indian cinema is beyond the scope of this chapter. Instead, by focusing on *KHNH*, I explore some of the ambivalent ways in which the text constructs and performs gender as it edits and reassembles the patriarchal universe of Indian cinema. I highlight themes in the movie that seem to offer a more progressive portrayal of gender and sexuality only to contain and constrain it within a male-ordered ideology. I argue that such ambivalence suggests the recognition of the Indian diasporic spectator who continuously attempts to negotiate narratives of home–abroad, margin–center and East–West that are precariously and restlessly balanced against each other. On the one hand, the uncertainty and instability of being migrant and/or minority leads the diasporic audience to find the aggressive valorization of and essentialized "Indian-ness" and gendered nationalist ideology promoted by Indian cinema as comforting and validating (Ram, 2002). On the other hand, living in the West, negotiating with its rhetoric of individualism, the inevitable inter-generational conflicts, and the globalized marketplace prompt uneasiness with the monolithic, reified constructions of gender and nation.

SUMMARY OF *KHNH*

The plot of *KHNH* revolves around a love triangle. The setting is New York, and we are first introduced to Naina (played by Bollywood super-star Priety Zinta), who is a second-generation Indian woman in her 20s. She lives with her mother, grandmother, younger sister, and brother. Her father is deceased, her mother struggles to make ends meet with her café, and Naina is studying for her MBA by attending night school. Naina's good friends consist of Sweetu and Rohit, who are both second-generation Indians like herself. Sweetu lives with her sister, Jas, who is the co-owner of the café with Naina's mother. Rohit, in contrast, comes from an affluent family, but he is determined to make it on his own in the city. Into their lives enter the protagonist, Aman, played by Bollywood's current leading male star, Shah Rukh Khan. Aman has come to New York to seek treatment for his heart condition. However, he keeps his illness a secret and infuses everyone with his *joie de vivre*. Naina falls in love with Aman, and Rohit falls in love with Naina. Knowing his heart condition is fatal, Aman, who also is in love with Naina, chooses to keep his feelings secret and instead attempts to bring Naina and Rohit together. After a series of emotionally charged scenes and situations, Naina and Rohit get married, and Aman finally succumbs to heart failure.

MOTHERS, DAUGHTERS, SISTERS, FRIENDS

The central role played by women in *KHNH* is demonstrated by the preponderance of female characters and plot developments that revolve around female relationships. After the opening monologue, Naina's mother, Jenny, is introduced. She is talking on the phone with the bank manager attempting to convince him to extend her loan so that her café business can survive. She struggles to choke back her tears as Naina enters. They are united in their grief as Naina has just been immersed in her own sorrow related to the loss of her father. The intergenerational thread of associations includes Lajjo, Naina's paternal grandmother, and Gia, Naina's younger sister. These associations are not a celebration of women's support and mutual sustenance. Rather, Jenny and her mother-in-law, Lajjo, are caught in a toxic relationship of mutual, bitter distrust. However, a crucial aspect of the plot development is the resolution of their relationship, which eventually leads to a strong, supportive alliance that binds all three generations of women. The emphasis on female relationships is echoed in the fact that the coffee shop is co-owned by two women, without any apparent male assistance or support.

Women collaborating and building community is clearly a strong theme in *KHNH*. The initial acrimony and anger that mark Jenny and Lajjo's relationship and taint the lives of Naina and Gia with misery and gloom are ultimately resolved. To emphasize the strong bond of women in this film, the concluding scene depicts Naina narrating her story to a now grown-up Gia. Naina has a young daughter playing in the background to remind the audience of future generations of women who carry with them the stories and experiences of their foremothers.

Although these narrative elements clearly indicate that *KHNH* is a story that places women at the center, it ultimately gives power back to the male character. Despite underlining women's roles and presence in this text, it is the male character, Aman, who assists in mending the relationships between the women. His intervention and the power of his arguments are eventually the key to unlocking the secrets that divided and isolated these generations of women. Similarly, although the coffee shop is owned by two women, it is a failing business until Aman steps in with his fresh, new, vigorous marketing ideas. Aman thus emerges as a benevolent force working in the background to bring peace, harmony, stability, and even prosperity in the lives of these women. The fact that his name means "peace" is not a coincidence. Placing Aman as peacekeeper and savior thus robs *KHNH* of its potential to truly be a progressive, feminist text.

WOMAN AS SUBJECT

By depicting several generations of women, *KHNH* presents a narrative of progression. Lajjo, the grandmother, is caught in a world of traditional values and unyielding orthodoxy. Jenny, the mother, on one hand subscribes to a conventional model of sacrificing motherhood and on the other demonstrates an unusual sensitivity in understanding human relationships in a changing world. Naina, the American-born daughter, is invested with cosmopolitan markers, from swinging her Burberry handbag, sipping her Starbucks latte and munching a low fat bagel, to jogging through Central Park. These signs are supposed to signal to the audience that she is situated in the metropolitan West and, as her narrative voiceover informs us, she associates her self-reliance and skeptical outlook with New York. Representing the second-generation Indian diaspora, Naina is a product of two worlds. Naina's character is clearly an improvement on the way in which women of the Indian diaspora have been typically represented. Usually, the Indian woman brought up in the West is portrayed as superficial and licentious, her depravity associated with being Western. Inevitably she is transformed and disciplined, becoming "good," and exemplifying purity and sanctity. Sometimes she is presented as culturally unsullied, demonstrating that despite being situated in the West, her Indian selfhood is untainted.

KHNH reassembles such stock images of the Indian diaspora by presenting Naina as a second generation Indian American woman who successfully shuttles back and forth between the inner world of the Indian diasporic community and the outer world of the Western metropolis. Her journey is symbolized by the musical score in the opening scene, where the strains of a Mozart symphony give way to the drumbeat of *Punjabi bhangra*[2] music as she approaches her home located in an Indian enclave in Brooklyn. With relative ease she navigates the borders of cultural difference as she does the "disco" at a club, attends salsa dancing classes, and effortlessly participates in traditional Indian engagement and wedding rituals. She exemplifies the acculturation strategy of integration as she comfortably participates and accepts her bicultural identity. The demonization of the West seen in movies set in the diaspora is minimized in *KHNH*, so that Naina's transformation is not presented as a movement from being Western and corrupt to becoming Indian and virtuous, nor is she presented as an embodiment of traditional Indian womanhood. Instead, her development is depicted as being a personal, individual journey where she learns how to deal with her own inner demons. There is no narrative of return in *KHNH*, where the immigrant longs for the idealized India. Nor is Naina's character employed as a cipher for the nation. When introducing herself, her voiceover proclaims, "I am Naina Katherine Kapoor, and this is my story." Naming here is significant as her name reflects both her Hindu and Christian heritage. Indian cinema often erases minority voices by conflating being "Indian" as being "Hindu." India is a multicultural nation where different religious, linguistic and ethnic communities jostle together. By defining the Indian self as the opposite of the Western self, Bollywood submerges these regional, religious, and local differences. Hinduism, which is the dominant but not exclusive religion in India, is then made to symbolize the essential Indian character. This inscription of the Indian nation as a Hindu nation employs gender as its vehicle to communicate itself as moral, spiritual, and respectable. By emphasizing Naina's Catholic genealogy, inherited through her mother Jenny, an Indian Christian, *KHNH* resists coding her as a sign for the Indian/Hindu nation.

In the final scene, Naina once again locates herself as the narrator of the film with her last words: "I am Naina Katherine Kapoor Patel, and this was my story." The addition of Patel refers not just to her marriage to Rohit, but also emphasizes his regional identity as a Gujrathi. By emphasizing such regional and religious diversity through her name, *KHNH* belies the common strategy of eclipsing local and minority identities in favor of a universal Hindu/Indian national self. Furthermore, the refusal to subscribe to the characteristic woman/nation formula of Indian cinema points to a shift in the way *KHNH* represents the diasporic subject. By highlighting the individual and the personal, *KHNH* attempts to mediate gender without the refracting lens of nationalist rhetoric.

Woman as subject in *KHNH* is further signaled by the fact that the movie opens with Naina's voice narrating the story. She introduces us to the various characters and sets the stage for the plot to unravel. Her voice returns in the concluding scene and we realize that the narrative has just been told as a flashback. The use of a female narrator who states in her introductory monologue that this is her story is a device that situates the woman as subject in *KHNH*. Feminist film critics have written extensively about woman as object in the male-centered universe of mainstream western cinema and deplored the absence of woman as subject (Kaplan, 1983; Mulvey, 1989; Silverman, 1983). Indian cinema similarly is dominated by the male subject (Chakravarty, 1993; Virdi, 2003). By introducing Naina as the chief protagonist and narrator, *KHNH* offers us a woman-centered story. As the plot progresses, it is Naina who develops, changes, and transforms. Her voiceover is woven through the narrative informing the audience about her psychological transformation. Furthermore, she introduces the other characters, comments on them, and situates their place in this retrospective narration. In the final scene, she completes her tale and reflects on her life, emphasizing her primacy as the film's narrator and subject.

Although Naina is certainly the subject of this narrative, she is not the agent. In other words, she does not initiate action or move the plot forward. Instead, the prime agent of this narrative remains the chief male character, Aman. He acts as the puppet master and the plot progresses because of him. He is the one who forces Naina to look within and change, resolves conflicts between various characters, saves Jenny's café and, most importantly, submerges his own feelings for Naina and plays cupid to Naina and Rohit. So although female subjectivity is clearly introduced in *KHNH*, male agency is still preserved. The male center is restructured, but the larger male order of mainstream Indian cinema remains intact.

Ultimately, it is Aman—in Pygmalion-like fashion—who effects Naina's transformation from being pessimistic and repressed to becoming optimistic and uninhibited. Although the use of the male protagonist as the eventual and inevitable puppet master limits the progressive potential of the film, *KHNH* nevertheless unsettles the prototype of the gendered nation.

RECASTING MASCULINITY/
REASSIGNING SEXUALITIES

Embedded in Indian cinema's construction of the nation are masculinity, heterosexuality and the affirmation of traditional marriage and family.

As Virdi (2003) explained, Indian cinema's narratives "are unfailingly centered on a hero and heroine, who together constitute its fundamental templates in which masculinity is the flip side of femininity" (p. 87). Although Aman clearly controls the action and has a god-like role in *KHNH*, several features of the film suggest a reconfiguring of patriarchy through the recasting of masculinity and a comic reassignment of sexuality. For one thing, the male characters in the film in sheer number and importance are outmatched by the female characters. Additionally, hypermasculinity, which is typical in Bollywood cinema, is notably absent. There is no villain for the hero to vanquish, restore order, and demonstrate his power. Instead, would-be male rivals Amit and Rohit quickly become supportive friends. Such portrayals of male friendship are not unusual for Indian cinema. Several Indian movies underscore the relationship between two male heroes. *KHNH* similarly portrays male friendship in the Bollywood tradition and then uses a comic subplot where Aman and Rohit are misconstrued to be lovers by the maid, Kantaben. Recognizing this and then reveling in shocking Kantaben, Aman takes every opportunity to perpetuate the misunderstanding. Although gay characters have been used to add comedy in Bollywood films, such an overt and self-conscious spoof on sexuality that uses the primary male protagonists is rare.

Subverting masculinity is further effected by the (non)representation of father figures in *KHNH*. Rohit is the only young person to have a father, and he is infrequently present. When his father does enter the narrative, he is portrayed as understanding, emotional, and indulgent. He brushes away his tears when Rohit and Naina get engaged. When Kantaben informs him of Rohit's alleged homosexuality, he makes a concerted effort to understand his son's preference. Similarly, Chadda, Aman's uncle who comes close to being the other father figure in the film, is relegated to the margins and shown either mildly flirting with or being intimidated by Lajjo. For audiences familiar with Indian cinema, the fact that the role of Chadda is played by the actor Dara Singh further emphasizes the theme of de-masculinization. Dara Singh, a former professional wrestler, earned fame in Bollywood by playing "strong man" characters. Performing his own stunts, he was cast in mythological and/or fantasy roles that depicted his physical prowess. In *KHNH*, we see an aging Dara Singh playing the role of the elderly Chadda who shyly nurtures a desire of Lajjo and hides behind Aman when she so much as gazes sharply at him. The comedy achieved by Chadda's character and the related subplot relies on the presentation of masculinity as tamed, defanged and declawed.

Parodying sexuality and marginalizing fathers might partially disrupt the heteronormative, hypermasculine world of Indian cinema.

However, these interruptions are deceptive. Although an overt, dominant father figure may be absent, Aman—with his power to rearrange everyone's lives—plays surrogate patriarch. Similarly, although Aman pretending to kiss Rohit may tickle the audience, homosexuality is still trivialized as mere grist for the comic mill.

CONCLUSION

In this chapter, I point out instances of how *KHNH* refuses patriarchal discourses while simultaneously confirming the male-centered structure of Indian cinema. Previous movies set in the diaspora have all reinscribed a patriarchal, nationalist ideology and demonized the West in an attempt to reaffirm an essentialized cultural identity. Additionally, the female body served as the site where this discourse of an essentialized Indian identity was etched. In contrast, *KHNH* declines to place the nation center stage. In this movie, a woman is the narrator and primary subject, normative heterosexuality and aggressive masculinity are comically disrupted, and women do not obviously embody cultural purity to redeem the nation. Similarly, we do not witness a hero who challenges the villain in order to secure the stability of the nation. For instance Aman, the Indian from India, and Rohit, the American-born Indian, are not presented in dichotomous terms in which Aman is presented as morally superior and culturally authentic.

By resisting an overt narration of the nation, the representation of gender is similarly released from being a symbol for nationalism and national identity. Instead, an individuated, global, migrant, hybrid portrayal of the Indian woman emerges in *KHNH*. However, to celebrate *KHNH* as a text that radically challenges the construction of the virtuous, dutiful, and obedient female of the typical Bollywood narrative would be an error. As I have shown in my analysis of *KHNH*, the text continually subverts its own progressive potential by firmly anchoring a powerful male as an omniscient and omnipresent force that propels the plot to its harmonious conclusion. Nevertheless, the emergence of a new kind of gendered representation in *KHNH* indicates an unsettling of the category of woman that is worth examining.

Like many popular culture texts, *KHNH* is a site of struggle where the status quo is both resisted and reaffirmed. In her insightful study, Virdi (2003) presented a historical analysis that reads popular Indian cinema as a narrative of India's social history. She considers the corpus of Indian cinema to show how the film texts project a "powerful nationalist rhetoric" (p. 206) while at the same time revealing the tensions and the oppositions to such depictions of the nation. In *KHNH* such ambivalences and resistance is apparent as the hegemony of the gendered nation is questioned to give way to a more transnational staging of identity.

Unpacking the gaps and slippages in the ways in which women are mediated in such a popularly consumed film text is imperative if we are to understand the global context of Bollywood. *KHNH* clearly attempts to present a story about "Indians" in a globalized context without overly relying on the nation as a trope to build its narrative. The re-editing of the typical gendered nationalist script in *KHNH* suggests ways in which Indian cinema is attempting to incorporate a transnational dimension. As the Indian cinema industry increasingly recognizes the global context of its spectators, new ways to perform and assemble narratives related to gender, sexuality, the family and the nation are being imagined and invented.

NOTES

1. The term diaspora, a Greek word meaning "dispersion," originally described the Jewish communities that were forcibly exiled out of their homeland in ancient Palestine. It is currently employed to refer to communities composed of exiles, refugees, and immigrants.
2. Originally a traditional folk music from the punjab region in Northern India, Bhangra has been reinvented as popular fusion music that is immensely popular in both the Indian diaspora and in India.

REFERENCES

Appadurai, A. (1999). Globalization and the research imagination. *International Social Science Journal, 51*(160), 229–39.

Chakravarty, S. (1993). *National identity in Indian popular cinema, 1947-1987* (1st ed.). Austin: University of Texas Press.

Courtright, P. (1995). Sati, sacrifice, and marriage: The modernity of tradition. In L. Harlan & P. B. Courtright (Eds.), *From the margins of Hindu marriage: Essays on gender, religion and culture* (pp. 184–204). New York: Oxford University Press.

Das Dasgupta, S. (1993). Feminist consciousness in woman-centered Hindi films. In The South Asian Women's Descent Collective (Ed.), *Our feet walk the sky.* San Francisco: Aunt Lute Press.

Ganti, T. (2004). *Bollywood: A guidebook to popular Hindi cinema.* New York: Routledge.

Jain, M., & Chowdhary, N. (1997, August 4). NRIs in films: Coming home. *India Today,* p. 20.

Kaplan, A.(1983). *Women and film: Both sides of the camera.* New York: Methuen,

Kingsley, D. (1993). *Hinduism*. Upper Saddle River, NJ: Prentice Hall.

Malhotra, T., & Alagh, T. (2004). Dreaming the nation: Domestic dramas in Hindi films post- 1990. *South Asian Popular Culture, 2*(1), 19–28.

Mishra, V. (2002). *Bollywood: Temples of desire*. New York: Routledge.

Morley, D., & Robins K. (1995). *Spaces of identity: Global media, electronic landscapes and cultural boundaries*. New York: Routledge.

Mukhi, S. (1998). Underneath my blouse beats my Indian heart: Sexuality, nationalism, and Indian womanhood in the United States. In S. D. Dasgupta (Ed.), *A patchwork shawl: Chronicles of South Asian women in America* (pp. 186–205). New Brunswick, NJ: Rutgers University Press.

Mulvey, L. (1989). *Visual pleasures and narrative cinema*. London: Macmillan.

Power, C., & Mazumdar, S. (2000, February 28). Bollywood goes global. *Newsweek International*, p. 52.

Ram, A. (2002). Framing the feminine: Diasporic readings of gender in Indian cinema. *Women's Studies in Communications, 25*(1), 25–52.

Saidullah, J. K. (1992). *Shakti*—the power of the mother: The violent nature in Indian mythology and commercial cinema. *Canadian Women's Studies, 13*(1), 37–41.

Sen, R. (2003). *Different trees, same wood: The transnational politics of identity underlying Bollywood's coming of age in Hollywood*. Paper presented at the annual convention of the National Communication Association, Miami, FL.

Silverman, K. (1983). *The subject of semiotics*. New York: Oxford University Press.

Thomas, R. (1989). Sanctity and scandal: The mythologization of Mother India. *Quarterly Review of Film and Video, 11*(3), 11–30.

Vasudev, A. (1983). The woman: Vamp or victim. In A. Vasudev & P. Lenglet (Eds.), *Indian cinema superbazaar* (pp. 95–100). New Delhi, India: Vikas Publishing.

Virdi, J. (2003). *Cinematic imagination: Indian popular films as social history*. New Brunswick, NJ: Rutgers University Press.

9

"I am *Cenicienta* (Cinderella) and I'm Choosing My Prince"

Reality TV Adapts an Old Fairy Tale for the New Millennium

Susana Kaiser

It has been presented as the fantasy dream to millions of women around the world: find your prince and be the one whose delicate foot fits into the crystal slipper. Cinderella and her prince will marry and live happily ever after! Her voice trembling, she looks her prince in the eyes and confesses: "From the moment I saw you, I knew you were the man of my life. I've been warned that you are a womanizer, but I take the risk. I pick you." *Cenicienta* (Cinderella), a beautiful, Mexican-American woman from Texas, chooses Alejandro, a handsome, Spanish man from Barcelona, as her prince. *Cenicienta* listened to her heart, and her heart won over her fears. But they don't marry and live happily ever after—at least not yet. Rather, they leave together in one of the two brand-new cars they have won.

This version of the Cinderella fairy tale was enacted in a Spanish-language reality TV show, *La Cenicienta*, which was created for the Latin@[1] community within the United States. *A* takeoff of *The Bachelorette*, it aired during 6 weeks in September and October 2003, on the Spanish-language network Telemundo.[2] The conclusion of the show is a reenactment of—and twist on—the story of Hernán Cortés, the Spanish conqueror of Mexico, and *La Malinche*, the indigenous slave who became his lover, translator, and collaborator. From their union, the first *mestizo* was said to have been born. The story of the first *mestizo* as an outcome of conquest prompts us to consider the issue of *mestizaje*, or racial miscegenation, in the context of *La Cenicienta*. Mixture and hybridity are central to several of the themes addressed in this show. In fact, La Cenicienta combined two TV genres: reality TV and *telenovela*, which are Latin-American soap operas. Its hybridity also is related to the cultural construction of the "Latino" identity or "Latinoness" of the show's 20 participants, each one representing variations of *mestizaje*, with their inherent connotations about cultural characteristics, nationalities, identities, class, gender, race, and ethnicity.

Cenicienta was Minerva Ruvalcaba, 24 years old, twice divorced, and mother of 2-year-old Vanessa. The scenario was a fantasy castle in Palm Springs, California, complete with moat and drawbridge. *Cenicienta* scrutinized, tested, discarded, and selected her Prince Charming among 20 candidates of diverse ages, ethnic backgrounds, education and occupations, accurately depicting the heterogeneity within the category "Latino." They included business entrepreneurs, a pop singer, a lawyer, a teacher, a fashion model, and a writer. Either they or their ancestors were from Colombia, Cuba, Argentina, Spain, Mexico, or Ecuador. Despite the competition, the bonding between the men was constantly showcased. They shared a house, practiced sports, cooked, and even talked about their feelings concerning romance and family.

Cenicienta had some help in picking her prince. Her family, represented by her mother, also named Minerva, and her brother Sergio, participated in the selection process. *Cenicienta*'s father stayed in Mexico and couldn't be in the United States because of problems with *la migra* (immigration authorities). You cannot get more real than that—this is certainly a "real-world" issue for many Latin@s. The advising team had also a *madrina* (godmother), two girlfriends (Karla and Selma), a Catholic priest, and an astrologer. Each of them played specific roles in selecting the prince.

The event was a delightful opportunity for "gluing" myself to the tube and watching a succession of contradictory messages combining an apparent openness with the perpetuation of several clichés about female to male relationships, and a full catalogue of homophobic and racist stereotypes. Additionally, the show brought up issues of class, generational gaps, immigration, and relationships between the United States and Latin America. And it exposed fissures in the notion of Latino unity and *Latinidad*, an umbrella label for the Latin@ culture and condition. But I also argue that we should credit the show for creating a realm for the showcase and discussion of several controversial issues within the Latin@ community.

My discussion of the show is informed by the many questions that I kept asking myself while watching it. Overall, I was interested in the representations of Latin@ women and men and in how these representations either reinforced or challenged stereotypes. Another concern was the selection and portrayal of specific Latin@ "values." This was necessarily linked to how the show addressed issues of class, race, ethnicity, gender, and gender relations, as well as its conceptualization of family and religion. Because it was presented as reality TV, I was also paying attention to how "real" the show was in comparison with the reality of Latin@ experiences in the United States and to how real-life issues intruded into the fantasy world of the TV show. In what follows, I first discuss some theoretical concepts framing my analysis. I then summarize the characteristics of the show, including information about the participants. I follow this by focusing on the dynamics of the selection process, its outcome and the implications of *Cenicienta's* decisions.

FRAMING THE ANALYSIS—
CONCEPTUALIZING HYBRIDITY

The network promoted the show—as "the first reality series that shows the world how to fall in love, Latina style" (Elber, 2003). Telemundo ratings do not fare well in comparison to Univisión, which continues to dominate Spanish-language television viewers. But *La Cenicienta* was one of the highest-rated prime-time series for the network and improved its time-slot rating by 77% (Livsey, 2003).[3] Strategies for reaching large audiences included prime time broadcast five days a week, the traditional *telenovelas* slot—as well as closed-captioning in English, as many Latin@s speak English at home, in particular the younger generations. This links with the first issue for framing the analysis.

Reality TV or *Telenovela?*

The distinctions between television genres are difficult to decipher. As Neal (2001) noted, genres are becoming ambiguous and there is a growing hybridization. Hill (2005) discussed a process of "intensive cross-fertilization," which consists in the sharing of different elements amid genres and creates new genres. This mixing of old genres such as soap operas or contests is an important development, and reality TV is a prime example of this increasing hybridity (Creeber, 2001; Olsson & Spigel, 2004). Among the characteristics that reality TV shows share is the presumption that they are about real—usually ordinary—people caught on-camera living real-life situations, unscripted, and with minimal editing.

Telenovelas are the Latin American version of soap operas. The genre has a strong connection to oral culture and traces its origins to the readings at Cuban *tabacaleras* (cigar factories) and the Argentine circus and *radioteatro* (theater plays broadcast by radio). Some characteristics of *telenovelas* include being closed serials that run for a limited time period (generally 150 episodes); being broadcast during prime time 5 or 6 days a week; and having a target audience that consists of females and males of different ages.[4]

La Cenicienta was marketed and presented as reality TV. As such, it illustrated the inherent hybridization of the genre but also shared characteristics particular to *telenovelas*. In addition to its broadcast at the *telenovela* slot, *Cenicienta's* daughter was the big secret hidden from the potential Prince Charming. This is a typical *telenovela* parenthood plot, where things are never as they appear to be and where stories of "the mother who is not the mother" or "the uncle who is the father" are constant ingredients. Navarro (2003) argued that hiding the daughter, a decision made by producers to avoid alienating the "princes," worked as a *telenovela* cliffhanger. It was unknown who would win or if the winner would accept the single mother.

The network targeted the *telenovela* audience and integrated the show into an online forum dedicated to *telenovelas* (Telenovela World, 2003). The opening comment in the forum, 3 weeks before the show aired, announced that Telemundo would present *La Cenicienta*, an original serial where "romance and telenovela weave with the real life of Minerva Ruvalcaba, a beautiful single mother who is given the opportunity of choosing the love of her life among 20 suitors." It further invited audiences to appraise the tasks awaiting *Cenicienta*: "Give us your vote and share with us your opinion; do you think that it's easy for a Latina single mother to start over her life in this society?"[5] It also asked if it was possible for the family to help her choose the man of her life and if the family's voice could be stronger than the voice of Minerva's heart.

Latin@s: Pan-ethnicity, Multiple Identities and Hybridity

Latin@s include those who were in the United States before the Pilgrims arrived, those who were "crossed over by the border" when sections of Mexico became parts of the United States with the end of the Mexican-

American War,[6] and those who keep arriving from different Latin-American countries. Thus, we are talking of a diverse group, of a wide variety of races and ethnicities, social classes and levels of education, belonging to different waves of arrival, and having multiple reasons for migrating. Once in the United States, this heterogeneous group acquires this new Latin@ identity, which is added to the many others they carry.[7] However, as Oboler and Dzidzienyo (2005) noted, in particular about first-generation immigrants, national and ethnic differences do not disappear automatically when they settle in the United States, even when they adopt the homogenizing label of Latin@s.

In matters of race and ethnicity, the diversity of the group ranges from the indigenous populations of the Americas to the Spanish, Portuguese, and other European conquerors, including the millions of Africans brought as slaves, Asians, and Arabs. Moreover, race and ethnicity are experienced differently in the United States and in Latin America, with further differences within each country. Race matters are not the same in Brazil than in Argentina or Guatemala. Across the Americas, racisms are pervasive but often invisible. "White" is positioned and lived as superior. Although we talk about a dominant "racial democracy" in Brazil or Venezuela, as Dulitzky (2005) noted, it is a "region in denial" (p. 39).

As Hall (1996) said, race is the "floating signifier."[8] Migrations illustrate how racisms float. For example, Latin Americans who are not discriminated against in their own countries may face discrimination when arriving in the United States; Puerto Ricans may be White in the island and seen as Black in the United States (Oboler & Dzidzienyo, 2005). Furthermore, immigrants bring with them racism that is rooted in their countries of origin and shapes racist attitudes within Latin@ communities, in particular toward those of darker skin (Sawyer, 2005). Thus, in discussing the racism of *Cenicienta*'s Mexican American family, we should be aware that, in Mexico, there is denial and discrimination against the Black population (Vaughn, 2005).

Latinas: Virginity, Sexuality, Motherhood

The fact that many Latino men still want to marry a virgin, as producers of the show argued, brings up the virgin–whore dichotomy. Commenting that few societies prize female virginity as Latin@ do, Stavans (1998) noted that virgins are considered pure, good women whereas prostitutes are "hedonistic" and bad women. However, as Del Castillo (1999) observed, "Virginity (mental, physical, or whatever it may mean for us) is more an obsession created by and for the use of men than an actual feminine state of being" (p. 22).

Discussions of virginity merit some remarks about the education and socialization process of Latina girls. According to Villenas and Moreno (2001), Latina mothers reify patriarchy and, in the advice they give to their daughters, imply that "one is part of the community in gender-specific roles as daughters, single women, mothers, and wives" (p. 676). However, recent studies (Denner & Guzmán, 2006) suggest that, in interaction with their mothers, Latina adolescents are contesting traditional and oppressive gender-role expectations. This challenge becomes a dialectic process: "While mothers are teaching their young daughters culturally specific expectations about sexual behavior, they are also learning from their daughters about how to liberate themselves from traditional Latino gender roles" (p. 232). Hence, a process of transformation goes on within the Latin@ communities.

But how are Latinas and these gender roles represented in the media? For Ramirez Berg (1998), three basic stereotypes are endlessly reproduced and recycled in different forms. They are the half-breed harlot, the female clown, and the dark lady—a range of nymphomaniac whores, unthreatening and asexual funny characters, and mysterious, virginal women. Where does *Cenicienta* fit here? She is both a mother, albeit single, and a woman assertive in her sexuality. Valdivia (2000) said there are different single mothers: those who never married, are widows or divorced. In discussing the role that social class and race play in mainstream film representations of how the mother became single, she noted that there are good and bad single moms. Good single moms are usually represented as sexless widows, bad single moms are generally divorced and actively sexually. Valdivia thus pointed to representations of motherhood and sexuality as a binary situation where sexual activity conflicts with good parenting. I argue that *Cenicienta*, a sexually active, divorced mother, challenges this mother to whore dichotomy and the dominant, stereotypical, binary representations of single motherhood. In negotiating sexuality and motherhood, she becomes another hybrid in the show.

Latinos: Machismo, Homosexuality

Much has been said about Latinos' machismo. Castaneda argues that, "machismo is complex and multifaceted and too often, in Anglo-American interpretations, reduced to self-aggrandizing male bravado that flirts with physical harm to be sexual" (cited in González, 1996, p. xiii). Stavans (1998) traced its roots to the conquest of America and the story of La Malinche and Cortés: "The primal scene of the clash with the Spaniards is a still-unhealed rape: the phallus, as well as gunpowder, was a crucial weapon used to subdue. Machismo as a cultural style endlessly rehearses this humiliating episode" (pp. 228-229).

But how macho are the Latinos? What about homosexuality? Homosexuals may be the targets of great hostility, but they have always been present in the Latin@ community. In describing how Latino machos fervently praise their virility, Stavans (1998) warned: "[We] have adopted the armature of our Spanish conquerors: Hispanic men are machos, dominating figures, rulers, conquistadors—and also, closeted homosexuals" (p. 230). Thus, we should look at gender representations in the show, and the related dynamics involved in the selection process, aware that *Cenicienta's* family upheld dominant and traditional gender roles. They valued an ideal macho Latino prince and showed their distrust for anything suggesting that a candidate was not a "real man."

THE SHOW: ITS CHARACTERISTICS

U.S. census figures indicate that a single mother heads 28% of Latino families with children. Yet, many Latino men still want to marry a virgin. According to Navarro (2003), the show's producers wanted to change the way society sees single mothers as shamefully marked, and they convinced the network that the virginal Cinderella ideal needed updating.

This is a progressive twist that addresses the reality of single motherhood within the Latin@ community. It also is consistent with Latin-American *telenovelas*, which regularly incorporate everyday life issues and current political and socioeconomic events into their plots.[9] Be it political corruption, crime, or riots, productions often reflect what is going on in their countries. Similarly, *La Cenicienta* was connected with the real world, with religion, race, childrearing, and immigration issues of concern and debate. This marks a difference with the show's Anglo counterpart, *The Bachelorette*, where, as Douglas (2002) argued, nothing from the real world, such as money or racial attitudes, was allowed to enter the fantasy.

Another related element was the promotion of *Latinidad* as an imagined socially and culturally constructed concept. *La Cenicienta* was a showcase of heralded—and often stereotypical—real and imagined Latin@ "values," such as the centrality of the family and the importance of religion. There was consistent reinforcement of the notion that *Cenicienta's* was a typical Latino family. This also was present in online summaries linked to the Telemundo site (see Episodios, 2003). Moreover, the inclusion of a Catholic priest to interview candidates was a strong sign of the weight religion had for *Cenicienta's* family, even when Catholicism is not the only religion practiced by Latin@s. Priests are standard characters in *telenovelas*, where they act as consultants, advisors, judges, and the embodiment of knowledge. The secrets that people confess to them are common ingredients in the plots.

Karmen the astrologer neutralized the weight of Catholicism. She embodied the esoteric and supernatural, the magic potential to see beyond what is visible. She offered another assessment of the candidates, meeting with them before their first date with *Cenicienta*. We can argue that her presence both reinforced stereotypes of Latin@ reliance on magic and tarot readings, and illustrated the co-existence of traditional religious practices with other spiritual rituals.[10]

The *madrina*, or godmother, was Eva Tamargo, a popular television host. *Madrinas* are like second mothers and important members of the extended family. Within the Catholic religion, when children are baptized, they have a godmother and a godfather who make a life commitment to protect the children, including assuming the responsibilities of the biological parents if something happens to them. Her presence guaranteed *Cenicienta* an unconditional mentor, confidante and ally who would lovingly and dispassionately advise her in this quest to find the ideal prince.

As for the two friends, they were very different. Selma, the less attractive one, appeared as a mature young woman in an interracial/ interethnic relationship with an Anglo man. Her own Cinderella story is that she came to the United States from Honduras and was cleaning houses to support herself and her baby when one of her clients fell in love with her and subsequently married her.[11] Quite the opposite, Karla was a very attractive single woman characterized as a playgirl constantly emphasizing her sexuality in her dress, behavior, and relationship to the participants.

CHOOSING THE PRINCE: THE SELECTION
AND ELIMINATION PROCESS

The selection and elimination process was multifiltered, comparable to competitions where contestants have to fulfill several consecutive tasks. It was not enough to seduce *Cenicienta*— suitors also had to win over her daughter and pass examination with the family, the friends, the priest, and the astrologer. The first filter was that of the family, represented by her mother and her brother Sergio. The astrologer met with all the candidates before their first date with *Cenicienta*. Her friend Karla interviewed all participants who were not eliminated by the family. The priest interviewed the six finalists.

During the 6 weeks that this reality show about inter-Latin@ dating lasted, Latin@ unity and shared identity were constantly challenged and their flaws uncovered. *La Cenicienta* exposed what Zazueta Martínez (2004) referred to as inter-Latino prejudice and the culture clashes related to differences ranging from religion, countries of origin, and skin color. Hence, the show illustrated fissures in the concepts of pan-ethnicity, Latino unity and homogeneity within the culturally and commercially constructed notion of *Latinidad*.[12]

Family: Mother and Brother as Filter 1

Cenicienta had not been smart or lucky in choosing previous husbands. At 17, against her family's advice, she had married a 35-year-old Spaniard who made her very unhappy and forced her to return to her family's house. She then married a Mexican singer with whom she had a baby, but he wasn't the man she was expecting. The "Cinderella complex"[13] was revisited: fear of independence was here fear of making new mistakes for having been too independent in the past and ignoring what mom and dad had said. *Cenicienta* was apparently convinced that the only way to find a good husband, and a father for her daughter, was to stop listening to her heart and start paying more attention to what her family had to say. Moreover, in explaining why the family had a role in the selection process, the network's president argued that, "In true Latino fashion, you're not just marrying the bride; you're marrying the entire family" (Elber, 2003).

The family made the initial moves by eliminating the first eight contestants. The selection process became a true "inquisition" (Episodios, 2003). As a participant in the online forum noted, the family questioned contestants similar to the way Simon Cowell disparages singers on the hit TV show *American Idol*. Family "filters" revealed zero tolerance toward other races, ethnicities, and/or religions. Mother and brother reinforced traditional gender roles and patriarchy, relying on ideal and stereotypical male values, suspicious of anything that didn't conform to their preconceptions and aspirations for *Cenicienta* and her daughter. They did not want a Black man or a Jewish "prince," neither a fashion model nor someone who wore earrings.

Although it was obvious that some of the 20 candidates did not interest *Cenicienta* at all, information about those who made it through the family's first cut illustrates the many types of Latinos that the show's producers thought should compete for her.[14] The family's questions, objections, and rejections illustrated Latino prejudices in relation to inter-Latino dating.

The winner, Alejandro, a bartender, initially was eliminated by the family and later reincorporated thanks to the magic of the *madrina's* wand. *Cenicienta* had an obvious connection with him, but the family was critical because of their memories of how much she had suffered with her Spanish husband. Pablo, one of the three finalists, was a Mexican-American school teacher; the family initially opposed him because he didn't make enough money to give *Cenicienta* what they wanted for her and her daughter. Bernardo, the third finalist, was an Argentinean student and actor. The family didn't like him because he was 2 years younger than *Cenicienta*. Daniel, a Jewish-Mexican engineer, was opposed by Minerva's Catholic family because they disapproved of interfaith couples. Lázaro, a Black Cuban-American marketing consultant, was rejected because the family opposed interracial relationships. Joseph, who was born in the United States and was the show's only non-Latino candidate, was a production editor; the family saw him as belonging to another culture. Edwin was an Ecuadorian, a sexually liberated party guy who had worked as a model. They family didn't like him because of what they considered to be his apparently loose morals. Johnny, a Cuban-American professional scuba diver who loved motorcycles, had been involved with gangs in the past; the family distrusted him for his adventurous life and his multiple tattoos and earrings. Hernán, a Uruguayan pop singer, was questioned by the family because he wore skirts during some musical performances and dyed his hair—questionable behaviors, according to Minerva's brother. Francisco was a Salvadoran-Mexican and the successful owner of a business; the family liked him because he was responsible, mature, and could provide for Minerva.

Overall, the Prince Charming candidates were open-minded and had no prejudices about religion, race, nationality, language, or age. This was a marked contrast with *Cenicienta's* family, which was full of prejudices. They didn't like Mexicans (although they were Mexicans), gringos, Argentineans, Jews, Spaniards, Cubans, men who loved their mothers, men who were successful, older men, or younger men.

A major filter was in the "cultural" differences marked by the family as between themselves as Mexicans and the "other Latinos." A set of stereotypes was present in comments such as "Argentineans are too liberal," "Who does this Spaniard think he is, Antonio Banderas?" or "Cubans are different." In other words, *Cenicienta's* Mexican family managed to insult most other Latin American countries and passed horrible comments and judgments. Interestingly, when confronting her family and stressing her interest in dating candidates of a different race/ethnicity, religion, or nationality to whom she was obviously attracted, *Cenicienta* often used the term "culture." At times, it appeared as a metaphor for her physical attraction to a suitor through comments such as, "I want to know more about his culture."

The family's racism became evident in their screening of Lázaro, the Black Cuban-American. They said one racist thing after the next. Among their less inflammatory questions was: "Why are you looking for a White woman?" They even asked Lázaro, the son of an interracial marriage between a White man and Afro-Cuban woman, why he wanted to commit the same mistake as his parents. In the end, Lázaro auto-eliminated himself with a goodbye speech denouncing the family's racism, questioning their "whiteness" and highlighting the mestizaje of Latin@s—including pointing to how proud of their origins the other contestants were and reminding the family of the discrimination most Latin@s face. He further suggested to the family that if they ever felt discriminated against as Latin@s, they should remember his face. The surprised family claimed that they were not racists and had "Black friends." *Cenicienta's* mother's defense included pointing out that her hairdresser was Black. Even the *madrina* asked the family how was it possible that being Latin@s, and having suffered discrimination in the United States, they could discriminate against Lázaro because of his skin color.

Stereotypical beliefs of what a man should be and how he should look were also present in the screening process. Mom and brother articulated their opinions with remarks such as "He dyes his hair, he must be gay." "He wears earrings and has tattoos, there's something strange." "He is a fashion designer, and that's a woman's business." They made clear that *Cenicienta* needed a man who looked like a "man" and worked in a "man's" job—whatever that means. The family's homophobia reached its peak when Edwin, the fashion model—ergo too liberal and maybe gay—asked *Cenicienta* if she had ever kissed a woman. The mother was outraged when her daughter reported details of the date. She voiced her indignation, facing the camera and asking: "What does he think, that my daughter is a lesbian?"

Immigration, a central issue within the Latin@ community, was ever-present in the show. Minerva's father couldn't come to the United States from Mexico because he had a visa problem, and stories of crossing the border and settling in the United States were common experiences for most of the contestants. Nevertheless, her mother and brother were very suspicious that some of the candidates were primarily interested in the benefits in immigration status that winning the show could provide. They discussed their perception that Alejandro, the Spaniard chosen as "prince," wanted "papers" and was looking for a way to legalize his situation. Although Alejandro was perceived as belonging to a higher social class, the Mexican-Americans were aware of *Cenicienta's* superiority and power as a "legal" U.S. resident.

Second Phase of Screenings:
The Additional Filters

And what about the other members of the "selection committee"? Why did *Cenicienta* rely on them? Except for the brother and the priest, the advisers were women. The show's producers provided a variety of women, ranging from friends to an astrologer, and highlighted the relevance their recommendations would have over *Cenicienta*. We can see here a promotion of the roles that sisterhood and women's advice might play among Latinas.

Karmen, the astrologer, was responsible for exploring the candidates' past and future through esoteric means, such as palm and card readings. Before their first date with *Cenicienta*, contestants had a session with her. This was intended to "see" what was in their future: jobs, travels, a woman, true love, maybe *Cenicienta*? The inclusion of an astrologer, however, undoubtedly reinforced the stereotype of Latin@s as superstitious believers in the occult and the supernatural.

Father Alberto Cutié interviewed contestants to assess their moral qualities according to the Catholic values so important for the family. Cutié, a very popular TV and radio host within the Latin@ community who has his own Web site and writes for several newspapers, appeared on the show in its fifth week, when only six participants remained. It was time for more in-depth scrutiny of the potential winners and to advise *Cenicienta*. The priest wanted to know if the men were ready to marry, what they liked about *Cenicienta*, and what they thought about her family. He asked for opinions about virginity (an irrelevant issue for the participants) and brought up the issue of domestic violence, asking if they would be capable of beating a woman. In advising *Cenicienta* and her family, he acknowledged the racism within the Latino@ community and the problems that interracial couples may face. Furthermore, he bluntly stated his concerns about the tattooed candidate who had been involved with gangs in the past, and the Spaniard he perceived as a "playboy."

Cenicienta's friend Selma, the Latina married to an Anglo, participated in the family discussions and constantly reinforced the idea that happiness was possible between people from different cultures and ethnicities. But her interaction with the candidates was minimal. On the other hand, *Cenicienta*'s friend Karla played a main advising role in matters of sex. She interviewed the men in the hot tub, checking their physiques in bathing suits and asking about their sex life, preferences, fantasies, and intimacy issues— including spicy questions about their erogenous zones, their first sexual experience, their "skills" as lovers, even the "myths" about Black males—obviously alluding to the male sexual organ. Karla's reports to *Cenicienta* were conversations seemingly out of the TV serial *Sex and the City*, a markedly nonconservative ingredient of the show.

Moreover, *Cenicienta* discussed her sexuality and talked constantly about the need for "chemistry" with her future prince. She did this in conversations with her advisers and through voiceover reflections while wandering around the "palace." This is a positive portrayal of Latinas that challenges stereotypes and asserts their right to a sexual life without compromising being a good mother. *Cenicienta* had no reservations about passionately kissing those candidates to whom she was attracted. In post-date meetings with her family, she continually reaffirmed her sexuality with comments related to physical attraction that she felt or did not feel toward particular candidates. This included details about their kisses, although her family worried there was too much kissing with the different men. When the family pushed for candidates they thought would be good for her, Minerva firmly rejected them if there was no chemistry.

But a good lover wasn't enough for *Cenicienta*. She and her advising team were very pragmatic in addressing the challenges of single motherhood. So her daughter Vanessa, who appeared in the show when only six participants were left, became another filter. Once the big secret was revealed, *Cenicienta* brought Vanessa on a date with each of the finalists to check their qualities as potential dads. In addition to seducing the mother, the prince had to accept and seduce her daughter. Interestingly, during the family reunions after the disclosure of the daughter, her brother Sergio kept insisting that *Cenicienta* had to choose the candidate that was the best for her as woman and mother. Even the tradition-bound brother acknowledged that, in addition to being a mother, *Cenicienta* was, first of all, a woman.

To reinforce the centrality of family within the "Latin@ culture," and the concept that one also "marries the family," producers added one more component: the families of the three finalists. Pablo's Mexican family—his mother and younger brother—lived in the United States. The parents of the other two potential princes traveled—Alejandro's from Barcelona and Bernardo's from Buenos Aires. These encounters showed how differences of class, culture and education were perceived by *Cenicienta*'s family, shaped the meetings, and affected their opinions about the candidates. The meeting with the Spanish parents was relaxed and friendly; they evidently created a good impression on *Cenicienta*'s mother and brother. The Mexican family immediately connected with *Cenicienta*'s—there was talk, and crying, about the struggles, sacrifices, and what they went through in coming to and settling in the United States. With the Argentine parents, the meeting was polite but distant;

Cenicienta's mother found them cold and arrogant. The elimination of the Argentinean highlighted their reputation among many Latin Americans of Argentineans being snobbish and full of themselves. As in a typical *telenovela* scene, the camera followed Bernardo as he was leaving the palace, a tango playing in the background. In marked contrast to the other candidates, who left sad and almost crying, Bernardo exited proclaiming, "I have many women waiting for me."

FOOD FOR THOUGHT:
WHICH MESSAGES DID THE SHOW CONVEY?

We should give credit to the show for discussing on-camera several polemical issues, including disclosing many "dirty secrets"—such as racism, homophobia, and the lack of unity and solidarity—within the Latin@ community. But the messages were contradictory and confusing. Although certain topics were addressed from a progressive standpoint—for example, having a single mother as heroine—others were approached from conservative positions.

The show aimed to neutralize the family's extremely conservative discourses through the more open-minded perspectives of *Cenicienta*'s godmother and friends. Each episode had a brief epilogue in which *Cenicienta* and her *madrina* discussed the events of the day, with *Cenicienta* posing questions such as, "*Madrina*, is it possible to be happy with a man from another race?" This usually reaffirmed *Cenicienta*'s independence and her right to decide over the opinions of her family, friends, priest and astrologer. The politically correct *madrina* would always reaffirm the concept: "It's your voice, your life—stand up for what you believe and want."

I did some incursions into the online chatroom.[15] Browsing through *Cenicienta*'s forum gave me the opportunity to explore how fans of the show were reading and evaluating the issues discussed throughout the selection of "the prince," and how different perspectives impacted discourse about "Latin@ values," race, ethnicity, gender, family and religion. As postings suggested, the show opened spaces for discussion of controversial issues. Several participants in the forum noted that the program portrayed an ignorant and racist family and presented Mexicans in a very bad light, truly embarrassing to the community. They suggested that producers held a low opinion of the Latin@s and considered them ignorant and primitive. Postings particularly ridiculed the "homophobic brother" for whom everybody and everything was "gay" and claimed that he was a bitter, closeted gay—*una jota disfrazada como vaquero* (a gay guy dressed as a cowboy).[16]

However, despite these progressive discursive openings, the show reproduced stereotypes about the Latin@ community and reinforced stereotypes about the ideals of femininity, masculinity, and relationships between women and men. The endorsement of traditional gender roles in reality TV has been analyzed by Maher (2004), who noted that the cable TV show *A Wedding Story*, which is supposed to display the diversity of modern couples, allows for some variety in class and race/ethnicity but focuses on mostly middle-class, white, heterosexual folks. I found comparable patterns in *La Cenicienta*. The age-old dream gets updated and re-interpreted, but without any major change to the traditional Cinderella fairy tale. The difference with Telemundo's show may be its portrayal of single motherhood and how it challenged machismo, patriarchy and the veneration of female virginity within the Latin@ community. According to Minerva Ruvalcaba (*Cenicienta*):

> None of the reality shows on the English channels would have given a woman like me, a single mother, a chance to go on television and look for love. . . . Many Latin men are very machista and wouldn't accept a woman like me. I am the opposite of what Cinderella is. But on the show I was treated like a princess and I realized that I deserve to be treated that way. (Fernandez, 2004)

Is there a real happy ending here? *Cenicienta*, speaking after having chosen her Prince Charming, asserted that she considered her family's opinions but, in the end, listened to her heart. She is happy because the show showcased a single mother in a good light and hopes to convey a positive message so that young girls will learn from her experience. But one of her most revealing comments is about how she sees herself 10 years from now: "It has always been my dream to get married in the church. I also see myself with one or two extra kids because Vanessa loves Alejandro" (Netimo.com, 2003). In the end, the fable has been adapted and updated, albeit without losing much of its original dream or reflecting significant changes in traditional notions of heterosexual romance. Prince Charming/Ideal Dad exists! He loves *Cenicienta* and her daughter. Now they can live together—children included—happily ever after.

ACKNOWLEDGMENTS

I thank Yeidy Rivero for her helpful feedback on an earlier version of this chapter, which was presented at the 2005 International Communication Association Conference in New York.

NOTES

1. Latin@ means both Latina/female and Latino/male. The Spanish language is gendered—feminine words end in "a" and masculine in "o." Plurals are determined by the male presence. For example, if you talk about 10 persons and nine are female but one is a male, the word is used with the masculine ending. Thus, there is a growing use of "@" to express both the masculine and feminine and correct this patriarchal imbalance. I use Latin@ when referring to both genders.
2. Telemundo is a subsidiary of NBC, which also promoted the show among its English-speaking Latino viewers (Navarro, 2003).
3. According to Nielsen Hispanic Television Index, for the period 10/30/03-11/26/03, ratings were 19.5 for Univisión and 5.1 for Telemundo (Livsey, 2003).
4. For *telenovelas,* see, among others, López (1995); Martín-Barbero (1995); McAnany and La Pastina (1994).
5. Posted in Spanish, my translation. Telenovela World. http://foro.telenovela-world.com (Accessed Nov. 27, 2003).
6. With the Treaty of Guadalupe Hidalgo, ratified by the Mexican Congress in 1848, Mexico ceded almost half of its territory to the United States in return for $15 million. This land included the current states of California, New Mexico, Nevada and parts of Colorado, Arizona, Utah and Oklahoma (Acuña, 2004).
7. At a personal level, I was an Argentinean before settling in the United States. I am now Latina and Argentinean.
8. Title of a lecture by Stuart Hall recorded in the video of the same name (Media Education Foundation, 1996).
9. See, among others: Martín-Barbero (1995); López (1995); Mazziotti (1993); Tufte (2000).
10. For example, *Santería,* popular in parts of the Caribbean, is rooted in the religious syncretism that resulted when the conquerors forcefully converted to Catholicism the indigenous and African populations.
11. Information posted in Telenovela World.
12. See, for example, Dávila (2001); Zazueta Martínez (2004); Rojas (2004).
13. The "Cinderella complex" is an unconscious desire, based primarily on fear of being independent, to be taken care of by others (Dowling, 1990).
14. Information about the candidates is from Telenovela Forum.
15. See Telenovela World.
16. This was before the release of the successful movie *Brokeback Mountain.*

REFERENCES

Acuña, R. (2004). *Occupied America: A history of chicanos.* New York: Pearson Longman.

Creeber, G. (Ed.). (2001). *The television genre book.* London: British Film Institute.

Dávila, A. M. (2001). *Latinos, Inc.: The marketing and making of a people*. Berkeley: University of California Press.

Del Castillo, A.R. (1999). Malintzin Tenépal: A preliminary look into a new perspective. In A. S. López (Ed.), *Latina Issues: Fragments of historia(ella) (herstory)* (pp. 2-28). New York: Garland Publishing.

Denner, J., & Guzmán, B. L. (Eds.). (2006). *Voices of adolescent strength in the United States*. New York: New York University Press.

Douglas, S. J. (2002, December). The face of post-feminist patriarchy. *In These Times*. Retrieved November 24, 2003, from: http://www.alternet.org/story/14670.

Dowling, C. (1990). *Cinderella complex*. New York: Pocket Books.

Dulitzky, A. E. (2005). A region in denial: Racial discrimination and racism in Latin America. In A. Dzidzienyo & S. Oboler (Eds.), *Neither enemies nor friends: Latinos, Blacks, Afro-Latinos* (pp. 39-60). New York: Palgrave Macmillan.

Elber, L. (2003). Telemundo to air "La Cenicienta," reality dating show. *Associate Press*. Retrieved November 24, 2003, from http://bayarea.com/mld/mercurynews/news/local/6389203.htm

Episodios, (2003). *Telenovela-World*. Retrieved April 3, 2005, from: www.telenovela-world.com/diane/laceninienta/Summary.HTM.

Fernandez, M.E. (2004, July 12). Reality takes a novela turn. *Los Angeles Times* Retrieved November 15, 2006, from http://www.nelygalan.com/press/latimes1.htm.

González, R. (1996). Introduction. In R. González (Ed.), *Muy macho* (pp. xiii-xx). New York: Anchor Books.

Hall, S. (1996). *Race: The floating signifier*. Northampton, MA: Media Education Foundation.

Hill, A. (2005). *Reality TV: Audiences and factual television*. New York: Routledge.

Livsey, A.J. (2003, December 8). Hispanic TV's new reality factor. I*Media Life Magazine*. Retrieved November 19, 2006, from: http://www.medialifemagazine.com/news2003/dec03/dec08/5_fri/news4friday.html.

López, A. M. (1995). Our welcomed guests: Telenovelas in Latin America. In R. C. Allen (Ed.), *To be continued . . . soap operas around the world* (pp. 256-275). London & New York: Routledge.

McAnany, E., & La Pastina, A. (1994). Telenovela audiences: As a review and methodological critique of Latin American research. *Communication Research, 21*, 828-849.

Maher, J. (2004). What do women watch? Tuning into the compulsory heterosexuality channel. In S. Murray & L Ouellette (Eds.), *Reality TV, Remaking television culture*. New York: New York University Press.

Martín-Barbero, J. (1995). Memory and form in the Latin American soap opera. In R. C. Allen (Ed.), *To be continued . . . soap operas around the world* (pp. 276-284). London & New York: Routledge.

Mazziotti, N. (1993). *el espectáculo de la Pasión. Las Telenovelas Latinoamericanas*. Buenos Aires: Colihue.

Navarro, M. (2003, September 8). Latino TV embraces reality show. *New York Times* (www.nytimes.com).

Neal, S. (2001). Introduction: What is genre? In G. Creeber (Ed.), *The television genre book.* London: British Film Institute.

Netmio.com. Retrieved November 24, 2003, from http://www.netmio.com/channel_detail/.

Oboler, S., & Dzidzienyo, A. (2005). Flows and counterflows: Latinas/os, Blackness, and racialization in hemispheric perspective. In A. Dzidzienyo & S. Oboler (Eds.), *Neither enemies nor friends: Latinos, Blacks, Afro-Latinos* (pp. 3-36). New York: Palgrave Macmillan.

Olsson, J., & Spigel, L. (Eds.). (2004). *Television after TV: Essays on a media in transition.* Durham, NC: Duke University Press.

Ramirez Berg, C. (1998). Stereotyping in films in general and of the Hispanic in particular. In C. Rodriguez (Ed.), *Latin looks: Images of Latinas and Latinos in the U.S. media* (pp. 104-120). Boulder, CO: Westview Press.

Rojas, V. (2004). The gender of Latinidad: Latinas speak about Hispanic television. *Communication Review, 7*(2), 125–153.

Sawyer, M. (2005). Racial politics in multiethnic America: Black and Latina/o identities and coalitions. In A. Dzidzienyo and S. Oboler (Eds.), *Neither enemies nor friends: Latinos, Blacks, Afro-Latinos* (pp. 265–280). New York: Palgrave Macmillan.

Stavans, I. (1996). The Latin phallus. In R. González (Ed.), *Muy macho: Latino men confront their manhood* (pp. 145-164). New York: Anchor Books.

Telenovela-World. *La Cenicienta* on-line forum. Retrieved November 27, 2003, & May 17, 2005, from http://foro.telenovela-world.com/n4/list.php?f=208.

Tufte, T. (2000). *Living with the rubbish queen: Telenovelas, culture and modernity in Brazil.* Luton, UK: University of Luton Press.

Valdivia, A. N. (2000). Clueless in Hollywood: Single moms in contemporary family movies. In A. Valdivia (Ed.), *A Latina in the land of Hollywood and other essays on media culture.* Tucson: The University of Arizona Press.

Villenas, S., & Moreno, M. (2001). To valerse por si misma between race, capitalism, and patriarchy: Latina mother–daughter pedagogies in North Carolina. *Qualitative Studies in Education, 14*(5), 671-687.

Vaughn, B. (2005). Afro-Mexico: Blacks, Indígenas, politics, and the greater diaspora. In A. Dzidzienyo & S. Oboler (Eds.), *Neither enemies nor friends: Latinos, Blacks, Afro-Latinos* (pp. 117–136). New York: Palgrave Macmillan.

Zazueta Martinez, K. (2004). Latina magazine and the invocation of a panethnic family: Latino identity as it is informed by celebrities and Papis Chulos. *The Communication Review, 7,* 155-174.

Part V

Limited Resistance

10

Structuring the Status Quo

The L Word and Queer Female Acceptability

Rebecca Kern

Dramas in the media age of reality programming are becoming harder to find on network television. On any given evening during prime time, a viewer may turn on the television to find one or two dramas—rarely on the same network. As network television includes more reality programming, prime time cable, notably pay cable networks such as Showtime and HBO, have recaptured the drama format. Previously, dramas have only included queer[1] characters as secondary members of the cast. However, these two networks have included dramas that appear to speak directly to minority audiences, primarily queer audiences. One drama in particular, *The L Word*, appears to focus its themes and characters for a queer female audience, yet has gained popularity within mainstream culture.

The L Word, a commercial-free drama on Showtime Networks Inc., is about the lives of six self-identified lesbian and bisexual female friends in Los Angeles. The importance of a drama such as *The L Word* is that it is the first show to date to focus on queer women and queer issues. Additionally, Ilene Chaiken, the show's producer and director, and many of the episodic writers are self-identified lesbians. The show continues to receive significant media hype, including advertising and newspaper and magazine articles in many major U.S. cities. *The L Word* has even been deemed a "revolutionary" (Bolonik, 2004; Franklin, 2004) and "groundbreaking" (Ostrow, 2004) television program by writers in print media, as the show presents queer women who are not secondary or invisible characters and who are not presented as women dressed as men.

Television programming, even on pay cable networks, cannot exist without a large enough viewing audience. *The L Word*, which began in January 2004, has achieved at least 1 million viewers, and the third season saw a significant ratings increase[2] (Showtime, 2006). In addition, Showtime Networks has sold more than 200,000 DVDs of the second season (Showtime, 2000).

How, then, does *The L Word*, as a nonmainstream drama, attempt to be of interest to a mainstream audience? Does *The L Word* follow the structural patterns of mainstream dramas? Does it, as Raymond (2003) suggested, show "queer" female characters and themes in ways that make the show more palatable by "normalizing 'queer' to a mainstream audience" (p. 100)?

An understanding of the structure of *The L Word* at different levels provides some insight into how it helps construct normative ideas of femininity and female sexuality. Foucault (1978) argued that audiences gain power through knowledge and discourse. However, meanings and understandings are in constant flux, especially when elements of the discourse are in opposition to each other. Although explicit femininity is in direct contrast to popular notions of queer women as masculine, it does follow dominant and generally acceptable ideals of the proper woman. And although *The L Word* definitely makes queer females visible in the mass media, the nature of this visibility is at issue. Does this increased visibility bring with it a greater awareness of the reality of multiple queer female identities, or does it encourage the ideal of femininity and heterosexuality while eroticizing lesbian sexuality? This is significant in that the supposed resistant possibilities for a text such as *The L Word* may be subsumed by the need for audience appeal and economic growth by the network and the media industry in general.

This chapter explores whether *The L Word*, as a queer drama, maintains the status quo of dominant ideologies on gender and sexuality in society. In order to understand the structural layers of *The L Word*, it is necessary to examine a sequence of consecutive episodes, known as a "strip." According to Newcomb (1991), strips provide overall context and environment to the structure of the episodic text. Using discourse analysis, I examine three consecutive episodes—episodes 6, 7, and 8—of

The L Word from the first season for their structure within the strip and as individual episodes. I argue that the themes and characters on *The L Word* follow a structure that highlights the dichotomies of good and bad, inside and outside society, and other sociocultural dichotomies. These structural dichotomies are common elements in television dramas. Additionally, this chapter illustrates how normative structures of femininity and heterosexuality are a part of the show's discourse through the presentation of its queer female characters. I conclude with a discussion of how the media can be more resistant by upsetting and altering the structural elements inherent in television dramas.

STRUCTURING DRAMATIC TELEVISION TEXTS

Basic structural elements such as good versus bad, strong versus weak, and metropolitan versus pedestrian consistently structure the plots for television dramas and movies. These oppositional social dichotomies arise as competing areas of culture come into conflict, and they are reflected in the structure of television dramas.

One important area of oppositional ideologies is in the social constructions of gender and sexuality. Oppositional political, economic, and other social ideologies create binaries—male–female, masculine–feminine, and heterosexual–homosexual. Geraghty (1991) argued that all genres show a connection to the political and economic state of a culture, and that each genre structures a gendered world of public and private space, of masculinity and femininity. These designations of public and private also apply to sexuality, as society tends to consider sexuality a private event and homosexuality a secret and erotic event, especially in regards to women.

Levels of meaning taken from television texts, according to Hall (1993), derive from codes of culture and the codes within the series narrative. Codes are forms of selective traditions, such as appropriate gender roles, patriarchy, and hetero-normativity, which are embedded within communicative processes. The intersection of codes from varying environments creates what Newcomb (1991) called a "collision of ideologies," and the "dialogic nature of the television medium" (p. 76) is both influenced by and influences ideological conflict. The series is an example of the dialogic nature of television; by examining the series, its codes are made visible.

Newcomb described the television strip, or series, as the "basic unit of analysis to understand the concept of dialogue even in the primary examinations of the television text" (p. 80). The strip provides a starting point for investigating the narrative text as a whole. Many viewers follow the continuing dialogue of a dramatic series, so the strip is a necessary element when looking at the ideological structure of a text. As Newcomb (1991) stated, "A series [the strip] is an object in evolution" (p. 78), and the episodes within the series speak to an overarching dialogue that only the series can provide.

The three consecutive episodes examined here provide a continuing narrative, character and plot development, and a base for exploring the ideological codes within the televisual medium and dramatic format. However, it is important to bear in mind that these three episodes are part of a larger strip consisting of the entire first season and the multiple seasons in which The L Word has been on the air. Thus, although the three episodes examined here are not necessarily representative of the first season or of the entire series, they are sufficient to understand something about the nature of the show's structure and its construction of lesbian identity. Additionally, each of the three episodes was written and directed by different people. As the episodes are from the first season of The L Word, the character and plot development are in their introductory stages.

The series has several characteristics that follow traditional dramatic strips, such as soap operas. The first is that the primary opening scene always follows the ending scene of the previous episode, which helps the movement or energy of the strip. Second, the series follows the same six primary characters and their relationships to each other. Secondary characters float in and out of the episodes. Geraghty (1991) noted that through screen shots and storylines, the show is structured to keep the viewer interested. She also noted that soap operas center on the female protagonist, producing a communal feeling. However, unlike daily soap operas, The L Word airs weekly (Sunday at 10 p.m.) for 1 hour and only runs for 13 weeks per season. In this way, The L Word is similar to crime dramas, which air weekly with new episodes in blocks corresponding to television sweep periods.[3]

THE EPISODE

A series is not a series without the individual episodes structuring the overall narrative. "For if we choose to study a television series," Newcomb (1991) stated, "every episode of a series is part of the larger dialogue involving every other episode" (p. 78). The episodes within a series speak to a greater narrative structure filled with ideological differences and sociocultural codes. Looking at a series of episodes begins to illustrate patterns of ideological content and context.

Each episode of *The L Word* consists of seven scenes, with the longest scene first and the shortest scene last. The last scene of each episode sets up the beginning of the following week's episode. Each episode also begins with a story "short" that does not involve any characters from the show but eventually has a connection to the plot of the episode. The story shorts deal with a queer issue and run for approximately 1 to 2 minutes. As with traditional serial dramas, before the start of an episode there is a recap of the previous plot's highlights. However, there are differences between *The L Word* and other dramatic television forms, such as soap operas and crime dramas. Soap operas run daily, and the plot of the show moves from episode to episode, creating a longer narrative. However, there is no recap of the previous episode. Crime dramas, although including the same characters week to week, do not usually follow a narrative from episode to episode. *The L Word* episodes are part of a larger dialogue, which airs weekly. Another structural difference between traditional dramas and *The L Word* is advertising. Prime-time and daytime dramas on network and cable television are always interspersed with commercials. *The L Word* is on Showtime, a pay cable network (viewers pay a monthly fee for service) that is commercial free, so the episodes run as uninterrupted narratives.

THE L WORD PLOT

The structure of the plot on *The L Word* is consistent across episodes. Two or three primary storylines run parallel, and an additional one or two secondary storylines connect at various points in each episode. As previously stated, each episode also begins with a story short that is separate from the overall narrative of the show but does have a connection to the specific episode. To understand the plot structure of the three episodes discussed in this chapter, it is necessary to illustrate the thematic connections within and among episodes. This includes the use of an external story to begin each episode. It is also necessary to examine the structure of the plot and characters as examples of how dominant ideologies on gender and sexuality play out in *The L Word*.

STRUCTURING FEMININITY, STRUCTURING HETERO-NORMATIVITY

The ideal, appropriate gender roles for women and men are hegemonic constructions bound to popular understandings of sexual and gender difference. Tied to these understandings are dominant conventions of femininity and masculinity, and specific gendered behaviors and attributes that define difference.[4] Butler (1990) defined *gender* as "an identity tenuously constituted through time, instituted in an exterior space through a stylized repetition of acts" (p. 140). It is through these stylized repetitions of bodily acts that the body becomes a site of discursive practice, a text. Femininity plays out through the body and the temporal and spatial conditions of feminine practice. Susan Brownmiller (1984) defined femininity as, "in essence, a romantic sentiment, a nostalgic tradition of imposed limitations. . . . Femininity always demands more. It must consistently reassure its audience by a willing demonstration of difference, even when one does not exist in nature" (pp. 14-15). Hollows (2000) similarly noted that feminine identity is a "meaning that is made and remade in specific historical conditions" (p. 31).

MARRIAGE AND MONOGAMY

In Episode 6, titled "Lawfully" (2004) the introductory "short" deals with two men engaging in oral sex in a public bathroom. One of the men is an undercover police officer who arrests the other man. The short is set in 1976, and the social connection is not evident unless the viewer knows the history of the 1970s gay rights movement and Stonewall.[5] The primary storyline of this episode six follows the continuing narrative of Tim, a secondary character, and Jenny, a primary character. Four out of the seven scenes of this episode focus on this relationship. Tim and Jenny are engaged to be married. However, Jenny has shown increasing interest in a lesbian named Marina. After Tim walks in on Jenny and Marina involved in an intimate act, he leaves. Jenny later finds him and begs for his forgiveness, stating that all she wants is to be his wife. Tim and Jenny get married that night in Tahoe,[6] but before Tim will consummate the marriage, he asks Jenny to shower. While Jenny sleeps, Tim takes off his wedding band, places it on the nightstand and leaves the motel. On his way home, he is pulled over for speeding by a police officer—the same officer in the introductory "short." Tim explains that he has just gotten married and left his wife in a motel because of her infidelity with a woman. The officer, sympathetic, lets Tim go without a ticket.

Many ideological constructs of gender and hetero-normativity are at play in these scenes. First are the dominant values of marriage and monogamy. Jenny begs Tim to marry her: "Don't leave me, because if you leave me, I think that I will die. I love you and I want to be your wife" (Scene 3). She portrays a highly emotional, helpless woman, one who cannot live without a man. In Scene 5, the camera focuses on the marriage bed. The room is dark, but Tim and Jenny are shown silently lying there, their bodies not touching. The symbolism of this, and the wedding band left behind, tells the viewer the marriage has ended. Tim, tormented by what he has witnessed and unsure whether he can trust Jenny, is presented as a sympathetic character who has been wronged. Even the police officer, when told Tim's story, sides with Tim against Jenny. He tells Tim: "Homos are dangerous" (Scene 7), and lesbians are particularly dangerous because they know how to satisfy other women better than men do. Later, Tim is shown to be distraught at having left Jenny at the motel without a way to get home; he tries to find her, even appealing to the police for help. Although he is portrayed as understandably hurt and angry over Jenny's infidelity, he is concerned for her safety and wants to make things right.

Jenny, on the other hand, is represented as untrustworthy, a conniving liar who is morally bankrupt. Not only does she cheat on her fiancé, but also lies to him about her relationship with Marina, claiming that the time he walked in on them was the first and only time they had sex. Tim, who finds out this is not true through a friend, asks Jenny when she returns 2 weeks later how often she had sex with Marina. She lies to him again, and at that point, Time has had enough: He throws her out of the house and throws her belongings on the lawn. Rebuffed by Tim, Jenny then goes to Marina and convinces her to take her in. They have sex, and it is unclear whether Jenny prefers being with Marina over Tim, or whether she is confused or even a sexual opportunist. When Jenny learns from Marina that her girlfriend, Francesca, is returning to town, she is upset and leaves Marina. Both Marina and Francesca repeatedly push the boundaries of their relationship by having sexual relationships with others. Jenny, having left Marina, now has nowhere to turn. Because she created this dilemma through her own actions, she appears to simply get what she deserves. Jenny is punished for her infidelity, lying and lesbianism. In this way, the structure of the plot reinforces normative ideals of sexuality, monogamy and marriage, while at the same time reinforcing the myth that lesbians and queer individuals only think about sex.

THE HETERO-NORMATIVE FAMILY

Conceptions of family are tied to popular understandings of marriage and monogamy. In *The L Word*, many of the scenes in Episodes 6, 7, and 8 focus on Tina's pregnancy and her seemingly perfect, 7-year relationship with Bette. Even Bette's sister, Kitt, thinks Bette has everything—a career, love, and family. Kitt says to Bette, "You [and Tina] have a solid marriage, like God chose you two to be together." Bette's father, however, is not accepting of their relationship and the pregnancy. In Episode 6, Bette and Tina take Bette's father to dinner to tell him Tina is pregnant. Bette's father refuses to acknowledge the baby as his grandchild because a donor inseminated Tina. He calls the child a "fictional creation." By itself, the story tells of an old-fashioned father unable to understand the changing landscape of American families. However, in Episode 7 ("Losing It, 2004"), at an herbalist's office, Tina bumps into her sperm donor, Marcus, and his current girlfriend. The girlfriend is apparently unaware that Marcus had been a sperm donor. Once she finds out, she becomes increasingly angry at the loss of the potential child with Marcus. The girlfriend then harasses Tina, claiming the child Tina is carrying is not hers and Bette's, and threatening to sue for custody. The dominant ideal of parents as male and female structures the theme of the plot, which highlights the oppositional binary of heterosexual and homosexual. It also draws on ideological beliefs concerning the definition of a proper family at a time of political concerns over same-sex marriage.[7]

In the first scene of Episode 8, three friends of Bette and Tina's go to their apartment to perform an "intervention." The three friends—Dana, Alice, and Shane—state their concerns that Bette and Tina are too wrapped up in the pregnancy and have become boring due to nesting behavior and obsession with all aspects of the pregnancy. In other words, the friends are telling the couple that they have become passive and are following tradition too closely. Ultimately, they tell the couple that starting a family has become "destructive" to their friendship. The underlying message of this storyline may well be that pregnancy and children are for heterosexuals because lesbians who chose to go have children may lose their friends and be rejected by the larger lesbian community. This reinforces the dichotomy between homosexuals and heterosexuals while at the same time positioning lesbian parents as clearly outside the mainstream by lesbian standards.

FEMININITY AND MASCULINE GENDER ROLES

Bette and Tina, as the primary couple on *The L Word*, follow many traditional structural elements, including gender-role practice. Although they are both women, Bette assumes a masculine gender position, and Tina the feminine position. This is evident in a number of different scenarios across the majority of Episodes 6 and 7. First, Bette is a driven professional, while Tina has given up her career to have a baby. In fact, Tina gave up her career as soon as she became pregnant. In this way, Bette takes on the active, masculine role, and Tina takes on the passive, feminine role.

Bette also takes on the masculine role in her handling of all of the couple's affairs. For example, before the couple goes to meet Bette's father for dinner, Bette rejects the outfit Tina has chosen as inappropriate and tells her, "Let me pick out something for you." In the next episode, Bette is seen as the chivalrous male figure when she rubs Tina's feet and offers to get her anything she wants. Later in the same episode, Bette has to go away on business, but Tina is too ill to travel. Bette later sends Tina gifts to make up for being gone. Not long after Bette leaves town, Tina is accosted at the herbalist's by Marcus's girlfriend. In an overly emotional moment, Tina leaves a distraught message on Bette's cell phone, telling her that she is not doing well. When Bette receives the message, she frantically tries to reach Tina by phone, but is unable to even leave a message because the message in-box is full. So Bette flies back to Los Angeles rather than attend the important dinner in her honor, explaining to her hostess that her partner is pregnant and there is a problem with the pregnancy. When Bette arrives home, she finds Tina surrounded by their friends at what looks like a party. Tina admits that she perhaps overreacted because of hormones, and Bette resignedly says that all that matters is that she and the baby are safe. In this scene, Tina takes on the role of the overly emotional, overwrought female, whereas Bette plays the role of the more capable, competent, and sensible breadwinner—who in more traditional stories is male.

The story of Tim and Jenny also shows structural evidence of gender binaries on *The L Word*. Tim, in a fit of anger and machismo, goes to Marina's home to confront her about her intimacy with Jenny. Tim yells at Marina, telling her she is "not honorable," and that she "preyed on Jenny." Tim then grabs Marina by the wrists, shakes her and pushes her, leaving bruises on her arms. Tim's display of aggression may be forgiven, for Marina has wronged him. Marina clearly is the villain, both for her unrestrained sexuality, as enacted in her relationship with Jenny, and her destruction of a marriage. Dominant ideologies of hetero-normativity are evident in the struggle between Tim and Marina. It follows similar dramatic themes of two males fighting over a female. In this way, Marina is also in the role of the masculine.

THE FEMININE AND THE EROTIC

Perhaps the most obvious forms of femininity are in the appearances of the primary characters themselves. Attached to this femininity is the sexualization of the lesbian female. All of the primary characters on *The L Word* are very feminine by traditional Western standards. They have long hair, wear make-up, are tall and leggy, and appear in revealing clothing. However, the femininity of the lesbian females seems heightened at specific moments throughout each episode. It is within these moments that the feminine is tied to specific discursive practices of the body and society's expectations of appropriate appearances for women.

Revealing clothing on television dramas is nothing new; soap operas incorporate sex and nudity frequently in their storylines. Brownmiller (1984) noted that "touches of nudity are another proof of feminine expression. It is chic to bare the skin, to play the tease, however unwittingly, between the concealed and exposed" (p. 95). In the intimate scene between Jenny and Marina in Episode 6, both women are still in their stockings and bras. Additionally, Jenny has her hair pulled in a bun, which is reminiscent of a ballerina. The stockings are sheer and the bras are black and lacy, and because of her hair, Jenny appears fragile and doll-like. Tim walks in on the two women during their state of undress, and as Marina goes to leave, she does not put her shirt back on over her bra. The viewer watches as a voyeuristic spectator, gazing into the eroticized sexual world of lesbianism. In Episode 8, at a party on a yacht, several women strip naked and join each other in a hot tub. Later in the same episode, another sexual encounter occurs between Jenny and Marina. In Episode 7, Dana—a professional tennis player—and her girlfriend Laura, have sex on a friend's couch while others in the room presumably are asleep nearby. The scene is set in the middle of the night, and the noises made by the women wake up the others, unbeknownst to them.

In another scene in Episode 6, Dana and her girlfriend are talking to Dana's publicity agent. The agent seems to think that Dana's lesbianism is purely erotic as he asks, "Hey, if you two would ever like to mix it up, let me know." In a later episode, he tells her she is "fucking hot." He then tells Dana that to be a spokesperson for Subaru,[8] she cannot be gay in public because "out and proud doesn't sell cars," but that she "can become a lez" [lesbian] when she retires. The agent also tells her that for the publicity dinner with Subaru that evening, she must go with her male doubles partner because she needs to remain "consistent" in public. Dana arrives at the party in a short, tight, sleeveless, pink taffeta dress and heels, with her male doubles partner on her arm. These scenes uphold hetero-normativity and femininity by insisting that it is only acceptable to be gay in secret, and that femininity must always be retained. It is not possible to be famous and queer in this scenario. While out on a date with her girlfriend, Dana imagines others in the restaurant are looking at them with disapproval. By Episode 8, Dana ends her relationship with her girlfriend, choosing what she believes she must do for her career over being true to herself. In this way, she validates the hetero-normative beliefs of her agent.

The opening shorts in Episodes 7 and 8 also uphold hetero-normativity and the erotic devaluation of lesbian sexuality. For example, the opening short of Episode 7 shows two teenage girls who work in a fast food restaurant kissing and groping each other. Their manager, a young man in his 20s, watches them from behind the glass of the office door. While the viewer cannot see more than his face as he watches the girls, it can be assumed from his expressions and heavy breathing that he is masturbating. Later in the same episode, the viewer finds out that one of the girls committed suicide after the manager told their parents what he had witnessed. This example shows how the dominant, patriarchal culture views lesbian sexuality—it is considered pornographic. The opening short of Episode 8 ("L'Ennui") also shows a lesbian sexual encounter—however, with a slight twist. In this short, Marina's girlfriend Francesca, a seamstress, is seducing a woman she is fitting for a dress, caressing the woman's leg as she runs her hand up under the skirt she is pinning, again demonstrating lesbians as predatory and hypersexualized.

The thematic elements in *The L Word* illustrate how dominant, hetero-normative ideologies intertwine with non-traditional texts. The queer women on the show are sexualized through the stories. And dominant ideas concerning marriage, femininity, family, sexuality, and gender difference are ideologically constructed within *The L Word* to limit the potential for resistance.

STRUCTURING THE STATUS QUO

There is no doubt that *The L Word* gives queer women visibility in the mass media. This is evident through the program itself, the media coverage the show has received in newspapers and magazines around the world, and extensive advertising. This visibility is progressive in the sense that queer women previously were either excluded or limited to secondary characters on television.[9] However, the representation of the lives of queer women follows traditional dramatic television structures and dominant ideological codes of Western culture. This is significant because the show has gained popularity through mass advertising and articles in mass-market publications. In other words, the show has been marketed to more than just a queer female audience. In order for *The L Word* to maintain mass appeal, the show structure must correspond to dominant ideologies to attract and maintain a mass audience.

Illustrations of these structural elements are evident on the surface level in the series and episodes themselves. The structure of a text begins to uncover the ideologies it possesses. As Newcomb (1991) discussed, the series and the episodes within a series are "objects in evolution" (p.

78) and highlight ideological conflict. The episodes of *The L Word* even follow structural elements of soap operas and other women's texts. These fundamental structures assist in upholding gender differences and femininity as well as hetero-normativity.

The characters and themes on *The L Word* are perhaps the most telling illustrations of femininity and hetero-normativity. As Hollows (2000) argued, the mass media reiterates culture, and the binaries created from ideological conflict. The program structure of *The L Word*, and the structure of the show's themes and characters, sustains the dominant ideals of female femininity and hetero-normativity in Western society. The six queer women on *The L Word* are all very feminine, which is evident through the structure of the characters, especially in their appearance and relationships in various social arenas. However, they also appear as sexual predators, as in the cases of Marina and Francesca, or hypersexualized like Dana and her girlfriend. The sexuality of these women is put on display to create a voyeuristic glimpse into the erotic.

The concern here is that while *The L Word* may be trying to increase overall knowledge and visibility of queer women, traditional ideologies about women and heterosexuality are still structuring the text. In order for the text to have more resistant sociocultural possibilities, the structure of the text needs to break from the dominant—in a sense, to begin to create new cultural media histories, ones that can perhaps change the structure of nontraditional texts. The hope then is that viewers will take away more than the status quo.

NOTES

1. The usage of queer is an umbrella term as used in queer theory to include all non-heterosexual and transgender individuals.
2. The number of viewers is based on subscriber information only, and does not include viewers who are not subscribers. Showtime has not released the ratings for the third season as of the writing of this chapter.
3. Sweep periods occur four times a year, usually during September, November, February, and May.
4. Behaviors and attributes associated with gender include clothing, beauty practice, displays of emotion, and bodily comportment. Names, colors, and motherhood also create gender difference.
5. In 1969, the Stonewall Inn, a gay and drag queen bar on Christopher Street in the West Village of New York City, was raided by police. The raid resulted in a riot that galvanized the gay rights movement.
6. Lake Tahoe, Nevada.
7. At the time of this writing, only three states have approved any form of same-sex unions—Vermont, Massachusetts, and Connecticut. In many states,

there is political support for a constitutional amendment that would ban gay and lesbian marriages. A number of states already have rewritten the definition of marriage in their constitutions as only valid between a man and a woman.

8. Subaru has consistently been a supporter of gay and lesbian organizations and events, and it has used queer men and women in its advertising.

9. *Ellen* was an exception to this. However, after Ellen DeGeneres came out as a lesbian on her television program, ABC canceled her show due to advertiser complaints, even though her coming-out episode was highly watched.

REFERENCES

Bolonik, K. (2004, January 12). Not your mother's lesbians. *New York, 37*(1), 19–23.

Brownmiller, S. (1984). *Femininity*. New York: Linden Press.

Butler, J. (1990). *Gender trouble*. New York: Routledge.

Foucault, M. (1978). *The history of sexuality: An introduction*, volume 1. New York: Vintage Books.

Franklin, N. (2004, February 2). L.A. Love: *The L Word* brings lesbian life to the small screen. *The New Yorker, 45*, 80–82.

Geraghty, C. (1991). Soap opera and utopia. In J. Storey (Ed.), *Cultural theory and popular culture: A reader* (pp. 317-325). New York: Prentice Hall.

Hall, S. (1993). Encoding, decoding. In S. During (Ed.), *The cultural studies reader* (pp. 507–517). New York: Routledge.

Hollows, J. (2000). *Feminism, femininity and popular culture*. Manchester: Manchester University Press.

Lawfully (2004). *The L Word* (R. Troche, Writer, D. Minahan, Director, I. Chaiken, Producer). New York: Showtime Networks, Inc.

L'Ennui (2004). *The L Word*. (I. Chaiken, Writer, T. Goldwin, Director, I. Chaiken, Producer). New York: Showtime Networks, Inc.

Losing It (2004). (G. Turner, Writer, C. Virgo, Director, I. Chaiken, Producer). New York: Showtime Networks, Inc.

Newcomb, H. (1991). On the dialogic aspects of mass communication. In R. Avery & D. Eason (Eds.), *Critical perspective on media and society* (pp. 68–87). New York: Guilford.

Ostrow, J. (2004, January 18). Sex not what sells series about lesbian community (electronic version). *The Denver Post*, A Section, p. F-01.

Raymond, D. (2003). Popular culture and queer representation: A critical perspective. In G. Dines & J. Humez (Eds.), *Gender, race, and class in media: A text reader*. Thousand Oaks: Sage.

Showtime Networks Inc. (2006, February 2). *More Love! More Lust! More Longing! Showtime's The L Word® returns for a fourth season*. Retrieved September 14, 2006, from http://www.sho.com/site/ announcements/060202lword.do.

11

The Burden of History

Representations of American Indian Women in Popular Media

S. Elizabeth Bird

In Summer 1995, U.S. toy stores were flooded with dolls, books, playsets, costumes, and games carrying the name of Pocahontas, the Indian princess. The Walt Disney marketing juggernaut was selling images of American Indians as never before, and the face and body of an Indian woman in particular.[1]

The animated feature, *Pocahontas*, was the first mainstream movie in history to have an Indian woman as its leading character. It seemed ironically appropriate that this role was a cartoon—the ultimate in unreality. For although women from other ethnic groups have had varied, but definite success in transforming stereotypical media representations, American Indian women have continued to appear in a limited range of roles and imagery. More than a decade after Disney's *Pocahontas*, there has been little significant change in that situation. Indeed, it is striking that the most pervasive representations of Indian women in contemporary U.S. culture are stereotypical images in such places as comic books, advertising, toys, "collectables," and greeting cards.

The mainstream media visibility of American Indians in general has declined since the 1990s, a decade that saw a rise in "Indian" movies and a few TV shows, following the unexpected success of *Dances With Wolves* in 1990. Even in that decade, Indian women were conspicuous by their absence, appearing (with some exceptions) in small, supporting roles, as loyal wives or pretty "maidens," while the plot lines belonged to the men. To understand why this happened, and to interpret the current state of representation, we must understand one basic point: Mass images of American Indians are images created by White culture, for White culture, and the representation of Indian women carries the double burden of stereotyping by both ethnicity and gender. American Indians have only recently (although quite successfully) begun to influence the production of images of themselves, and the range of available imagery of Indians is remarkably small.

This was demonstrated eloquently in the classic work by Berkhofer (1979):

> the essence of the White image of the Indian has been the definition of Native Americans in fact and fancy as a separate and single Other. Whether evaluated as noble or ignoble, whether seen as exotic or downgraded, the Indian as an image was always alien to the White. (p. xv)

As Berkhofer noted, interest in American Indians has ebbed and flowed over time. Depending on the era, the Indian male has usually been either the "noble savage" or his alter ego, the "ignoble savage." As White cultural images of themselves change, so does the image of the Indian change—now becoming everything Whites fear, in the person of the marauding, hellish savage, then becoming everything they envy, in the person of the peaceful, mystical, spiritual guardian of the land who was in vogue in the 1990s. However they are pictured, Indians are the quintessential Other, whose role in mass culture is to be the object of the White, colonialist gaze. And a central element in that gaze has been a construction of the Indian as locked in the past.

WOMAN AS PRINCESS OR SQUAW

Although this limited view of Indians has affected the representation of both men and women, it has curtailed the presentation of women more. Again, to understand that, we need to go back in time to see how the current imagery developed. Just as male imagery alternates between nobility and savagery, so female Indian imagery is bifurcated. From early times, a dominant image was the Indian Princess, represented most thoroughly by Pocahontas, the 17th-century sachem's daughter who, according to legend, threw herself in front of her tribe's executioners to save the life of colonist Capt. John Smith. Even before this, the Indian Queen image had been used widely to represent the exoticism of America, evolving into the dusky princess who "continued to stand for the New World and for rude native nobility" (R. Green, 1975, p. 703).

As Tilton (1994) described it, the Pocahontas/princess myth became a crucial part in the creation of a national identity: "On a national level . . . it had become clear by the second decade of the nineteenth century that Pocahontas had rescued Smith, and by implication all Anglo-Americans, so that they might carry on the destined work of becoming a great nation" (p. 55). The Indian princess became an important, nonthreatening symbol of White Americans' right to be here because she was always willing to sacrifice her happiness, cultural identity and even her life for the good of the new nation. Endless plays, novels, and poems were written about Pocahontas, extolling her beauty and nobility, and illustrating the prevailing view of the princess—gentle, noble, nonthreateningly erotic, virtually a White Christian, and yet different because tied to the native soils of America. As Tilton explained, the Princess Pocahontas story enabled the White United States, but especially the South, to justify its dominance, providing a kind of origin myth that explained how and why Indians had welcomed the destiny brought to them by Whites.

The "Indian princess" as a stereotype thrived in the 19th century and into the 20th. For example, Francis (1992), in his study of the "Imaginary Indian" in Canadian culture, described the late 19th-century success of author and poet Pauline Johnson, the daughter of a Mohawk chief. Dressed in a "polyglot" costume of ermine tails, knives and beads, the "Mohawk princess" declaimed melodramatic tales of doomed love between Indian women and White men. Audiences "saw in her the personification of Pocahontas. . . . The original Miss America, Pocahontas came to represent the beautiful, exotic New World itself. Her story provided a model for the ideal merger of Native and newcomer" (pp. 120-121). Similarly, Deloria (2004) described the fascinating career of early 20th-century Creek singer Tsianina Redfeather, who, as a classic buckskin-clad princess, entranced audiences with her mixture of musical refinement and Native identity.

But just as popular imagery defined White women as either good or bad, virgin or whore, so it forced images of Indian women into a similar bipolar split. According to R. Green (1975), the Indian "princess" is defined as one who helps or saves a White man. But if she actually has a sexual relationship with a White or Indian man, she becomes a "squaw," who is lower even than a "bad" White woman. The squaw is the other side of the Indian woman—a drudge who is at the beck and call of her savage Indian husband, who produces baby after baby, who has sex endlessly and indiscriminately with Whites and Indians alike. R. Green documented the sad history of this image in popular songs and tales of the 19th century, and King (2003) offered a thorough analysis of the multiple derogatory connotations of the word, arguing that "it is best understood as a key-word of conquest" (p. 3). The perception of Indian women as sexual conveniences is demonstrated with graphic horror in the eyewitness accounts of the 1865 Sand Creek massacre of Cheyenne, after which soldiers were seen to move the bodies of Indian women into obscene poses, and to cut off their genitals for display on their saddle horns (Jones, 1994).

The inescapable fact about this dual imagery of Indian woman is that the imagery is entirely defined by Whites. From early contact, White observers brought their own categories and preconceptions to indigenous American cultures, and "authoritative" sources defined the role of the Indian woman in ways that bore little relationship to reality. Thus, James Hall and Thomas McKenney (who was the chief U.S. administrator of Indian affairs from 1816 to 1830) wrote in 1844: "The life of the Indian woman, under the most favourable circumstances, is one of continual labour and unmitigated hardship. Trained to servitude from infancy, and condemned to the performance of the most menial offices, they are the servants rather than the companions of man" (McKenney & Hall, 1844/1933, p. 199). No actual Indian culture saw women in these limited terms; in fact the range of Indian cultures offered a variety of roles for women, many of them holding a great deal of honor and prestige.[2] As Denetdale (2001) pointed out, for example, "In contrast to popular stereotypes about Native American women that have cast them into the dichotomies of princess and squaw drudge, the few Navajo women in the historical record are noted as autonomous and self-assured" (p. 1). The complexity of these roles has been elided from both mainstream history and popular culture because they were not comprehensible to white culture. Thus, as R. Green (1975) argued, stereotypes of male and female American Indians "are both tied to definition by relationships with white men, but she (woman) is especially burdened by the narrowness of that definition" (p. 713).

THE WESTERN AS DEFINING GENRE

As popular media evolved, the definitions of Indian women remained oppressively narrow. As I have noted, representations of Indians have stayed locked in the past, and the popular genre that has ensured that is the Western (Leuthold, 1995). Western film and television simply took over where dime novels and Wild West shows left off, endlessly reliving the myth of the late 19th-century frontier. The Western genre was hard on American Indians, imprisoning them in their roles as marauding savages, and later as noble, doomed braves. Although we think of Westerns as "cowboys and Indians," during the great era of Western film from the 1930s to the 1950s, actual Indian characters were surprisingly rare. Rather, they appear as yelling hordes, scenery, or in occasional bit parts. And, as Tompkins (1992) pointed out, the Western is overwhelmingly male, dealing with male quests and challenges. Women may be there as an incentive or a reward, but they are not subjective participants in the story. Indian women, above all, disappear. If they surface occasionally, they are minor plot devices, like the character from the famous 1956 western *The Searchers*: "Her name was 'Look.' This woman is treated so abominably by the characters—ridiculed, humiliated, and then killed off casually by the plot—that I couldn't believe my eyes. The movie treated her as a joke, not as a person" (p. 8).

Thus, in the "golden age" of the cinema Western, the "squaw" was the most common image of Indian women. At the same time, the sacrificing princess stereotype was still salient, as it had been at the birth of cinema. Marsden and Nachbar (1988) described the princess image in such early films as the 1903 *Kit Carson*, in which an Indian woman helps Kit escape and is killed by her own chief. "For the next 10 years this romantic figure, young, beautiful and self-sacrificing, would come to the aid of Whites almost as often as the savage Reactionary would murder or capture them" (pp. 609-610). Although Pocahontas herself is portrayed in many movies, the theme is replayed in other guises—*The Squaw's Sacrifice* (1909), *The Heart of the Sioux* (1910), *The Indian Maid's Sacrifice* (1911), *The Heart of an Indian* (1913). As Deloria (2004) put it, in these films, Indian women offered White men "access through marriage to their primitive authenticity and their land. Having transformed their white partners, the Native spouses then voluntarily eliminate themselves so that reproductive futures might follow White-in-White marriages" (p. 84).

From the 1920s to 1940s, the portrayal of the princess declined. She returned with the "sensitive" Westerns of the 1950s and beyond, led especially by director Delmer Daves' *Broken Arrow*, released in 1950. This told the story of a White man (played by James Stewart), who in the course of setting up a peace accord with Apache chief Cochise, falls in love with and marries Sonseeahray, or "Morning Star" (played by Debra Paget), an Apache woman who is, naturally, a princess. Sonseeahray dies, after being shot by a white man who is breaking the peace, but, as always, her death is not in vain. As the Stewart character speaks over the final scenes in the film, "The death of Sonseeahray put a seal on the peace." The Princess figure again went into decline in the 1960s, seeming outdated and of less importance to White culture. Although the graphically obscene dimension of the "squaw" did not translate into the movie era, the remnants of it remained in the few, tiny roles for Indian women in Westerns from the 1950s onwards. Without the princess stereotype, White culture had only the squaw, and she was by definition unimportant and uninteresting.[3] Like her princess predecessor, the newer squaw was devoted to a White man, but she had even less importance to the plot, and was easily sacrificed if necessary. As Marsden and Nachbar (1988) pointed out, none of the famous "Indian" movies of the early 1970s had substantial roles for women: "*A Man Called Horse* (1970); *Little Big Man* (1971); *Jeremiah Johnson* (1972); and *The Man who Loved Cat Dancing* (1973)—all have Indian women married to Whites who die either during the film or in the background of the film's story" (p. 614).

Thus, the most obvious and overwhelming aspect of portrayals of American Indians (male and female) is that these portrayals reflect a White gaze. Ironically, this has become even more pronounced in recent years, even as portrayals of Indians have become more "authentic," in terms of accurate detail, language, and above all, the use of Indian actors. When non-Indian Hollywood stars played Indians, there were occasional films that purportedly saw events from the point of view of an Indian character. Thus, in Robert Aldrich's 1954 *Apache*, Burt Lancaster is cast as Massai, an Apache warrior who first defies White authority, but eventually learns to farm, and sets the stage for peace. His wife, a classic Indian princess, also played by a White actress, Jean Peters, is a woman who sacrifices everything, and almost dies for love of Massai. ("If I lost you, I would be nothing," she mourns at one point in the film.) Like the casting of Debra Paget and Jeff Chandler in *Broken Arrow*, these many ludicrous casting choices are insulting, consigning actual Indian actors to minor roles.

However, contemporary filmmakers, aware that it is no longer acceptable to cast Whites as Indians, seem to have simply abandoned central roles for Indian characters. Clearly, this is an economic as well as a cultural decision—no Indian actor apparently has the drawing power that Burt Lancaster or Jeff Chandler had in their era. Inevitably, the lead roles go to White characters playing White roles. Even the television movie, *The Legend of Walks Far Woman*, (1982) would probably not have been made without a star like Raquel Welch in the (Indian) title role. Thus, ironically, although Hollywood now realizes that Indian roles must be played by Indian actors, those actors often find themselves playing only side-kick roles. The films look more "authentic" now, but as Leuthold (1995) wrote, issues of representation go far beyond accurate detail into "questions of whether (Indian) women are depicted with a full sense of humanity" (p. 178). One device producers have used is to

create a central role for a White actor to play a mixed-blood Indian—
Tom Berenger in *At Play in the Fields of the Lord* or Val Kilmer (who does
have Indian heritage) in *Thunderheart* (1992). But, once again, there have
been none of these roles for women; the female role in *Thunderheart*,
played with conviction by Sheila Tousey, is small and, predictably, ends
in death.

CONTEMPORARY MEDIA REPRESENTATIONS
OF INDIAN GENDER

Meanwhile, Indian men have fared somewhat better in media depictions. It is not insignificant that the most recent collection of essays on
the *Hollywood Indian* (Rollins & O'Connor, 2003) rarely mentions women.
Indian men also have been consigned to the past, defined by the
Western genre. But Westerns are about men, and Indian men since the
1950s have had roles as side-kicks to the hero. Most significant, however, Indian men were the focus of the wave of fascination with things
Indian that first crested in the 1960s and 1970s when the counter-culture
embraced Indians (Brand, 1988). Although mainstream media interest
subsided somewhat in the 1980s, the Indian "wannabee" phenomenon
was gaining momentum in New-Age-tinged popular culture (R. Green,
1988b), and rose again in the 1990s, this time in a more mainstream, eco-
logically minded form. The Indian elder who is wise beyond white
understanding first began to appear in films like *Little Big Man* and *One
Flew Over the Cuckoo's Nest* (1975), and returned in force after *Dances
With Wolves*. In the 1990s, as never before, Indians were chic—mystical,
wise, earth-loving, and tragic. New Age culture appropriated Indian
religious practices, clothing, music, and myths, whereas Indian-inspired
art and design became all the rage.[4] In this trend, Indian culture is yet
again commodified and made the object of White consumption, as it has
been for centuries (Castile, 1996).

   This fascination is consistently associated in popular imagery with
Indian men—artists, warriors, shamans. Indeed, in a study of male
Indian imagery in film, romance novels, and other popular media, Van
Lent (1996) convincingly shows that the image of the Indian male
became an important cultural icon in the 1990s. Perhaps in response to
cultural uncertainties about "correct" male roles, the Indian man, usually placed in a "dead" historical context, bifurcated in a slightly new way.
Young men are handsome and virile, with the potential for decisive
action when pressed, yet tender, loving, and vulnerable. Thus, Indian or
mixed-blood men prove incredible lovers for White women in romance
novels, whereas Indian women are invisible. Handsome young Indian

men fight alongside White heroes in 1990s movies like *Dances With Wolves, Last of the Mohicans,* and *Squanto.* Meanwhile, older men act as wise sages in the same period pieces, and they provide a similar spiritual dimension in more contemporary films like *Free Willy, Legends of the Fall* and even *Natural Born Killers.* They were stereotypical roles, they were usually subordinate to White storylines, and they served White cultural needs—but at least they were there (Bird, 2001).

In contrast, roles for Indian women in mainstream film and television have been meager at best. It is instructive to look, for example, at the Indian woman who became most familiar on both the large and small screen in the 1990s. Tantoo Cardinal, a Metis (mixed-blood) woman from Canada, had roles in several movies, including *Black Robe, Dances With Wolves,* and *Legends of the Fall.* She also played a recurring role in the television series *Dr. Quinn, Medicine Woman,* to which I return later; first, I consider Cardinal's movie roles.

In *Dances With Wolves,* Cardinal plays Black Shawl, the wife of Kicking Bird, the medicine man who befriends Lt. John Dunbar, the lead character played by director Kevin Costner. Black Shawl is a definite advance on the sacrificial princesses of the past—she admonishes her husband when he is too curt with his ward, Stands with a Fist, and nudges him into authorizing the marriage of Dunbar and Stands with a Fist. Kicking Bird and Black Shawl are permitted an enjoyable sex life, and their marriage is seen as warm and loving. Nevertheless, it is clearly a minor, supporting role. The lead female role is Stands with a Fist, a White woman who has been adopted into the tribe. This fact does make it plausible that she can speak English, and thus can interpret for Dunbar and Kicking Bird. However, one wonders why some other device did not occur to Michael Blake, the author of the book and screenplay, that would have made a Lakota woman a central character.

In *Black Robe* (1992), Cardinal again plays the wife of a more prominent character, although with less humor and light relief. Her character is killed midway through the film. The one other role for an Indian woman in the film is that of the chief's daughter Annuka, with whom a young subsidiary character falls in love—an unrewarding role played by Sandrine Holt, who is Eurasian, not Native American. The film, although praised by critics for its accuracy, misrepresented the important role of Iroquoi women in political decision making (Churchill, 1994). Worse, perhaps, it resurrected the squaw in Annuka. Churchill commented on "Annuka's proclivity, fair and unmarried maiden though she is, to copulate voraciously with whatever male she happens to find convenient when the urge strikes. More shocking, she obviously prefers to do it in the dirt, on all fours" (p. 128). Only when she falls in love with Daniel, a young Frenchman, does she learn how to enjoy love and the civilized "missionary position." Once again, the message is that sexuality among Indians is casual and animal-like, although an Indian can be uplifted by a real love relationship with a White.

Legends of the Fall (1994) is a classic example of Indian identity being appropriated to add mystery and resonance to White characters' life problems. The film is narrated by Gordon Tootoosis as a Cree elder who frames the life of hero Tristan Ludlow (played by Brad Pitt). Cardinal plays Pet, an Indian woman married to a hired hand on the Ludlow ranch. She is clearly loved and respected, but speaks hardly at all. Eventually, her daughter (played by Katrina Lombard) marries Tristan, but is killed in a random act of violence, setting in motion a new twist in the main, White characters' lives.

Cardinal has spoken about her supporting roles and the frustrations that go with them: "If you've got those small roles, you're there on the (production) set but you're barely ever used" (cited in Greer, 1994b, p. 152). She describes building the characters in her mind, giving them histories and trying to make the experience more fulfilling this way: "You have to give yourself a reason for being there, a whole history where you live, what the whole place looks like, what your everyday life is like" (p. 152). One can only think how frustrating it must be for other Indian women, having to do their best with tiny, underwritten, and stereotypical roles. For example, Kimberley Norris, an Indian woman who had a small role in the 1980s TV miniseries *Son of the Morning Star*, reports how she was told to redo a scene in which she wept for the slain leader Crazy Horse. Instead of her tears, she was told, "Let's do it again and just take it with that dignified stoicism of the Indians" (cited in Greer, 1994a, p. 144). As Norris commented, "That was a real quick lesson in their perception of how we don't have those natural human emotions" (p. 144).

THE DUAL BURDEN OF GENDER AND RACE: DR. QUINN, MEDICINE WOMAN

Even in the 1990s and into the 21st century, American Indians are still rare on popular television, largely because of the demise of the Western as a major TV genre. They did appear occasionally, frequently as stereotypical "mystical wise men," in action adventures such as CBS' *Walker, Texas Ranger*, where the supposedly part-Native hero (Chuck Norris) was advised and inspired by his Indian uncle and mentor on a semi-regular basis. *Northern Exposure*, which ran on CBS from 1990 to 1995, did succeed in challenging some stereotypes, and I shall return to that show later.

Aside from *Northern Exposure*, the only other show that included Indians as regular characters over a sustained time period was CBS' *Dr. Quinn, Medicine Woman*, a frontier drama set in the late 1860s. Generally despised by critics for its formulaic and sentimental predictability, and dismissed by Jojola (2003) as "an awful, awful, apologist's series" (p. 19), *Dr. Quinn* nevertheless proved very successful, lasting several seasons in the 1990s. The show featured a crusading woman doctor, Michaela Quinn (played by Jane Seymour), who fought the bigotry and sexism of the people of Colorado Springs on a weekly basis. The show was especially popular with women, and one reason for this was its essentially feminist point of view (Bird, 2003; Dow, 1996). Created and produced by Beth Sullivan, the show was populated by a cast of strong women, surrounded by a group of rather weak and bigoted men. As Dow suggested, the show took many of the standard Western formulas, such as the hero battling for justice, and transformed the hero into a woman. And unlike traditional TV Westerns, American Indians were included in the form of a Cheyenne village. However, these Cheyenne were largely anonymous, functioning as plot devices to showcase the central White characters. Indeed, *Dr. Quinn* illustrated perfectly the point that the Indian of popular culture is a White creation (Bird, 1996).

Perhaps most striking of all, the show had not one strong female Cheyenne character. In fact, *Dr. Quinn* threw into sharp focus the double burden of race and gender stereotyping that erased Indian women from popular imagery. It demonstrated that in popular media, the traditional, restricted images of White women have often been challenged and transformed; virtually all the strong characters were women, with men generally presented as ignorant buffoons (with the exception of the glamorous Indian "Wannabe," Sully, Michaela's love interest). Yet even within this context, there was no space for a significant Indian woman. The Cheyenne, although presented "authentically," and generally favorably, were not well-drawn characters with their own stories. Rather they were beautiful, serene, and spiritual, reflecting the 1990s fascination with New Age-tinged mysticism.

The one Cheyenne who had a significant presence was medicine man Cloud Dancing, the epitome of the stoic, strong, noble male Indian, who suffered horrendous personal losses with dignity and forgiveness, fitting right into a permitted role for Indian men—the noble wise man. There was no such role allowed for his wife, Snowbird, played until the character's death by the long-suffering Tantoo Cardinal. Her main role was to look wise and wifely, offering smiling advice to Cloud Dancing, just as she did as Kicking Bird's wife in *Dances With Wolves*. Mostly, however, she appeared briefly to allow *Dr. Quinn* to make a point—she suffered a miscarriage so that Michaela could become indignant about the Indians' lack of food; she looked on as Michaela vaccinated Indian children, uttering lines like, "You bring us strong medicine."

Cardinal must have had shows like *Dr. Quinn* in mind when she commented, "Native people are not brought into the foreground, or even accepted as an everyday part of life, not anywhere in the American media. It is rare, rare, rare that you see anything about Native people as human beings" (Greer, 1994b, p. 153). Other Cheyenne women drifted around the village, smiling and carrying babies. In one memorable episode, the show displaced Indian women completely, while trying to use their cultural experience to make a 1990s moral point. It focused on a woman who is the sole survivor of an Army raid on her Cheyenne village. She is brought to town, where she faces the ignorance and racism of the local people, and meanwhile proves to be a temporary rival for Sully's affections. This story offered a chance to develop a Cheyenne female character more fully, and yet this was avoided—the woman is White, and was merely raised Cheyenne. She fits perfectly into the pattern of White female Indian adoptees or abductees that we have seen in movies from *Soldier Blue* to *Dances With Wolves,* drawing on the long popular tradition of the captivity narrative (Bird, 2001). In this context, the White woman essentially stands in for the Indian woman, apparently making the character more interesting for White viewers, who can vicariously enjoy "going Indian," without having to engage with a real Indian woman. Toward the end of the 1994-1995 season, the producers of *Dr. Quinn* apparently found the strain of incorporating Indian characters too much, bringing to the screen the real historical massacre of Cheyenne at the 1868 "battle" of Washita. Snowbird and most of the villagers died, and Snowbird's dying words to Michaela were typically designed to assuage White guilt: "One day, perhaps many seasons from now, my people and your people will come to understand each other and no longer be afraid." After that episode, audiences saw Indian land being sold off, and the Cheyenne largely disappeared from the program. The notion that viewers might have been interested in following the fate of the survivors apparently did not occur to the producers.

RETURN TO POCAHONTAS

So it seems that by the mid-1990s, living, breathing Indian women had become so invisible and irrelevant that the only way mainstream White culture could insert an Indian woman back into the cultural picture was to return to Pocahontas—and make her a cartoon. And despite being touted as a feminist rendering of the tale, with Pocahontas as a free-spirited, courageous, and strong-willed young woman, the story clearly echoed the old imagery. Pocahontas persuades her father to make peace, although it is not clear why this is in her best interests. Even though she loses her lover, she learns to recognize the inevitability of "progress," a crucial and guilt-reducing element in the White image of Indians. In the cartoon, Disney tells us also that Pocahontas taught John Smith respect for nature, implying that she had a profound impact on how the nation developed—representing a kind of collective fantasy that is strikingly close to the sentimental image of Pocahontas embraced in the 19th century. Disney's version harks back to Victorian imagery in other ways— the cartoon character is notably voluptuous and scantily clad, as were the earlier images. As R. Green (1988a) pointed out, "the society permitted portrayals to include sexual references (bare and prominent bosoms) for females even when tribal dress and ethnography denied the reality of the reference" (p. 593). Combining "superwoman" imagery of women as both strong-willed and eminently desirable to men, alongside the current image of Indians as guardians of the Earth, "Disney has created a marketable New Age Pocahontas to embody our millennial dreams for wholeness and harmony" (Strong, 1996, p. 416).

"Our dreams," of course, refers to White dreams, for *Pocahontas* was still a White fantasy. Indeed, as Tilton (1994) wrote, "We might argue that if one were to formulate the narrative from an Indian perspective, Pocahontas would have to be presented as an extremely problematic character" (p. 90). Yet Disney's *Pocahontas* breathed new life into an Indian Princess stereotype that never really disappeared. We still see it, on Pocahontas-inspired merchandise in gifts shops and flea markets— "collector plates," dolls and figurines, greeting cards, and gaudy artwork. The image lives on in local legends about Indian maidens/princesses who leaped to their deaths for love of a handsome brave or a White man (DeCaro, 1986). But it has nothing whatever to do with the lived experience of American Indian women in the late 20th/early 21st centuries. As R. Green (1975) argued, "Delightful and interesting as Pocahontas' story may be, she offers an intolerable metaphor for the Indian-White experience. She and the Squaw offer unendurable metaphors for the lives of Indian women" (p. 714).

Not surprisingly, then, *Pocahontas* did not break ground for innovative representations of American Indian women. Indeed, in many ways, the film marked the high point of mainstream media's interest in exotic female Indian identity. Into the 1990s, interest waned; *Dr. Quinn* and *Northern Exposure* ended, and the mini-boom in Westerns spawned by *Dances With Wolves* fizzled out. Richard Attenborough's *Grey Owl* (1999) told the story of Englishman Archie Belaney, who masqueraded as an

Indian in Canada in the 1930s and became an international sensation as an environmentalist speaker and writer. Starring Pierce Brosnan, it was conceived as a major movie, but was not well received. The film is worth noting because it did have a significant role for an Indian woman. Annie Galipeau portrayed Anahareo, Grey Owl's common-law wife, who in reality encouraged him to write and market the books that made him famous, and clearly was a major force in his life. Unfortunately, in the movie she is presented as a young woman who, although strong-willed, will go to almost any lengths to win over and keep her Indian wannabe partner.

By 2006, the mainstream media interest in American Indian themes had all but disappeared, as evidenced in the lukewarm reaction to critically acclaimed director Terrence Malick's 2005 film *The New World*. The movie, which experienced serious production delays, was billed as "an epic adventure set amid the encounter of European and Native American cultures during the founding of the Jamestown Settlement in 1607," in which we witness "the dawn of a new America" (www.the-newworldmovie.com). The movie starred Colin Farrell as John Smith, Christian Bale as John Rolfe, and 14-year-old newcomer Q'Orianka Kilcher as Pocahontas, in yet another retelling of the classic legend. Despite its highly bankable cast and esteemed director, *The New World* made little impact. Many critics praised its stunning and evocative cinematography, but it lacked dramatic punch. The film perpetuated the fiction of a physical love affair between Smith and the "princess," and in an odd way it seemed to echo the style of the Disney cartoon, as much of the film involves Pocahontas educating Smith on the beauty of nature and her perfect, harmonious culture. The filmmakers were constrained by the discomfort of showing the 14-year-old Kilcher and 27-year-old Farrell as lovers, so the love story depends on endless scenes in which the two exchange lingering looks, platonic embraces, and rather chaste-looking kisses, while frolicking in the pristine Virginia scenery. Kilcher, whose heritage is part indigenous Peruvian, presents Pocahontas as strong, striking and independent-minded, although totally consumed by love. The film cannot escape the problematic nature of the story, in that she asserts her independence by effectively renouncing her family and tribe, and throwing in her lot with the English, resulting in her banishment. And despite numerous decorative roles for Indian extras, there are few Indian roles of any consequence, and none for other women, most of whom float mutely around the camp. Only one matters—the woman who helps create the "new America" that will largely exclude her own people. Malick's relatively unsuccessful Pocahontas version seems to mark the end (for the time being) of the small wave of "Indian" movies and television.

BREAKING THE STEREOTYPE

Although mainstream popular culture still offers little subjectivity to the Indian, male or female, the impetus for change grew steadily in the 1990s and into the 21st century. The day of the blockbuster Indian movie seems over, but that was never the venue for innovation anyway; in mainstream movies Indians continue to be trapped in the past, or in a conception of Indians as "traditional." Instead, we may look for change in smaller, independent films, and nonmainstream television. More honest portrayals of Indian life have developed in such "small" movies as *Powwow Highway* (1989), which became a very popular video rental among American Indians, and "came closest to revealing the 'modern' Indian-self" (Jojola, 2003, p. 15). Writing in 1998, Jojola (2003), predicted that the cycle of blockbuster "Indian sympathy" films would have to wane before space could open up for innovation in Indian representation. "Such invention will only come when a bona fide Native director or producer breaks into the ranks of Hollywood" (p. 21). That moment came with the 1998 release of the critically acclaimed *Smoke Signals*, directed by Chris Eyre from stories by noted Spokane/Coeur d'Alene writer Sherman Alexie. As Cobb (2003) wrote, *Smoke Signals* breaks new ground in that it is ultimately about Indian people telling their own stories without any reference to White/Indian relationships: "*Smoke Signals* was not merely a part of the continuum of Native Americans and film; it was a pivot point" (Cobb, 2003, p. 226). Eyre went on to direct the more somber *Skins* (2001), while Alexie himself made *The Business of Fancy Dancing* (2002), which addressed the issues faced by a gay central character.

These productions, rooted in the reality of contemporary reservation life, have shattered the stereotypes of American Indian screen roles. At the same time, women have not had major roles in these films. Both *Powwow Highway* and *Smoke Signals* focus on road trips that tell the story of two male buddies. Female roles are by no means stereotypical, but are limited. *Skins* also concentrates on the relationship between two brothers, Mogy and Rudy, played by Graham Greene and Eric Schweig. There are three tiny female roles, two played by well-known actors, Lois Red Elk and *Northern Exposure*'s Elaine Miles. Michelle Thrush plays Stella, ostensibly Rudy's love interest, but the relationship (and Stella's character generally) is barely explored, with Thrush getting only a few minutes of screen time.

Women fared a little better in *Dance Me Outside* (1995), set on a contemporary Canadian reserve. Although the film's central characters are young men (Indian actors Ryan Black, Adam Beach, and Michael Greyeyes), there are several interesting and nonstereotypical female roles, notably girlfriend-turned-activist Sadie (played by Jennifer Podemski) and the hero's sister, Ilianna (played by Lisa LaCroix), who is torn between her old flame and a new, White husband. Finally, one other 1990s independent film deserves a mention—*Where the Rivers Flow North*. Jay Craven, the non-Indian director, co-producer, and co-writer, adapted it from a novella by Vermont author Howard Frank Mosher. Although not "about Indians" at all, it finally provided a major, co-starring role for an Indian woman—Tantoo Cardinal. This film tells the story of a couple, an aging White logger (Rip Torn) and his Indian housekeeper/common-law wife Bangor (Cardinal), as they fight against the acquisition of their land in the 1920s. Bangor is written as an Indian woman, and there are moments in the film where that is clear, such as when the developers' strong-man refers to her as a squaw. But her ethnicity is not the issue—her complicated, bickering relationship with Torn's character is. In a reversal of the usual pattern, the male character dies in his quest for independence, leaving Bangor alone, not victorious but at least surviving. The film, by its nature and subject matter, could never be a "big" movie, but at least it may point to the possibility of roles for Indian women that acknowledge their ethnicity while being "about" larger human issues.

Conventional wisdom also is challenged in other nonmainstream media. Independent documentary Indian filmmakers are telling their stories (Prins 1989; Weatherford, 1992), and Indian women such as Loretta Todd, Sandra Osawa, and Jolene Rickard have emerged as among the strongest of them (Ginsburg, 2003). Noncommercial television has also led the way to change; for instance the National Film Board of Canada produced many films, beginning with a series of four 1-hour television movies in 1986, called "Daughters of the Country," which told four different stories of Indian or Metis women from the 18th century to the present. Although still set in the past, these were extraordinary in that they told their stories from the point of view of the women. Suddenly, instead of a movie that gazes at Indians through the eyes of White settlers, soldiers or trappers, we saw those Whites as interlopers, whose ways are strange and alien. So accustomed are we to the standard way of seeing things, that it takes time to adjust. I found myself expecting to have the story of *Ikwe* told through the eyes of the White man she is forced to marry. Instead, he remains peripheral and, ultimately, dispensable. Life in the Ojibwa village is simple and mundane, concentrating more on survival and everyday tasks than on mystical ceremonies. The women who play the lead roles, such as Hazel King as Ikwe, or Mireille Deyglun as *Mistress Madeleine*, are neither voluptuous princesses nor dumpy squaws, but ordinary women who face human dilemmas not defined by their ethnicity.

Canada has also led the way in producing TV series and movies that represent contemporary Native experience, something that has not happened at all in the United States. Canadian Broadcasting Corporation series such as *The Rez* and *North of 60* have had a national impact that has transcended their identity as First Nation or "Indian" productions and made their stars nationally known. Native musicians have also had an impact, with singers such as Inuit Susan Aglukark and the Innu band Kashtin, who have also gone beyond an indigenous market.

U.S. network television went some way in expanding the imagery of Indian women in the CBS series *Northern Exposure*, which ran from 1990 to 1995. As Taylor (1996) wrote, *Northern Exposure*, which was set in contemporary Alaska, "casts its native population as alive, well, and flourishing, part of the dominant white society and modernity, yet still practicing traditional ways" (p. 229). As part of an ensemble cast, the show included two native Alaskan characters, Ed Chigliak (played by Darren E. Burrows) and Marilyn Whirlwind (played by Elaine Miles). Like all the characters on the show, neither was simple and one-dimensional, but rather displayed idiosyncratic, quirky characteristics. Marilyn was large, and yet was allowed to be sexual without being portrayed as "loose" or "squaw-like." At the same time, Taylor pointed out that the program was vague and inconsistent about Marilyn's cultural heritage; she seemed to move between the distinctly different Haida, Tlingit, and Athabascan cultures, whereas White characters are consistently rooted in specific ethnicities. "Television would never consider giving cajuns Russian accents, (or) putting Islamic women in bikinis," (p. 241), yet *Northern Exposure*'s producers moved Marilyn and Ed's tribal affiliation with abandon.

In the long term, it's doubtful if *Northern Exposure* had any major impact on mainstream portrayals of Indians. The show was so distinctive, dreamlike and "unrealistic" that it may be remembered as a unique and nonrepresentative moment in television. Yet when I asked Indian viewers to compare *Northern Exposure* and *Dr. Quinn*, which is ostensibly presented as more "realistic," they all agreed that *Northern Exposure* was more "real," reflecting a sense of identification with the Native Alaskans as human beings, rather than cardboard characters (Bird, 1996). In that respect, *Northern Exposure* was in a different class from any U.S. television show, before or since.

We also saw a hopeful sign in the 1994 Turner Broadcasting series on *The Native Americans*, which attempted to dramatize historic moments in Indian history in a series of feature-length TV movies. Although *Geronimo* and *The Broken Chain* were dismissed by at least one Indian critic as "feeble" (Merritt, 1994), the same writer had more encouraging words for *Lakota Woman: Siege at Wounded Knee*, a dramatization of the autobiography of Mary Crow Dog, who took part in the 1973 American Indian Movement (AIM) siege at Wounded Knee. The movie was made with a 90% Indian cast, and 40% of the crew were Indians, offering unprecedented opportunities for Indian people to gain experience in film-making techniques. Executive producer Lois Bonfiglio described the filming as "an extraordinary spiritual and emotional experience" for everyone involved. Indeed, the movie proved exceptional in that, like the smaller budget Canadian films, it told the story from the point of view of Mary Crow Dog, played by Irene Bedard (the voice of Disney's *Pocahontas*). The film does not glamorize Indian women—Mary is seen to sink into a life of alcoholism and promiscuity before being transformed by the message of AIM. Neither does it stereotype her as a degraded squaw; she is simply a human being, dealing with a set of problems and issues, many of which confront her because of her ethnic heritage. Although some may be cynical that Ted Turner and Jane Fonda were merely jumping on the Indian bandwagon (Merritt, 1994), *Lakota Woman* did offer an encouraging step in the right direction.

In 1996, HBO offered a groundbreaking mini-series *Grand Avenue*, based on the novel by Greg Sarris, which follows five generations of Pomo Indians as they leave the reservation to deal with life in Santa Rosa, California. Again, this production offers much more well-drawn roles for women than most feature films, giving rich opportunities to Irene Bedard, Sheila Tousey, and the inevitable Tantoo Cardinal. And perhaps the most high-profile effort of all has been the PBS *Mystery* productions of the very popular Tony Hillerman Navajo novels, starring Adam Beach and Wes Studi as Navajo police officers Jim Chee and Joe Leaphorn. An earlier film attempt to make one of the novels, *Dark Wind* (1993), which cast non-Native actors in the central roles, was widely derided. However, PBS signed Chris Eyre to direct *Skinwalkers* (2002) and *Thief of Time* (2004), which were much more successful. Although the main roles again were male, Alex Rice as lawyer/love interest Janet Peete and Sheila Tousey as Emma Leaphorn gave fine performances in rich, nuanced and nonstereotypical roles.

Meanwhile, American Indian women novelists and poets have worked hard to cast off the old imagery. Leslie Silko, Paula Gunn Allen, Joy Harjo, and others "have established a 'voice' and an 'identity' for the Indian woman which are grounded in the realities of the present, rather than the stereotypes of the past" (Tsosie, 1988). An interesting intervention in the world of comic book production, a notoriously stereotypical industry, is Bluecorn Comics, which produces *Peace Party*, a "multicultural comic book featuring Native Americans" and also maintains a comprehensive Web site with pages on stereotypes and how to combat them (www.bluecorncomics.com). Even so, the Peace Party series centers around two leading male characters, with women generally taking subordinate roles. Nevertheless, it can be hoped that eventually, just as White and African-American women now have at least some voice in creating mass imagery, American Indian women will break into the consciousness of the mass culture industry. As Tantoo Cardinal said, "We have to get to a place where our Native women have a sexuality, a sensuality, an intelligence" (cited in Greer, 1994b, p. 153). But the stereotypes of Indians, male and female, will be hard to shatter—their role as the exotic, fascinating "other" is so entrenched and so naturalized.

DOES IT MATTER?

Over the last 20 years or so, feminist media criticism has moved past earlier, simplistic studies of media imagery—the kind of study that described media portrayals and discussed whether they reflected reality or perpetuated stereotypes. Classic studies offered a rich discussion of female "resistant" and "subversive" readings, suggesting that women can find pleasure in a range of unexpected texts (see, e.g., Ang, 1985; Bird, 1992; Brown, 1990; Press, 1991; Radway, 1984). Additionally, as more women take part in the production of media—as scriptwriters, directors, producers, and actors—we see the opportunity to celebrate some of the huge advances that have been gained in the representation of women. As Cook (1993) wrote, these female media makers "speak for themselves and not necessarily for all women: but they insist on their right to speak differently, and for that difference to be recognised" (p. xxiii).

Yet overwhelmingly, these gains have been made by White and African-American women, with American Indian women still almost invisible in mass culture in other than stereotypical representations. Ironically, "Indianness" is pervasive in U.S. culture, as a style that has embraced particular icons, such as the ubiquitous dream-catcher, or Kokopelli, the South West's hump-back flute player, both of which now appear on everything from T-shirts to earrings. A contemporary restless quest for spirituality continues to fuel demand for sweat lodges, sandpaintings, and carved fetishes—all disconnected from specific tribal identity and context. Indians seem to be the last ethnic group that still can be freely stereotyped in the most grotesque ways. As recently as 2004, American Indians were outraged by a CBS Grammy Award broadcast featuring the hip-hop duo OutKast, who performed their hit "Hey Ya" against a backdrop of smoke, teepees, and other Indian pop culture symbols. Singer Andre "3000" Benjamin, in a lime-green "Indian" costume and wig, was backed by scantily clad, gyrating dancers in feathers and green "princess" outfits. An introductory voice-over intoned that "the Natives are getting restless." A staff writer for the newspaper *Indian Country Today* commented, "These may have been costumes to OutKast and the producers . . . but to American Indians they were the latest in a long line of insults, caricatures drawn from history" (http://www.indiancountry.com). The performance drew protests from many Indian nations, individuals, and well-known Indian voices, such as writer and columnist Suzan Shown Harjo. AIM member Vernon Bellecourt commented that the performance was analogous to portraying African Americans "with a grass skirt, a bone through their nose, a war lance in hand and balancing a watermelon and pork chop in the other" (www.bluecorncomics.com).

But does the limited picture of Indian women (and men) actually matter? After all, most people are surrounded by real men and women; they know that media imagery is not everything, and their understandings of gender are formed not only by media but also by day-to-day interactions. In many parts of the country, however, non-Indians never see or encounter a real, living Indian person (McGuire, 1992). Media representations take on an added power in this situation, filling a knowledge vacuum with outmoded and limited stereotypes, as several studies suggest (see Riverwind, n.d.). In my study of *Dr. Quinn*, for example, White viewers found the portrayal of the Cheyenne "authentic" and believable, especially when the Cheyenne behaved in ways that are, indeed, stereotypical—stoic, silent, and spiritual. It was these very aspects of behavior that Indian viewers found most problematic. Furthermore, one of the most striking findings in my later study (Bird, 2003), which offered participants the chance to create a hypothetical television show with an Indian character, was that White participants had a particularly hard time developing a nonstereotypical female role—even in a region of the country that has one of the largest populations of Native people. Perhaps the reality is trumped by the endless parade of buckskin-clad "princesses" on comic books, greeting cards, "collectables," and gift shop paraphernalia.

In 1993, Williams introduced an anthology that in many ways was a celebration of the transformations women have brought about in popular filmmaking. She presented the collection as the beginning of an answer to her own question: "So what happens when marginalised or repressed stories come to the fore? What happens when fantasies of power or tales of difference . . . become the conscious, overt, marketable stuff of mainstream cinema?" (p. xxv). When it comes to representations of American Indian women, the answer to this question is sadly clear. We don't know what happens, although the examples of independent film and television offer an encouraging way forward. More than a decade after Williams' question, American Indian men and women in the United States have little public identity as everyday Americans. Only when we find room for their tales will our mediated realities be finally able to break the lock of a mythic past.

NOTES

1. Although some prefer to use the term *Native Americans*, I have generally chosen to use *American Indians*, since this is the more commonly used self-description in Minnesota where I resided when first writing this.
2. Tsosie (1988) discusses the range of traditional roles for women in several indigenous cultures. For a discussion of accepted alternative female roles in specific cultures, see Lewis (1941) and Medicine (1983). Many Native American cultures also offered alternative social roles for men (see Callender & Kodrens, 1983). Foster (1995) describes how strong female roles have been erased from the historical literature on the Iroquois.
3. Indian actress Lois Red Elk commented in 1980 that of the many small roles she has played in her career, almost none of her characters was given a name (Leuthold, 1995).
4. For a discussion of appropriations of Native culture, see Whitt (1995) and Meyer and Royer (2001). A. Green (1991) took issue especially with White feminists who appropriate Indian spirituality.

REFERENCES

Ang, I. (1985). *Watching Dallas.* London: Methuen.
Berkhofer, R.F. (1979). *The white man's Indian.* New York: Vintage Books.
Bird, S.E. (1992). *For enquiring minds: A cultural study of supermarket tabloids.* Knoxville: University of Tennessee Press.
Bird, S.E. (1996). Not my fantasy: The persistence of Indian imagery in *Dr. Quinn, Medicine Woman.* In S.E. Bird (Ed.), *Dressing in feathers: The construction of the Indian in American popular culture* (pp. 245-262). Boulder, CO: Westview Press.
Bird, S.E. (2001). Savage desires: The gendered representation of American Indians in popular media. In C.J. Meyer & D. Royer (Ed.), *Selling the Indian: Commercializing and appropriating American Indian cultures* (pp. 62-98). Tucson: University of Arizona Press.
Bird, S.E. (2003). *The audience in everyday life: Living in a media world.* New York: Routledge.
Brand, S. (1988). Indians and the counterculture, 1960s-1970s. In W.E. Washburn (Ed.), *The handbook of North American Indians* (Vol. 4, pp. 570-572). Washington, DC: Smithsonian Institution Press.

Brown, M.E. (Ed.). (1990). *Television and women's culture: The politics of the popular.* Newbury Park: CA: Sage.

Callender, C., & L.M. Kodrens (1983). The North American berdache. *Current Anthropology, 24,* 443-490.

Castile, G.P (1996). The commodification of Indian identity. *American Anthropologist, 98*(4), 743-749.

Churchill, W. (1994). *Indians are us: Culture and genocide in Native North America.* Monroe, ME: Common Courage Press.

Cobb, A. J. (2003). This is what it means to say *Smoke Signals.* In P.C. Rollins & J.E. O'Connor (Eds.), *Hollywood's Indian: The portrayal of the Native American in film* (pp. 207-228). Lexington: University Press of Kentucky.

Cook, P. (1993). Border crossings: Women and film in context. In P. Cook & P. Dodd (Eds.), *Women and film: A sight and sound reader* (pp. ix-xxiii.). Philadelphia: Temple University Press.

DeCaro, F. (1986). Vanishing the red man: Cultural guilt and legend formation. *International Folklore Review, 4,* 74-80.

Deloria, P.J. (2004). *Indians in unexpected places.* Lawrence: University Press of Kansas.

Denetdale, J.N. (2001) Representing Changing Woman: A review essay on Navajo women. *American Indian Culture and Research Journal, 25*(3), 1-26.

Dow, B. (1996). *Prime time feminism: Television, media culture, and the women's movement since 1970.* Philadelphia: University of Pennsylvania Press.

Foster, M.H. (1995). Lost women of the matriarchy: Iroquois women in the historical literature. *American Indian Culture and Research Journal, 19*(3), 121-140.

Francis, D. (1992). *The imaginary Indian: The image of the Indian in Canadian culture.* Vancouver: Arsenal Pulp Press.

Ginsburg, F. (2003). Indigenous media: Negotiating control over images. In L. Gross, J.S. Katz, & J. Ruby (Eds.), *Image ethics in the digital age* (pp. 295-311). Minneapolis: University of Minnesota Press.

Green, A. (1991). For all those who were Indian in a former life. *Ms., 2*(3), 44-45.

Green, R. (1975). The Pocahontas perplex: The image of the Indian woman in American culture. *Massachusetts Review, 16*(4), 698-714.

Green, R. (1988a). The Indian in popular American culture. In W.E. Washburn (Ed.), *The handbook of North American Indians* (Vol. 4, pp. 587-606). Washington, DC: Smithsonian Institution Press.

Green, R. (1988b). The tribe called wannabee: Playing Indian in America and Europe. *Folklore, 99*(1), 30-55.

Greer, S. (1994a). Imagining Indians: Native people voice their concerns, beliefs, and action plans at Arizona film festival. *Winds of Change, 9*(4), 142-144.

Greer, S. (1994b). Tantoo Cardinal: A part of all nations: *Winds of Change, 9*(4), 150-153.

Jojola, T. (2003). Absurd reality II: Hollywood goes to the Indians. In P.C. Rollins & J.E. O'Connor (Eds.), *Hollywood's Indian: The portrayal of the Native American in film* (pp. 12-26). Lexington: University Press of Kentucky.

Jones, M.E., (Ed.). (1994). The military savagely destroys Indians: Testimony from U.S. Congressional investigations. In *The American frontier: Opposing viewpoints.* San Diego: Greenhaven Press.

King, C. R (2003). De/scribing squaw: Indigenous women and imperial idioms in the United States. *American Indian Culture and Research Journal, 27*(2), 1-16.

Leuthold, S.M. (1995). Native American responses to the Western. *American Indian Culture and Research Journal, 19*(1), 153-189.

Lewis, O. (1941). Manly-hearted women among the South Peigan. *American Anthropologist, 43,* 173-187.

Marsden, M.T., & Nachbar, J. (1988). The Indian in the movies. In W.E. Washburn (Ed.), *The handbook of North American Indians* (Vol. 4, pp. 607-616). Washington, DC Smithsonian Institution Press.

McGuire, R.H. (1992). Archeology and the first Americans. *American Anthropologist, 94*(4), 816-836.

McKenney, T.L, & Hall, J. (1933). *The Indian tribes of North America.* Edinburgh: John Grant. (Original work published 1844).

Medicine, B. (1983). "Warrior women": Sex role alternatives for Plains Indian women. In P. Albers & B. Medicine (Eds.), *Hidden half: Studies of Plains Indian women* (pp. 267-280). Lanham, MD: University Press of America.

Merritt, J. (1994). *Lakota Woman:* Authentic culture on film or exploitation. *Winds of Change, 8*(2), 90-93.

Meyer, C.J., & Royer, D. (2001). *Selling the Indian: Commercializing and appropriating American Indian cultures.* Tucson: University of Arizona Press.

Oneida Nation Response to OutKast Performance. (2004). Indian Country Today. Retrieved September 1, 2006, from http://www.indiancountry.com/content.cfm?id=1076426250.

Press, A. (1991). *Women watching television.* Philadelphia: University of Pennsylvania Press.

Prins, H. (1989). American Indians and the ethnocinematic complex: From Native participation to production control. *Visual Sociology, 4*(2), 85-89.

Radway, J. (1984). *Reading the romance: Women, patriarchy, and popular literature.* Chapel Hill: University of North Carolina Press.

Riverwind, J. (n.d). *The basic Indian stereotypes.* Retrieved September 1, 2006, from http://www.bluecorncomics.com/stbasics.htm.

Rollins, P.C., & O'Connor, J. E. (Eds.). (2003). *Hollywood's Indian: The portrayal of the Native American in film.* Lexington: University Press of Kentucky.

Strong, P.T (1996). Animated Indians: Critique and contradiction in commodified children's culture. *Cultural Anthropology, 11*(3), 405-424.

Taylor, A. (1996). Cultural heritage in *Northern Exposure.* In S.E. Bird (Ed.), *Dressing in feathers: The construction of the Indian in American popular culture* (pp. 229-244). Boulder, CO: Westview Press.

Thenewworldmovie.com. Synopsis of film *The New World.* Retrieved September 1, 2006, from http://www.thenewworldmovie.com

Tilton, R. (1994). *Pocahontas: The evolution of an American narrative.* Cambridge: Cambridge University Press.

Tompkins, J. (1992). *West of everything.* New York: Oxford University Press.

Tsosie, R. (1988). Changing women: The cross currents of American Indian feminine identity. *American Indian Culture and Research Journal, 12*(1), 1-38.

Van Lent, P. (1996). Her beautiful savage: The current sexual image of the Native American male. In S.E. Bird (Ed.), *Dressing in feathers: The construction of the*

Indian in American popular culture (pp. 211-228) Boulder, CO: Westview Press.

Weatherford, E. (1992). Starting fire with gunpowder. *Film Comment, 28,* 64-67.

Whitt, L.A. (1995). Cultural imperialism and the marketing of Native America. *American Indian Culture and Research Journal, 19*(3), 1-32.

Williams, L.R. (1993). Everything in question: Women and film in prospect. In P. Cook & P. Dodd (Eds.), *Women and film: A sight and sound reader:* (pp. xxiv-xxix). Philadelphia: Temple University Press.

Part VI

Finding Progress

12

Power(Puff) Feminism

The Powerpuff Girls As a Site of Strength and Collective Action in the Third Wave

Rebecca C. Hains

In 1998, Cartoon Network launched an animated program about a superhero team. In each episode, the "good guys" fought the "bad guys," saving their city from the menacing threat of destruction.[1] But there was a twist: Its superheroes were not guys, but girls. *The Powerpuff Girls* featured crime-fighting 5-year-olds Blossom, Buttercup, and Bubbles, the products of a laboratory experiment. Seeking to create the perfect little girl, Professor Utonium devised a formula that called for eight cups of sugar, a pinch of spice, and a tablespoon of everything nice ("The Rowdyruff Boys," 1998). However, a drop of "Chemical X" fell into the mixture, creating an explosion from which the Powerpuff Girls were born[2] —with "ultra-superpowers."

During the show's 8-year tenure on Cartoon Network, these kinder-garteners held an unusual daily routine. In addition to learning how to play nicely with other children, doing their chores, and spending time with their father, the professor,[3] they fist-fought any monstrous villain who threatened the city of Townsville and defended the public good, all while wearing cute little dresses, white tights, and Mary Jane shoes. This combination of "power" and "puff" made the show unique. As *Powerpuff* creator Craig McCracken explained, "I just thought it was cool to see these cute little girls being really tough and really hardcore" (cited in Weinkauf, 2002, n.p.).

At the height of *The Powerpuff Girls'* popularity, more than 2 million viewers agreed.[4] Half of these viewers were male, which disproved the canard that boys will not watch shows featuring female lead characters. In 2001, Brian Weinstock, vice president of boys creative at toy-licensee Trendmasters, explained, "We've always been really excited about the boy aspect of the show. . . . They watch the show and tell us, 'These girls kick butt!'" (Ebenkamp, 2001, p. 26). *The Powerpuff Girls* thus paved the way for an explosion of children's television shows about strong girls.[5] The cartoon's strong, 24.5% adult following was also uncommon (Hager, 2002), and with such wide-reaching appeal, *The Powerpuff Girls* was at the heart of a merchandizing empire worth nearly $1 billion (McAlister, 2002). Sales of licensed products continue today, although they target a narrower market of young girls.

The Powerpuff Girls also garnered its share of critical acclaim: It was nominated for four Emmy awards, winning one for Individual Achievement in Animation (Advertiser Staff, 2000; TV.com, 2006), and *TV Guide* named it one of the top 10 new kids' shows (Reed Business Information, 2000). Between 1999 and 2005, *The Powerpuff Girls* was also nominated for nine Annie Awards, the animation industry's equivalent to the Emmy Awards. The show won two Annies in 2001—one for its musical score and one for production design (TV.com, 2006).

Although *The Powerpuff Girls* is no longer on the air, the Powerpuff Girls have become symbolic of Cartoon Network (analogous to how Mickey Mouse is the Disney empire's most symbolic character). For example, at the May 2006 Electronic Entertainment Exposition (E3) in Los Angeles, California, The Game Factory announced the release of several children's video games based on Cartoon Network television shows (PR Newswire, 2006). Although none of the games had an obvious connection to *The Powerpuff Girls*, The Game Factory's E3 exhibit featured employees dressed as the Powerpuff Girls—and men attending E3 waited in line to have their photographs taken with these icons.[6]

In short, *The Powerpuff Girls'* reach, critical acclaim, and iconic status made it a significant popular cultural text whose importance continues today. However, the wealth of press coverage hailing the Powerpuff Girls as feminist icons increases the cartoon's significance (see, e.g., Corliss, 2001; DeRogatis, 2002; Havrilesky, 2002; Hopkins, 2002; McAlister, 2002; Sicilano, 2001). I agree with much of this press coverage, but I submit that *The Powerpuff Girls* was never a straightforward feminist text. It contained many contradictory messages about strength and femininity, in part because it represented a negotiation between two conflicting forms of Third-Wave feminism: (a) girl power, which reclaims the girlish and argues that girls can simultaneously be pleasurably feminine and powerful, and (b) power feminism, which argues that feminism should conceive of women not as victims of patriarchal society, but as empowered individuals.

Over the past 30 years, studies have consistently found that children's programming depicts its characters in limiting gender stereotypes, with boys featured more frequently, more prominently, and in a wider range of settings and activities than girls (see, e.g., Barner, 1999; Browne, 1998; Signorielli, 1989; Sternglanz & Serbin, 1974). Although this gender stereotyping seems to have decreased across time (Thompson & Zerbinos, 1995), the Powerpuff Girls' nonstereotypical behavior stood out. As Ogletree, Mason, Grahmann, and Raffeld (2001) noted in their content analysis of *The Powerpuff Girls*, the girls were generally "androgynous, combining traditional masculine and feminine behaviors" (p. 311). Likewise, Potts' (2001) study of Powerpuff viewers confirmed that the show appealed to many viewers—male and female, youth and adults—because the girls wielded power without relying on sex appeal, a tactic typical of other shows' strong females. The Powerpuff Girls could successfully buck stereotypical female behavior because of their cartoon-world's cultural context: Their fellow cartoon characters also resisted gender norms on a regular basis. As Havrilesky (2002) commented:

> [I]t makes complete sense in a world without gender-role stereotypes that these superheroes never tout their appeal as females or decry the unfairness of being girls. Why should they, when their daddy [a single parent] is a mommy, their boss is their boss's [the mayor's] female secretary, and their foes are always ultimately conquerable without the help of outside forces? That our heroes' girlishness is beside the point might just be the most revolutionary aspect of the show. (n.p.)

Although their girlishness may have been "beside the point" in their cartoon world, their girlishness was a critical aspect of their reception in the real world. The Powerpuff Girls' big round eyes and high-pitched voices contributed to a highly gendered, hyperfeminine presentation. This was juxtaposed with the stereotypically masculine behaviors in which they engaged. Given the media's frequent depictions of passive, "female" behavior, this remarkable combination constituted a denaturalization of the constructed dichotomy of male versus female—or of "power" versus "puff." It repositioned strength and power as viably coexistent traits in females.

McCracken indicated that the juxtaposition of the girls' femininity and their powerful behavior reflected and contributed to modern feminist thought. In interviews, he often highlighted the show's Third-Wave aura:

> [T]here's this kind of new feminism that's starting to rise up that isn't about denouncing things that are girlish. It's about embracing going shopping and buying shoes and wanting to be cute. You can embrace all that and at the same time still be really powerful. There seems to be a lot of that happening today, and I think the girls are a symbol of that new strength. (Weinkauf, 2002, n.p.)

It is unclear whether McCracken originally intended the girls as feminist symbols, but as he was a 20-year-old college student when he first created the Powerpuff Girls (Lloyd, 2000, n.p.), he more likely welcomed this reading afterward, in response to the positive Third-Wave reception *The Powerpuff Girls* received.

This chapter examines *The Powerpuff Girls* as a site of feminist discourse. It proposes that the cartoon still reflects and contributes to changes in the construction of female characters that resulted from Third-Wave feminism's girl power, which emphasizes girls' ability to be strong and successful while embracing girlishness. *The Powerpuff Girls* also reflects the ongoing Third-Wave dialogue about power feminism, which argues for equality while railing against the idea that women are victims of an oppressive patriarchy. As a still significant cultural text, *The Powerpuff Girls* demonstrates that fictional female characters can be both strong and feminine, for the characters' femininity does not undermine their strength, and they never become victims in need of rescue. Offering an overview of feminist thought and previous scholarship on mediated feminist discourse, this chapter assesses how *The Powerpuff Girls* as a text negotiates Third-Wave feminism, girl power, and power feminism.

SITUATING THIRD-WAVE FEMINISM

Although some debate exists about when Third-Wave feminism began, members of "Generation X"—people born in the 1970s and 1980s and who came of age in the 1990s—were the first to identify themselves as such. They grew up in the wake of Second-Wave feminism, enjoying the fruits of the Second-Wave's activism and immersed in the resultant rhetoric of equality of the sexes. Just like the Powerpuff Girls, they grew up expecting fair treatment and receiving it in many settings.[7] However, those identifying as Third-Wave feminists have seen that society does not always fully deliver on this promise of equality—not in the public sphere, and especially not in the home. As Allen (1997) noted:

> We grew up hearing "you can be anything you want to be," and yet we knew also that the world didn't welcome high-achieving girls as it did boys. We knew women had the right to have any job that a man could have, and yet we saw few female auto mechanics, engineers, and athletes. We heard about valuing everyone for their contributions—including stay-at-home dads as well as career women—but nonetheless we observed men going to work, pooh-poohing the concept of raising kids, and women either staying at home exclusively or holding a job *and* doing all the housework on top of that. (n.p.)

As a result of such experiences, Third-Wave feminists emphasize redressing issues of equality, particularly in the personal sphere. According to *The Third Wave: Feminism for the New Millenia*, Third-Wave feminists "are putting a new face on feminism, taking it beyond the women's movement that our mothers participated in, bringing it back to the lives of *real women* who juggle jobs, kids, money, and personal freedom in a frenzied world" (n.p.). In other words, they focus on individual empowerment, not on organized activism.

Within this broad conception of the Third Wave, many feminisms exist. As Lotz (2001) illustrates, the Third Wave's nuances are just as complex as those of the Second Wave (pp. 113, 117-118). Because a thorough exploration of its manifestations extends beyond the scope of the chapter, I focus on the two forms of Third-Wave feminism that most clearly manifested in my viewing of *The Powerpuff Girls*: power feminism and girl power.

Power Feminism

Power feminism arose as a backlash against the idea that women are victims of patriarchal institutions. Indeed, the term *victim* (Siegel, 1997) has been a key source of tension between Second- and Third-Wave feminists. For example, the radical feminist Germaine Greer famously declared, as a result of her economic and psychological analysis, that marriage is a form of slavery. Numerous members of the radical feminist group the Redstockings echoed this sentiment. Separatist feminists further suggested that women should sever their ties with men, at least for a time, in pursuit of personal growth free from oppressive restraints. However, radical and separatist perspectives sound puzzling and anti-male to younger, nonradical women: Because of the equality gains made in the Second Wave, many Generation-X era women and men find an emphasis on women as victims of the patriarchy foreign to their lived experiences.[8] They recognize that inequalities such as the wage gap still exist, but do not feel that they have been victimized by men.

Given this perspective, postfeminists such as Paglia (1992), Wolf (1993), Roiphe (1993) and Sommers (1994)[9] have spoken out against what has been called "victim feminism," which they say has unhealthily encouraged women to take on a victim's identity. In arguing for a move toward power feminism, some of these women have used tactics and approaches that are often problematic and which in many ways consti-tute a backlash (such as Roiphe's attempts to disclaim date rape,[10] and Paglia's essentialist view of human sexuality[11]). In its less problematic manifestations, however, power feminism "sees women as human beings—sexual, individual, no better or worse than their male counter-parts—and lays claim to equality simply because women are entitled to it" (Wolf, 1993, p. xvii). It calls not for revolution, but for effecting change on a more personal level, and it suggests that feminism needs to be something women can enact in their daily lives. Similarly, the Powerpuff Girls' work improved their city not just by working in tandem with Townsville's authorities, but also in daily interactions with others.

Authors like Wolf conceive of power feminism as dichotomously opposite to what she sees as the Second Wave's so-called victim femi-nism. However, calling so much of Second-Wave feminism "victim fem-inism" polemically and problematically pits one form of feminism against another, falling into the trap of "competitive either–or thinking, the belief that the self is formed in opposition to an other" (hooks, 1984, p. 31). *The Powerpuff Girls* writers deftly avoided this trap at times, as when the show exposed the false dualities of masculinity and feminini-ty, and of "power" versus "puff," but fell into it at other times, as when they pitted the girls' empowerment against an unflattering caricature of radical separatist "victim" feminism.

Girl Power

Despite power feminism's problematic opposition to Second-Wave femi-nism, power feminism has inspired many Third-Wave feminists and has strong connections with the girl power phenomenon. They are similar in their de-emphasis on organized activism and valuation of individual empowerment. But girl power emphasizes consumerism, for its messages of empowerment are found in popular culture texts and artifacts that present girl power as the fluffy, pleasurable suggestion that girls can do (and buy) anything they choose. Because girl power is commodified, sold, and consumed, it has manifested in popular music (such as the Spice Girls), movies (*Legally Blonde*), and television shows (*Buffy the Vampire Slayer*). Perhaps because the media typically imply that "feminism" is a dirty word, those who embrace the girl power of popular culture often choose not to call themselves feminists, even if they believe in equality.

Material culture is also a key site of girl power, typified by the tiny pink T-shirts that say "Girls Rule!" and sparkly makeup packaging. The conflation of empowerment, consumption, and personal appearance suggests that because girls can be both feminine and strong, they can wear whatever they want—frilly pink lace or purple fishnet stockings—without negating their power. The range of appearances endorsed by sites of girl power is mainly limited to normative femininity, which is problematic (Hains, 2004). However, rhetoric encouraging women's freedom of appearance is the chief aspect of girl power that McCracken discussed when he said that women can "be sexy and be feminine and be typically girlish, and still be a feminist" (Havrilesky, 2002).

The playful engagement with performing femininity permeates Third-Wave feminism beyond girl power. However, the goals and ideals of the Third Wave are so similar to those of the Second Wave that one young woman at the June 2001 National Women's Studies Association conference declared, "As far as I can tell, the Third Wave is just the Second Wave with more lip gloss" (cited in Dicker & Piepmeier, 2003, p. 3). Critics have commented that Third-Wave feminism's persistent focus on appearance is overly personal and troublingly apolitical, detracting from more serious equality issues.[12] Indeed, the obsession with representation has been critiqued as a major weakness. Baumgardner and Richards (2000) conceded to this point's validity, but they also appreciated its rationale as a political statement: Second-Wave feminists such as Betty Friedan emphasized "professional seriousness" in demeanor and appearance to encourage men to stop disrespectfully and belittlingly referring to them as "girls." By embracing the "girlie," Third-Wave feminists rescue the term and concept of "girl," claiming it as their own—as others before them have done with the terms "bitch," "queer," and "nigga" (pp. 137, 400). In this vein, Hopkins (2002) noted:

> Today, "fighting like a girl" is something to be proud of. Girls are fighting back, not just against male violence but also against restrictive stereotypes of feminine passivity. Today's girls don't just want the tough action hero, they want to be the tough action hero. They

might play at being "girly," but they have become all they ever wanted in a man. (p. 11)

Thus, in an era that assumes female equality, this embrace of girlishness rebels against "the idea that girls and power don't mix" (Baumgardner & Richards, 2000, p. 137). The argument is that, at least to a certain point, valuing girlishness empowers girls much like the Second-Wave empowered women.

The Powerpuff Girls draws heavily from girl power and reflects power feminism's influence. These conceptions will provide a useful context for discussing The Powerpuff Girls as a symbolic representation of Third-Wave feminism. First, however, let us turn to a brief history of feminist discourse in the mass media.

FEMINIST DISCOURSE IN THE MASS MEDIA

In the 1960s, during what Douglas (1994) called a "context of prefeminist agitation" (p. 125), a new type of woman appeared on television. Samantha of *Bewitched* (1964-1972)[13] and Jeannie of *I Dream of Jeannie* (1965-1970) possessed supernatural powers that their men sought to contain within the home. Discourse and public debate of the time informed this supernatural-containment metaphor for the subordination of women's equality, riding the heels of Friedan's (1963) *The Feminine Mystique* and women's lobbying of the Kennedy Administration for respect and rights (Douglas, 1994). Thus, the shows were complicated, contradicting one another and, frequently, themselves. Samantha and Jeannie's illicit use of their powers often suggested that "female power, when let loose in the public sphere, is often disruptive to male authority, but sometimes it also bolsters that authority. These colliding messages made *Bewitched* and *I Dream of Jeannie* simultaneously cautionary and liberatory" (Douglas, 1994, pp. 136-137), warning women that their excursions from the domestic sphere might not be well received—but perhaps also inspiring them to act on their feelings of empowerment.

Then, in the 1970s, television shows began to reflect advances made by Second-Wave liberal feminists, for many activists had called for changes to women's depictions in the media. Mary Richards of *The Mary Tyler Moore Show* (1970-1977), an unmarried career woman, pioneered the televisual construction of women who independently negotiate life, without husbands. She differed from unmarried women featured in earlier shows; Connie Brooks in *Our Miss Brooks* (1952-1956) and Ann Marie in *That Girl* (1966-1971) were actually focused on finding a man (Taylor,

1989). In contrast, Mary Richards wanted what many feminists of her era wanted: independence, a steady job with a salary, a place of her own, and the ability to make it on her own (Dow, 1996). As such, she became an icon of Second-Wave liberal feminism.

Mary Richards' independence may have been to Second-Wave liberal feminism what female "toughness" is to the Third-Wave. Just as Mary exemplified liberal feminism, some potential icons for Third-Wave power feminism and girl power have emerged in recent years—characters who are both clearly feminine and physically strong, like *Buffy the Vampire Slayer* (1997-2003),[14] the *Charmed* sisters (1998-2006), and Sydney on *Alias* (2001-2006). As Hopkins (2002) noted, "It appears that after decades of feminist critique, images of weak girls are finally losing currency" (p. 11). These modern warrior-women embody physical strength that has been scarce in depictions of women and girls. Tough men abound in action-adventure films, television dramas, cartoons, and comic books, but women usually play the weak, helpless victim. This is significant, for stories influence our constructions of reality, assigning and structuring social meaning (Shanahan & Morgan, 1999). The abundant stories about strong men and weak women have marked strength as masculine and weakness as feminine, binding gender to nongendered concepts. Thus, the media's recent representations of physically strong women are as significant as the 1970s depictions of women not as passive dependents, but independent and free.

In light of the trend toward depictions of strong, nearly invincible women, feminists such as Durham (2003) argued that this area has opened up for study, for "the Buffies and Sabrinas of contemporary pop culture have shifted social understandings of girl-oriented media in some significant way: No longer does this genre occupy 'the margins of what counts as intellectually serious'" (p. 25). Likewise, Inness' (1999) argued, "Anyone interested in gender roles in the United States needs to reflect on the construction of the tough girl because she suggests a great deal about changing gender identities" (p. 9). Significantly, Inness' analyses of tough women in *The Bionic Woman* (1976-1978), *Charlie's Angels* (1976-1981), the *Terminator* movies (1984, 1991) and *The X-Files* (1993-2002) indicate that in the media, a woman's femininity undermines her strength. Furthermore, texts about tough women often suggest that their strength is anomalous, emphasizing most women's helplessness. Thus, such texts engage in hegemony, conceding that women may be strong but reinforcing the ideology of women's weakness. This polysemy is common in the media; many shows contain multiple and conflicting messages. Those interested in the changing constructions of gender must note the prevalence of hegemony in most texts about physically strong women—and its near-absence from *The Powerpuff Girls*.

METHODOLOGY AND THEORY

In this essay, I offer a feminist cultural analysis of the constructions of female strength and feminism in *The Powerpuff Girls*. I draw on discourse analysis (Casey, Casey, Calvert, French, & Lewis, 2002), which, as Duke and Kreshel (1998) argued, is an appropriate method for analyzing gender constructions in the media:

> Every day, we participate in the discourse of femininity: in an infinite number of ways, we create and perpetuate an understanding of what it means to be a woman in our society. The mass media are fundamental in this cultural process of social construction and representation of the feminine. (p. 48)

I conducted my analysis using grounded theory, taking notes on recurring themes across *Powerpuff Girls* episodes. Over the course of my research, I viewed 105 of the 117 *Powerpuff Girls* episodes aired by Cartoon Network as of May 2004. I then turned to online fan-written transcripts for an understanding of the remaining episodes.[15] Through this approach, I sought to develop a holistic appreciation of the show while exploring the specific ways in which *The Powerpuff Girls* contributes to and reflects Third-Wave discourse.

This chapter focuses on five episodes that emerged as key exemplars of the show's discourse about feminism and female strength: "The Rowdyruff Boys" (1999), "The Boys are Back in Town" (2003), "Members Only" (2002), "Slumbering with the Enemy" (2000), and "Equal Fights" (2001). I discuss these episodes individually, but in terms of their dialogue within the entire series. Newcomb's (1991) interpretation of Bakhtin's dialogic theory argues:

> If we choose to study a television series every episode of a series is part of the larger dialogue involving every other episode. We see characters repeat their 'statements' through a range of plot issues. (p. 78)

Dialogic theory also acknowledges that as a text, a television show expresses numerous attitudes and behaviors within characters and across episodes. Characters' relationships become multivocal in relationship to each other; behavioral contradictions and surprising reactions to one another contribute to the entire text's polyvocality. Thus, an analysis of individual episodes in the context of the complete series will reveal how *The Powerpuff Girls* constructs strong girls, and elucidate its part in the ongoing mediated conversation about tough girls and feminism.

READING THE POWERPUFF GIRLS

Two broad themes emerged from my viewing of *The Powerpuff Girls*: the repositioning of power as a nongendered concept by subverting the idea that power belongs to men; and the depiction of group power and collective action as a subversion of the traditional conception of the superhero as a societal outsider acting alone. The cartoon suggests that heroism is the result of group efforts, empowering everyone in the community to participate. Within the show's discourse, these themes coalesce through an overt discussion of feminist thought that offers clear evidence for its embrace of Third-Wave feminism and, specifically, girl power and power feminism. Its characters explicitly reject a caricature of victim-oriented separatist feminist rhetoric, instead embracing equality and empowerment.

Girl Power in Behavior and Heroism

The Powerpuff Girls' girlie appearances and high-pitched voices clearly show they are female. However, in behavior, they are not always stereotypically feminine; their power and physical prowess break the stereotype of passive femininity, for they are ultimately stronger and tougher than the other characters. The self-sufficient heroes regularly emerge victorious from physical and intellectual battles with all of their foes. Unlike the women in *Charlie's Angels*, the girls do not have a Charlie to give orders; the helpless, hapless mayor of Townsville calls them in terrified distress whenever danger looms, and the girls determine their own course of action. Furthermore, as Inness (1999) noted, "Most women on television come across as highly incapable, unsuited to be heroes because they are helpless in emergencies" (p. 100). Thus, in opposition to helpless heroines, the Powerpuff Girls do not become victims when a battle intensifies. For example, although Mojo Jojo captures Blossom in "Not so Awesome Blossom" (2002) as a lure to trap the other girls and the professor in his lair, Blossom saves them all, foiling Jojo's plans—and beating him up for good measure. Likewise, in "Cop Out" (2000), when an enemy lowers the girls into a vat of acid and they cry for help, no one saves them; they emerge unscathed, realizing that acid won't hurt them.

In defeating their foes, the Powerpuff Girls do not resort to the trickery or deception so common in previous mediated texts about strong women. Inness (1999) noted that because 1970s American culture was, as it is today, "deeply troubled by toughness in women," the toughness of characters such as Charlie's Angels and Jaime, the Bionic Woman, "had to be made to seem less consequential and less controversial than it actually was . . . through the use of masquerade and disguise" (p. 47). Therefore, these women often used heightened appearances of femininity and seduction as crime-fighting techniques. This actually served to undermine their toughness, making it more palatable to viewers.

The Powerpuff Girls do not normally employ seduction and disguise. Although they always appear feminine, their femininity is of the cute-little-girl variety, lacking sex appeal—after all, they are 5 years old. In only one anomalous context do the girls hesitantly resort to a kindergarten version of the seduction technique: In "The Rowdyruff Boys" (1999), while in the County Jail, Mojo Jojo creates evil little-boy counterparts to the Powerpuff Girls from snips, snails, and puppy dog tails mixed together in a toiletbowl. Their parallel construction makes the boys an equal match for the girls, who lose a long battle. In the end, however, they are not defeated: At the suggestion of the mayor's shapely, feminine assistant, Ms. Bellum, the girls bat their eyelashes flirtatiously (see Fig. 12.1), then kiss the boys—which Ms. Bellum says is what little boys most fear. This suggestion is in some ways problematic, as it positions the girls' power within the context of the seductive power of adult women's sexuality, and the girls are ambivalent about enacting this technique. Buttercup's reply is, "Ewwww, gross." Yet the strategy works: Their kisses dissolve the boys into their original, harmless ingredients.

In traditional tough-women texts, such behavior undermines women's strength. For example, Inness' (1999) analysis revealed that

Fig. 12.1. The girls bat their eyelashes at the Rowdyruff Boys. Screenshot from "The Rowdyruff Boys" (1999).

because Charlie's Angels often depended on their sexiness to accomplish their goals, they appear "less tough and capable than they might if they depended on their brawn or brains to solve crimes" (p. 43). In this regard, a key difference between Charlie's Angels and the Powerpuff Girls emerges: Although the Powerpuff Girls use a kindergarten version of sexiness (flirty eyelashes and kisses) to defeat their enemies, it is not part of their crime-fighting repertoire. And why should it be, when—unlike Charlie's Angels—they have laser eye-beams and are essentially indestructible?

A later episode, "The Boys are Back in Town" (2003), presents the girls' second conflict with the Rowdyruff Boys. In some ways a revision of the earlier episode, which aired 4 years prior, it suggests that seduction is not an appropriate strategy. Him, the show's devil-figure, reconstitutes the Rowdyruff Boys to try to defeat the girls. However, he has "improved them" so that the girls' kisses make the boys larger and more powerful. In a turn of events ripe for psychoanalysis, the girls realize that insulting the boys' attempts at macho masculinity "shrinks 'em down to size" and defeats them.

Taken together, "The Rowdyruff Boys" and "The Boys are Back in Town" imply that the girls are more comfortable in their femininity than the boys are in their masculinity. In the former episode, the girls survive the kiss and the boys do not, casting the scene as a literal moment of girl power: The girls win not because of their superpowers, but because being a girl and performing normative femininity can itself be powerful in our society. The girls learn in the latter episode that a few well-targeted insults can easily shatter the boys' fragile masculinity, demonstrating that normative femininity is not the only way to bring bad boys down a peg: Girls are expected to be "nice," so subverting this norm by being as skillful as boys in wielding insults also works.

In dialogue with the show's overarching theme of power being accessible to girls is another episode called "Members Only" (2002). *The Powerpuff Girls* want to join the Association of World Super Men (AWSM, or "awesome," for short). The girls adore these super men, but when they apply for membership, they experience sexism for the first time. Although they pass the entrance exams, the men deny them membership. When the girls protest, Major Glory responds:

This is the Association of World Super Men! You're little girls. *We* are the men! The protectors, the hunters, the fighters, and the show-offs [*pounding podium*] and the noisemakers! *You* are little girls. *You* should be at home with your mommy, learning how to cook and clean, and . . . blah-blah-blah-blah-blah, whatever women stuff. So leave the superheroics to the super . . . *MEN!*

The girls return home angrily. Later, when the hypermasculine villain Mascumax attacks the association, the girls begrudgingly rescue them, easily defeating the men's nemesis, who bursts into tears. Afterward, the men of AWSM approach the girls sheepishly, and Bubbles says, "If you want us to join your club now, forget it!" The men explain that they were actually hoping to join the girls' club, because the girls are now *their* heroes. The girls exchange a satisfied glance. In the show's closing shot, the men wear dresses like the Powerpuff Girls', complete with white stockings and black shoes, as the "newly formed Society of Associated Puffketeers"—to comedic effect, of course.

Beyond sexism, why did the men refuse the girls' admission into AWSM? As Inness (1999) argued, the tough woman can make society uncomfortable because "she challenges the notion that there is a 'natural' connection between women and femininity and between masculinity and men" (p. 21). The girls' superior strength challenged the men's perception of power as men's domain, threatening their masculinity. Furthermore, as Fiske (1990) noted, anything that straddles binary categories becomes "anomalous" and therefore either sacred or taboo (p. 118). The girls, with a feminine appearance and masculine behavior, were at first "taboo," to be shunned and sent home. Observed Inness: "Our culture likes its girls to be girls and its boys to be boys" (p. 21). However, when the girls rescued the Super Men, they shifted in the men's eyes from the taboo to the sacred. They were suddenly heroes, saviors to be revered because of their inversion of the classic man-rescues-woman storyline.

In the episode's conclusion, all the super men have bent sex role expectations by wearing dresses and have become honorary girls—inverting the norm of strong women becoming honorary men (Clover, 1992). This significant visual statement means that although girls can dress like boys, the reverse is not true; seeing the men in drag is humorous for the audience. However, the men do not appear degraded by their cross-dressing. They flex their muscles and smile broadly, showing pride at being Puffketeers (see Fig. 12.2). In "Members Only," the

Fig. 12.2. The men of AWSM as "Puffketeers." Screenshot from "Members Only" (2002).

Powerpuff Girls challenge the notion that being a girl is degrading, for they single-handedly rescue a group of powerful, macho men from doom; in the end, the men want to be like them.

Community Empowerment and Collective Action

Just as *The Powerpuff Girls* presents a discourse oppositional to previous depictions of tough women and power as masculine, the girls differ significantly from traditional superheroes because they are part of society. Set-apart superheroes have a long tradition: Wonder Woman, Batman, the X-Men, Charlie's Angels, and Xena were all outsiders. Yet the Powerpuff Girls have a happy family life and participate in their community. Not external avengers of justice, they work within the system, taking action whenever the mayor or his secretary, Ms. Bellum, calls to report a crime or act of violence. They attend kindergarten like the other 5-year-olds, and have friends there. They do not live a double life featuring secret superhero identities in a Clark Kent/Superman fashion: Everyone knows who they are, and they behave the same in daily life as when fighting crime. These qualities combine to construct the Powerpuff Girls as superheroes who break the mold.

The girls further differ from classic superheroes because rather than wielding power in a hierarchal manner that would place them above everyone else, they empower their community by sharing power with them. Describing the typical effect that mythological heroes have had on their societies, Aisenberg (1994) argued:

> because classical heroes are figures fulfilling a god-given destiny, they stand above and beyond their fellow men. In their very perfection, their larger-than-life, nearly-god identity, heroes are inimitable, and therefore disempowering to more ordinary men, inhibiting them from becoming leaders. (p. 12)

Unlike this construction of the hero, the Powerpuff Girls do not mitigate the power of others. Instead, their toughness often inspires collective action by "normal" people in the cartoon, showing that they are, in fact, imitable.

This happens in several episodes, but perhaps the most interesting example is found in "Slumbering with the Enemy" (2000). The supervillain Mojo Jojo dresses in drag and calls himself "Mojicia" to crash the Powerpuff Girls' slumber party, where his disguise fools everyone but the girls. The girls worry that his presence might upset their friends and ruin the party, so—confident in their power to stop him as soon as he tries anything—they let him stay. In the morning, however, he emerges from the professor's laboratory, having stolen Antidote X, the Powerpuff Girls' kryptonite.[16] He douses the girls with it just before they reach him, rendering them unconscious. Mojo laughs madly and announces, "Thanks to Antidote X, I have finally defeated the Powerpuff Girls!"

When the slumber party guests realize that Mojicia is really Mojo, they run screaming. He shouts, "That's right! Scream! Cower! Fear me! Because now that the once-powerful Powerpuffs are now powerless, you have no one to protect you!" He then leans over the unconscious Powerpuffs and says with mock pity, "Look at you. You're just like your friends here. You are exactly the same as they are. Weak, helpless, and scared! You are now—dare I say it?—NORMAL LITTLE GIRLS! Useless, normal little girls who can't do anything, because they are normal!" He is unprepared when the "normal little girls" pummel him, striking him down with their pillows (see Fig. 12.3). He cowers; the Powerpuffs awaken and look on proudly. In the closing shot, several girls flex their muscles and glare fiercely as the narrator says, "So for the very first time, the day is saved, thanks to—the normal little girls!"

The normal girls' empowerment defies a long and problematic tradition of depicting women with strength as anomalous or unusual. Although shows like *The Bionic Woman* and *Charlie's Angels* progressively presented powerful women, the strength of their central characters highlighted the weakness of all other women. Thus, Charlie's Angels constantly rescued women too helpless to rescue themselves. If most women depicted couldn't face a threat, then the Angels "are the exception, not the rule" (Inness, 1999, pp. 44-45). In contrast, "Slumbering with the Enemy" reveals that most women and girls *are* strong: When the Powerpuff Girls are rendered temporarily unconscious, the normal

Fig. 12.3. The "normal little girls" defeat Mojo Jojo. Screenshot from "Slumbering with the Enemy" (2000).

little girls easily defeat Mojo Jojo on their own. *The Powerpuff Girls'* amazing strength does not imply that other females are weak; rather, there are degrees. As Mojo Jojo discovers when the slumber party guests interrupt his tirade, the normal little girls are not weak; they have normal levels of strength. Although they cannot individually defeat a supervillain, they have enough combined strength to topple a formidable foe. The episode suggests that you do not need superpowers to stand up for yourself, as long as you have a community of girls by your side.

Although this is a powerful feminist message, it does not mesh very well with the idea of Third-Wave feminism as an individual or personal movement. Therefore, I read it as a response to or critique of Third-Wave individualism, for it demonstrates the power of a collective sisterhood.

Thus, *The Powerpuff Girls'* discourse counters many other texts about strength and independence. It emerges as a site of community empowerment and collective action, offering the message that even without superpowers, women and girls can be strong. They need not sit by passively and become victims if a hero fails them. They can join together to emerge victorious, with or without their protectors' help. It also depicts more strong female characters than other shows do—little girls without superpowers with whom girl viewers can readily identify.

DISCUSSION: CONSTRUCTING FEMINISM
IN THE THIRD WAVE

In aggregate, the Powerpuff Girls' actions—including their powerful behavior, community involvement, and empowering of others—indicates their liberal feminist philosophy. They work within their society, not externally: They effect positive changes from within the system and with the approval of the city's mayor. They are not caricatured as man-hating feminists; they love and respect the positive male figures in their lives, including the kind but ineffectual mayor. These characteristics imply that the underlying Third-Wave ideology of *The Powerpuff Girls* is that men and women should be equal, and that equality can be achieved on a personal basis while working within society.

As if to confirm that this is the series' philosophy, a unique episode called "Equal Fights" (2001) presents an overt and politically charged discussion of feminism. Although the episode never uses the word "feminist" or "feminism," it negotiates various forms of feminism. "Equal Fights" features a villain, Femme Fatale, who wears a 1970s-style bellbottomed white jumpsuit and an eye mask, wielding a hand gun—all featuring the symbol for the female sex (   ). Her long blonde hair is styled straight and sleek as was the fashion in the 1970s (see Fig. 12.4), and when she is seen, disco-style background music further associates her with this era. A self-styled feminist bank robber, she only steals Susan B. Anthony coins, and assaults the men she robs with a barrage of insults.

Like the men of AWSM, Femme Fatale is a one-time guest character. However, her appearance contributes to the feminist thematic content of *The Powerpuff Girls*. According to Newcomb's (1991) interpretation of Bakhtin's dialogic theory, how the main characters in a text negotiate novel situations—such as conflicts resulting from the introduction of a guest star—offers insights into the text's ideologies (p. 77). In the case of "Equal Fights," the introduction of Femme Fatale raises serious conflicts between the Powerpuff Girls and the citizens they have vowed to protect, and it simultaneously highlights the conflicts within feminism discussed earlier in this chapter.

When the girls first encounter Femme Fatale, they overtake her quickly. As a diversionary tactic, however, Femme Fatale presents an argument grounded in a caricature of radical separatist feminist rhetoric. She comments on the scarcity of female superheroes. Only Wonder Woman stands alone; the rest act as mere "extensions of their male counterparts." She says this is for one reason only: "The man can't admit we're better than him, so he keeps us down!" Once she has the girls fuming about this injustice, she adds that oppressive men also dominate villainy. Therefore, just as the Powerpuff Girls are the only three female superheroes in Townsville, she is one of the only three female villains in Townsville—and the other two are in jail, "so they don't count." She concludes her argument with a plea for mercy rooted in women's solidarity. The girls agree to set her free, persuaded by the implication that Femme Fatale's life of crime is justified by women's oppression and her deliberate, radical separatist intent.

Fig. 12.4. Femme Fatale. Screenshot from "Equal Fights" (2001).

While Femme Fatale continues robbing Townsville, unchecked and unstoppable, the Powerpuff Girls' attitudes change dramatically. They see sexism everywhere, in places that it doesn't exist, for they have taken on the victim perspective that power feminists suggest has poisoned so many women. They have become the dupes of Femme Fatale's "bad" separatist feminism, the form most often (mis)represented by the mass media. The mayor's secretary, Ms. Bellum, and the girls' beloved kindergarten teacher, Ms. Keene, then talk with the girls about their attitude change. When Buttercup explains that they are not fighting Femme Fatale because "we girls gotta look out for each other," their mentors gently help the girls see that giving Femme Fatale free reign actually hurts the men *and* women of Townville—emotionally, financially and physically. This clarifies the show's ideological stance: Third-Wave feminism is not about overthrowing patriarchal institutions, or representing women as victims of men, or hating men. Rather, it supports the conservative stance that men and women are equal, and that females already have strength and empowerment at their disposal.

Thus, in the final scene of the episode, the girls stop Femme Fatale. As they corner her, they point out the irony of her theft of Susan B. Anthony coins, noting that Anthony became famous not only by breaking the law and voting in 1872, but for her reaction. Although the authorities were willing to treat her crime lightly because she was just a woman, "She demanded that she be sent to jail, just like any *man* who broke the law." Femme Fatale is at a loss for words, and Blossom says, "And that's exactly what we're gonna do to you!"

This dialogue presents the girls and their mentors as opposed to Femme Fatale, a caricature of radical feminism, and in so doing falls into the trap of constructing a false binary opposition that the show elsewhere so deftly exposes. As I have argued elsewhere, this is a problematic and offensive feminist move that perpetuates myths about "bad" feminism and polemically pits young feminists against their predecessors (Hains, 2004). For better or worse, this dichotomizing is part of *The Powerpuff Girls'* Third-Wave stance. Femme Fatale's empty rhetoric represents everything power feminists dislike about Second-Wave victim feminism, and positions the show as a Third-Wave text.

CONCLUSION

In one chapter, it is difficult to represent the multivocality and polysemy of *The Powerpuff Girls*. The show conveyed messages besides those presented here—including ideas about beauty and power, masculinity and villainy—and, as is common among media texts, some of its other messages may contradict those addressed here. Likewise, multiple readings of *The Powerpuff Girls* may exist among different audiences; this chapter makes no claims to reflect the possible interpretations. Given the rise of media texts that feature physically strong girls and women, and the media's attention on *The Powerpuff Girls* as a feminist text, however, this chapter's focus on dialogues of power and empowerment contribute to the growing body of literature about tough girls and Third-Wave feminism.

Although remarkably feminist, the show is simultaneously problematic. It fails to engage with the Third Wave's ideal of diversity. Third-Wave feminists such as Dicker and Piepmeier (2003) noted that "many Third Wavers realize [that] it's fine to engage with the world in a playful, individualistic way, but for that engagement to be informed by feminism, it has to take into account the power relations surrounding gender, race, class, and sexual orientation" (p. 18). Likewise, *The Third Wave Foundation* (2001) "strive[s] to combat inequalities that we face as a result of our age, gender, sexual orientation, economic status, or level of education" (n.p.). In contrast, the Third-Wave feminism in *The Powerpuff Girls* is White and middle class. The show's main characters are not racially diverse, and the girls live in a picturesque middle-class suburb of Townsville, not within the city. Perhaps because it airs on cable network Cartoon Network, its envisioned audience is White and middle class. However, the lack of representation in a show whose creator claims to embrace the "new feminism" is problematic.

Another complication: the show's medium. As discussed earlier, in most shows, tough women's strength tends to be undermined by their sexual appearance. In *The Powerpuff Girls*, although the girls were not drawn in a sexually appealing fashion like the girls on *Sailor Moon*,[17] their strength may have been undermined by the fact that they are characters in an animated cartoon, a genre that is typically considered trivial. But at the same time, this may have permitted the show's positive messages to be more readily received, for when viewers do not take something seriously, they may be more influenced by its messages. Its seeming innocuity may be as much a strength as a weakness.

On that note, can *The Powerpuff Girls*—or any mainstream media product—ever be a genuine feminist text? Feminism in a mass media text is commodified and sold to its viewers, who are then sold back to a text's advertisers. *The Powerpuff Girls* has spawned a vast merchandising empire, so the show's brand of girl power is quite literally sold to children through material culture in stores nationwide. Although girl power has permeated our culture and communicated the idea that girls can be feminine and powerful, its emphasis on the freedom to be feminine often translates into a freedom to buy products in pursuit of beauty and femininity—which is problematic and not particularly empowering. Indeed, the use of the "girl power" idea to move merchandise has only become worse since *The Powerpuff Girls'* inception. It has been used to sell everything from DVDs to deodorant. Given the terrible problems faced by women and girls in the United States and around the world today, the freedom to purchase commodities is a hollow freedom indeed.

The Powerpuff Girls' feminism is also rather conservative, making no call for action to redress the inequalities women continue to face. It tends to eschew the term *feminism* completely, perhaps because so many young people see feminism as a dirty word. Young women anxiously avoid being labeled feminists, even though they believe in equality. As Douglas (1994) lamented, "the main motto of women today is, supposedly, 'I'm not a feminist, but . . . '" (p. 270). Thus, it is no surprise that although the episode "Equal Fights" was ensconced in feminist discourse, the characters were never identified as feminist.

Despite this ambivalence, *The Powerpuff Girls* has many positive aspects. The show repositions power as nongendered, emphasizing the importance of group power and collective action and subverting the idea that strong women are exceptions to the norm. "The Rowdyruff Boys" and "The Boys are Back in Town" suggest that femininity can be a source of strength; "Members Only" depicts men happy to become honorary Powerpuff Girls; "Slumbering with the Enemy" extends power to everyday people; and "Equal Fights" negotiates feminist discourses unusual in popular culture. If changes in "the construction of the tough girl . . . suggests a great deal about changing gender identities" (Inness, 1999, p. 9), then *The Powerpuff Girls* constructs girls as less rigidly gendered, active, not passive, and tough, not weak. In the Third Wave, being a girl is not insulting, but empowering. While *The Powerpuff Girls* aired on Cartoon Network, it contributed to progressive ideas about girlhood—which, for a mainstream, commercial media text, is a remarkable thing.

NOTES

1. *The Powerpuff Girls* airs in 30-minute slots, each of which contains one 22-minute episode or two 11-minute episodes.
2. In creator Craig McCracken's original conception, the accidental ingredient was "a can of whoopass," and the girls were "The Whoopass Girls" (Cella, 2000).
3. Note that although the professor is the girls' creator, and they have a father–daughter relationship with him, they always call him "professor." As the professor is unmarried, they have no mother—although their kinder-

garten teacher, Ms. Keene, and the mayor's secretary, Ms. Bellum, provide them with strong female role models.

4. On September 8, 2000, an episode of *The Powerpuff Girls* broke a Cartoon Network record: It "posted a 3.4 rating, or 2.2 million households, making it the most-watched program in Cartoon's history" (Moss, 2000, n.p.).

5. Cartoons that have followed in *The Powerpuff Girls'* footsteps, featuring girls but also appealing to boys, include The Disney Channel's *Kim Possible* and Cartoon Network's *Totally Spies.*

6. Noted by the author in attendance at E3.

7. As Baumgardner and Richards (2000) noted, "We were a generation that was forced to experience equality when it came to the newly coed gym classes, and reveled in Title IX's influence on sports for girls. These products of culture are mundane to us, simply the atmosphere in our temporal tank" (p. 130).

8. This is reportedly less true, however, for women of color, sexual minorities and Third World feminists of the Third Wave (Lotz, 2001).

9. There is some debate as to whether or not these postfeminists are Third-Wave feminists. I argue that it depends on to whom you talk: One person's Third-Wave feminism is another person's postfeminism or feminist backlash. It also depends on whether postfeminism is being defined as "coming after feminism" or "postmodern feminism." I would consider the latter but not the former to be a form of Third-Wave feminism.

10. Roiphe argued that date rape is not actually rape, but rather sexual intercourse that a woman later regrets. She alleges that feminists have misused statistics on rape to create an atmosphere of fear, diminishing women's sexual confidence and instead instilling in them a victim's perspective.

11. Because of Paglia's essentialist position, in which she argues that there are inherent differences in male and female sexuality, she is often criticized for being pro-rape. This is because her arguments suggest that rape is inevitable and cannot be excised from the world.

12. Third-Wave feminist Erin Harde observed the personal nature of her own relationship with feminism, writing, "I think that whereas the Second Wave was more of a collective political movement, the Third Wave helps women work on a personal level . . . I am still coming to feminism on a personal level, but I eventually hope to contribute on a larger level" (Harde & Harde, 2003, p. 120).

13. All television show running dates are from TV.com, at http://www.tv.com.

14. For a discussion of Buffy's significance to feminism, see Owen (1999); for a discussion of gendered narratives of fear surrounding Buffy, see Jarvis (2001).

15. Fan-written transcripts, which include notations on visual and tonal aspects of each episode, are available at http://www.ppgworld.com/transcripts.

16. In the Superman comics and movies, a piece of kryptonite is a fragment of Superman's home planet, Krypton. Exposure to kryptonite is toxic to Superman, stripping him of his powers.

17. Sailor Moon is a popular Japanese girls' comic book (*manga*) that was later adapted into a cartoon series (*anime*) that aired on television in the United States and abroad. The complete series is available on DVD.

REFERENCES

Advertiser Staff and Wire Services. (2000, August 29). For Powerpuffs, whomping the bad guys is girl stuff [electronic version]. *The Honolulu Advertiser.*

Aisenberg, N. (1994). *Ordinary heroines: Transforming the male myth.* New York: Continuum.

Allen, K. (1997). The 3rd Wave: Who we are, and why we need to speak. Retrieved May 1, 2003, from http://www.io.com~wwwave/addresses/kimaddress. html.

Barner, M.R. (1999). Sex-role stereotyping in FCC-mandated children's educational television. *Journal of Broadcasting & Electronic Media, 43,* 551-564.

Baumgardner, J., & Richards, A. (2000). *Manifesta: Young women, feminism, and the future.* New York: Farrar, Straus & Giroux.

The Boys are Back in Town. (2003). *The Powerpuff Girls* (B. Larsen, C. Reccardi, Writers, P. Stec, Art director, R. Myers, J. McIntyre, Directors). Cartoon Network.

Browne, B.A. (1998). Gender stereotypes in advertising on children's television in the 1990s: A cross-national analysis. *Journal of Advertising, 27,* 83-96.

Casey, B., Casey, N., Calvert, B., French, L., & Lewis, J. (2002). *Television studies: The key concepts.* London: Routledge.

Cella, C. (2000). "Powerpuff Girls" creator McCracken discusses Bubbles & co.'s appeal. *Billboard, 112*(49), 111.

Clover, C.J. (1992). *Men, women and chain saws: Gender in the modern horror film.* Princeton, NJ: Princeton University Press.

Cop Out. (2000). *The Powerpuff Girls.* Cartoon Network.

Corliss, R. (2001, April 16). Go ahead, make her day [electronic version]. *Time Pacific Magazine,* p. 15.

DeRogatis, J. (2002, July 3). "Powerpuff Girls" fight the good fight. *Chicago Sun-Times,* p. 43.

Dicker, R., & Piepmeier, A. (2003). *Catching a wave: Reclaiming feminism for the 21st century.* Boston: Northeastern University Press.

Douglas, S.J. (1994). *Where the girls are: Growing up female with the mass media.* New York: Times Books.

Dow, B. (1996). *Prime-time feminism: Television, media culture, and the women's movement since 1970.* Philadelphia: University of Pennsylvania Press.

Duke, L.L., & Kreshel, P.J. (1998). Negotiating femininity: Girls in early adolescence read teen magazines. *Journal of Communication Inquiry, 22*(1), 48-71.

Durham, M.G. (2003). The girling of America: Critical reflections on gender and popular communication. *Popular Communication, 1*(1), 23-31.

Ebenkamp, B. (2001, June 11). Power to the puff people. *Brandweek, 42*(24), p. 36+.

Equal Fights. (2001). *The Powerpuff Girls* (L. Faust, Writer, D. Shank, Art director, R. Myers, C. McCracken, Directors). Cartoon Network.

Fiske, J. (1990). *Introduction to communication studies.* London & New York: Routledge.

Friedan, B. (1963). *The feminine mystique.* New York: Norton.

Hager, L. (2002). *What little girls are really made of: The Powerpuff Girls, citizenship, and quantum mechanics or, "Better pray for the girls."* Paper presented at Cultivating Knowledge(s): A Conference and a Celebration, University of Florida, Gainesville.

Hains, R.C. (2004). The problematics of reclaiming the girlish: *The Powerpuff Girls* and girl power. *Femspec, 5*(2), 1-39.

Harde, R., & Harde, E. (2003). Voices and visions: A mother and daughter discuss coming to feminism and being feminist. In R. Dicker & A. Piepmeier (Eds.) *Catching a wave: Reclaiming feminism for the 21st century* (pp. 116-137). Boston: Northeastern University Press.

Havrilesky, H. (2002, July 2). Powerpuff Girls meet world. *Salon.* Retrieved May 1, 2003, from http://archive.salon.com/mwt/feature/2002/07/02/powerpuff

hooks, b. (1984). *Feminist theory: From margin to center.* Cambridge, MA: South End Press.

Hopkins, S. (2002, February 19). Bam! Crash! Kapow! Girls are heroes now. *Sydney Morning Herald*, p. 11.

Inness, S.A. (1999). *Tough girls: Women warriors and wonder women in popular culture.* Philadelphia: University of Pennsylvania Press.

Jarvis, C. (2001). School is hell: Gendered fears in teenage horror. *Educational Studies, 27*(3), 257–267.

Lloyd, R. (2000, November 24-30). Beyond good and evil. *LA Weekly.* Retrieved June 21, 2004, from http://www.laweekly.com/ink/01/01/features-lloyd.php.

Lotz, A.D. (2001). Postfeminist television criticism: Rehabilitation critical terms and identifying postfeminist attributes. *Feminist Media Studies, 1*(1), 105-121.

McAlister, N. (2002, July 2). Powerpuff Girls battle villains on big screen. *Florida Times-Union*, p. C1.

Members Only. (2002). *The Powerpuff Girls.* (P. Rudish, Writer, R. Myers, C. McCracken, Directors). Cartoon Network.

Moss, L. (2000). "Powerpuff" quarter. *Multichannel News, 21*(4).

Newcomb, H. (1991). On the dialogic aspects of mass communication. In R. K. Avery & D. Eason (Eds.), *Critical perspectives on media and society* (pp. 69-87). New York: Guilford Press.

Not so Awesome Blossom. (2002). *The Powerpuff Girls.* Cartoon Network.

Ogletree, S.M., Mason, B., Grahmann, T., & Raffeld, P. (2001). Perceptions of two television cartoons: *Powerpuff Girls* and *Johnny Bravo. Communication Research Reports, 18*(3)307-313.

Owen, A. (1999). Vampires, postmodernity, and postfeminism: Buffy the Vampire Slayer. *Journal of Popular Film and Television, 27*(2), 24-31.

Paglia, C. (1992). *Sex, art, and American culture: Essays.* New York: Vintage Books.

Potts, D.L. (2001). Channeling girl power: Positive female media images in *The Powerpuff Girls. Simile, 1*(4).

PR Newswire. (2006). The Game Factory debuts new children's gaming titles at Electronic Entertainment Exposition. Retrieved July 26, 2006, from http://www.prnewswire.com/news/index_mail.shtml?ACCT=104&STORY=/www/story/05-09-2006/0004357742&EDATE=.

Roiphe, K. (1993). *The morning after: Sex, fear, and feminism on campus.* Boston: Little, Brown.

The Rowdyruff Boys. (1999). *The Powerpuff Girls.* (P. Rudish, C. Morrow, Writers, G. Tartakovsky, C. McCracken, Directors). Cartoon Network.

Shanahan, J., & Morgan, M. (1999). *Television and its viewers: Cultivation theory and research.* Cambridge, UK: Cambridge University Press.

Sicilano, J. (2001). Powerpuff Girls: Sugar, spice and a dash of feminism. *Cybergrrl: Voices of women,* TVGrrl Article 5161. Retrieved May 1, 2003, from http://www.cybergrrl.com/fun/tvgrrl/art5161.

Siegel, D.L. (1997). Reading between the waves: Feminist historiography in a "postfeminist" movement. In L. Heywood & J. Drake (Eds.), *Third wave feminism: Being feminist, doing feminism* (pp. 55-82). Minneapolis: University of Minnesota Press.

Signorielli, N. (1989). Television and conceptions about sex roles: Maintaining conventionality and the status quo. *Sex Roles, 21,* 341-360.

Slumbering with the Enemy. (2000). *The Powerpuff Girls.* Cartoon Network.

Sommers, C.H. (1994). *Who stole feminism? How women have betrayed women.* New York: Simon & Schuster.

Sternglanz, S.H., & Serbin, L. (1974). Sex role stereotyping in children's television programs. *Developmental Psychology, 10,* 710-715.

Taylor, E. (1989). *Prime time families: Television culture in postwar America.* Berkeley: University of California Press.

The Third Wave Foundation. (2001). Retrieved May 1, 2003, from http://www.thirdwavefoundation.org

TV.com. (2006). *The Powerpuff Girls.* Retrieved July 26, 2006, from http://www.tv.com/the-powerpuff-girls/show/3704/summary.html.

Thompson, T.L., & Zerbinos, E. (1995). Gender roles in animated cartoons: Has the picture changed in 20 years? *Sex Roles, 32,* 651-673.

Weinkauf, G. (2002, July 4). Powerpuff 'n' stuff: Animator Craig McCracken discusses his little whoopass chargettes. *New Times Los Angeles.* Retrieved May 6, 2003, from Lexis-Nexis database.

Wolf, N. (1993). *Fire with fire: The new female power and how to use it.* New York: Random House.

13

Feminism And Daytime Soap Operas

Elayne Rapping

for only in art has bourgeois society tolerated its own ideals and taken them seriously as a general demand. What counts as utopia, phantasy, and rebellion in the world of fact is allowed in art. There affirmative culture has displayed the forgotten truths over which 'realism' triumphs in daily life.

—Herbert Marcuse (1968, p. 114)

a work of art opens a void where . . . the world is made aware of its guilt.

—Michel Foucault (1965, p. 278)

It's Sunday night and my daughter is calling: "I hate that they have to kill off Eve," she moans, "although I don't blame her for wanting out of her contract—the show is definitely going downhill. And at least they're using her death to make a point about experimental drugs. The gay groups should be happy about that, if any of them are watching. Probably not. Even the rec.arts.tv.soaps.cbs crowd on the Internet seem to hate her, which I really don't get. She's the only interesting woman left on the show, and by far the most feminist. I mean once she goes, who will be left to really live a life that centers around female bonding and support. Her relationships with Harley and Lucy are just so neat. And she was the only one in the hospital who stood up for that poor nurse who was being sexually harassed by that creepy doctor what's-his-name and got the jerk fired. What do you think?"

We are having our usual weekly check-in call about the *Guiding Light*, the soap opera of choice among Pittsburgh women in the 1970s, when she was growing up, and the one to which we have remained loyal for almost three decades, through good times and bad. Neither of us lives in Pittsburgh now, but when we watch and discuss our soap opera, we still share a common community and a set of friends and neighbors about whom we care deeply, even as we laugh at their often ridiculously implausible lives.

But what's this about AIDS? The dying doctor, as you may know if you are a fan yourself, has died of a rare disease with no links to sex, drugs or blood transfusions. She has, it seems, picked up this virus while working as selflessly as Mother Theresa (and with as little political sophistication), as a doctor in a war-torn fictional nation.

Nonetheless, as Alison and I both understand, having followed and discussed the murky, contradictory, often subtextual politics of daytime soaps for so long, there is something progressive, in the most utopian sense of that word, about the conclusion of the storyline. The dying woman has made contact by way of the Internet with a colleague doing research on this disease, and has been secretly medicating herself with an untested drug. Her fiancé, himself a physician of the more usual, conservative variety, is adamantly opposed. But lo and behold, the cyber-researcher she has hooked up with is an old medical school pal of his—a woman who is representative of the many, admirable examples of female bonding, both professional and personal, in soap operas. This brilliant woman, for whom he has the utmost respect, convinces him—in a series of inspiring speeches of the kind Alison and I love to savor—of his fiancé's courage, her intuitive scientific acumen and her right to choose her own treatment. Men on soap operas often, and admirably, take moral and professional leadership from the wonderful women they love and/or work with. Eve even improves for a while on the treatment, but it is too little, too late, and she finally succumbs—as the contract of the actress who plays the role demands (and as we who follow the cyber-chat gossip have long known she would)—amidst sobbing friends, flashback clips of better days, and a eulogy in which it is predicted that her final act of medical courage will lead to an early cure for the disease. In Soapville, this is credible. For soap operas—and this is the quality that elicits the most derision from detractors and the most pleasure in fans—are highly unrealistic in a way that is, remarkably, often delightfully utopian.

The idea that bourgeois culture incorporates utopian visions and values, moments during which we are liberated from the constraints of realism and can glimpse in the distance a vision of that better world in which our often unarticulated heart's desires are fulfilled is not, of course, new. Media scholars have been aware of this since Fredric Jameson's (1990) seminal essay on "Reification and Utopia in Mass Culture." Nor is it news that popular culture, being taken so much less seriously than high art forms, has been the most powerful site of imaginative utopian protest. For as Jameson (1975) wrote elsewhere, it is in times like ours, when "our own particular environment—the total system of capitalism and the consumer society—feels so massively in place and its reification so overwhelming and impenetrable that the serious artist is no longer free to tinker with it" that popular forms—forms that are less "serious," less "massively in place"—assume "the vocation of giving us alternate versions of a world that has elsewhere seemed to resist even *imagined* change" (p. 64).

Although Jameson does not specifically mention soap opera, feminist media theorists have written extensively and insightfully about the utopian element in daytime soaps. Feminists have discovered in soaps a representation of "a world in which the divine functions;" a world that "exhorts the [real] world to live up to [women's] impassioned expectations of it," as Louise Spence (1995, p. 193) nicely put it. And John Fiske (1987), taking a somewhat different perspective, described soap opera as a genre in which "feminine culture constantly struggles to establish and extend itself within and against a dominant patriarchy . . . to whittle away at patriarchy's power to subject women and . . . establish a masculine-free zone from which a direct challenge may be mounted" (p. 197). Other feminist theorists have pointed to any number of specific soap conventions and teased out their utopian implications. It is often noted, for example, that through the incorporation of multiple subjectivities and points of view, and the use of multiple, open-ended narrative lines, readers are potentially empowered to question dominant patriarchal assumptions about family and gender norms and to resist hegemonic readings.[1]

But most of this work has focused on the way soaps represent and negotiate the traditionally feminine sphere of private life—the home, family and gender relationships, marriage and maternity, presenting their implicitly utopian social and political vision. Raymond Williams (1973) wrote that "community is the keyword of the entire utopian enterprise" (p. 212). And it is the sense of community—but of a feminized community closer to feminist visions of the future than to classic, literary utopias—that makes soaps so seductively addictive to so many women.

"The personal is political" is a classic, feminist slogan, and its meaning is particularly important to an understanding of what a feminist vision of community—and of women's roles with in that community—would be. Barbara Ehrenreich and Dierdre English (1978) eloquently articulated the vision and demands of that utopian worldview: "There are no answers left but the most radical ones," they wrote:

> We cannot assimilate into a masculinist society without doing violence to our own nature, which is of course *human* nature. But neither can we retreat into domestic isolation, clinging to an archaic feminine ideal. Nor can we deny that the dilemma is a social one . . . The Woman Question in the end is not a question of *women*. It is not we who are the problem and it is not our needs which are the mystery. From our perspective (denied by centuries of masculinist "science" and analysis) the Woman Question becomes the question of how shall we all—women and children and men—organize our lives together. (p. 323)

This statement still resonates for feminists—and still, unfortunately, remains unrealized. But on soap operas, in often bizarre, always complicated and highly contradictory ways, it is realized in ways that are often surprisingly satisfying.

How is it possible, in a form in many ways so hokey and even reactionary, for such progressive ideas to regularly appear? For one thing, soaps are presented from a female perspective which is, by its very nature, alterior. The private sphere, as has so often been noted, is privileged and valorized on soaps, and the things women do in that sphere are seen as central to the maintenance and proper functioning of human life. But what is less often noted is the effect this valorizing of private, feminine experience has on the representation of the public sphere. Soaps portray a world in which reality, as we know it, is turned on its head so that the private sphere becomes all important. But there is more to it than that. For in so privileging private values, soaps also construct a highly unrealistic but nonetheless prominent and important public sphere in which all institutions are forced to conform to private, feminine values.

The feminist idea that "the personal is political" is, of course, a critique of what had, since the rise of the industrial world order, been a sharp delineation between the male-driven public sphere, in which work, business and public affairs were handled, and the female-driven domestic sphere—the haven in a heartless world—in which the work of caring for and maintaining family relations, the socializing of children and the negotiation of emotional and spiritual matters, took place. In this scheme, issues of morality, and emotional and spiritual health were designated "female" concerns relevant primarily, if not exclusively, to the home and family life. The male world, by contrast, was understood to be ruled by the competitive, individualist values of the marketplace in which ruthlessness and greed and self-interest were largely accepted as inevitable, if not necessarily desirable. The need for men to return to the caring, nurturing, hearth and home where values such as caring, emotional openness, and mutual support and concern for the welfare of the group—in this case, of course, the nuclear or, at best, extended family or immediate[2] neighborhood community—was understood to be necessary.

Most popular culture genres elide this contradiction by foregrounding one sphere and hinting, usually only indirectly, at the contradictions between the values that prevail in those different worlds. Thus, westerns and crime genres focus on the male world of competition, aggression and violence and hold up, symbolically, an image of the personal, feminine sphere as a reminder of what has been sacrificed in the transcendence of male-driven public values. By contrast, family melodrama foregrounds the private sphere of marriage and family, even as it refers to the family-destroying values that inform the public sphere and that must be overcome (and this is rarely seen as possible) for personal happiness to be achieved.[3] Soap operas handily elide this contradiction and manage not to acknowledge or deal with it at all by ingeniously mapping out an entire public realm of political, economic, and legal events and institutions, as prominent as the personal, in which women and the concerns of the feminine operate as visibly and importantly as in the domestic. By so blurring the distinctions between the concerns of the two spheres, they alter the traditional representation of male figures—heroes and villains—and draw their male characters more fully into the life of the family and the emotions than other genres. Thus, even murderers and schemers are seen to be driven by obsessive love or family loyalties, just as are good doctors and lawyers. In this way, soaps create a world in which women are free to take their concerns for such values as compassion, cooperation, the valorization of spiritual and emotional concerns and perspectives into the marketplace, the workplace and the arenas in which law, justice, public health, and welfare and the business of maintaining democratic institutions are negotiated. And by extension, men themselves—now forced to operate in so feminized and humanized a public sphere—have no choice but to bring home the values by which they run their public lives.

In discussing feminist utopias, Fran Bartkowski (1989) noted that unlike most traditional male utopias, they incorporate "tacit rather than reified models of the state" (p. 15). What is "tacit" in feminist utopias, she suggested, and what distinguishes them from their male-defined counterparts, is a "discourse on the family" which sees the family as the "place where the inhabitants of the projected utopian state [are] formed" (p. 15). It is just such a discourse on the family, as the foundational root of social and political ideology that informs the vision of community and public life on soap operas. If home is where the heart is, on soaps, home is located everywhere. The gathering spots of soap geography—the restaurants, the health clubs, the diners and malls, even the hospital nurses stations and corporate office buildings—all serve as "homelike" environments. This is a world of public space which is family-driven in every arena. Its laws and policies are imbued implicitly with the values—"interconnectedness . . . nurturance, responsibility, and mutual respect" (Gilligan, 1982, p. 57)—which Carol Gilligan defined as informing the feminist moral universe that girls are socialized to maintain. On soaps, the binary split between private and public is virtually dissolved.

Thus, it is standard on soaps for police officers, district attorneys, and lawyers—and they tend to be equally divided between genders—to view their work in fighting crime, for example, as an extension of their roles as parents, keeping the city safe for their children, or wives and sisters and mothers. So thoroughly blurred are the sphere distinctions that there is *never* a contradiction between the two roles, never any possibility that one's role as a family member might clash with one's duty to defend a client or uphold the law. In fact, it is not uncommon, on soaps, for characters in these kinds of positions of authority to willfully ignore the law when their own sense of what is best for the safety of their loved ones is involved. And they are always, inevitably, judged to have been right—even heroic—in their judgment. On soaps, one's instincts about what is right for the family—no matter what the law might say—are always validated because the laws themselves, in their utopian idealism, are assumed, implicitly, to be in the service of such values.

Soaps, then, conform nicely to Angelika Bammer's (1991) description of feminist utopia. "Utopia," she noted, "identifies society as the site of lack." Unlike ideology, she explained, which "represents things as they are from the perspective of those in power . . . utopia is the opposing view of how things could and should be different" (p. 44). Soaps construct a world in which women—who do not, in any meaningful sense, participate in public policy formulation in reality—are allowed to "play house" with the world, to set up a public sphere informed by the values they are, in reality, enjoined to maintain and pass on (but only within the home and family of course).[4] Simone de Beauvoir (1961) once said that women were most grievously disempowered in not being allowed to "take responsibility for the world" (p. 49). On soaps, they are allowed to do just that. This is what is most empowering about the genre, because it is most at odds with the "common sense" to which women—and children—are otherwise exposed.

Of course, this is a somewhat unorthodox view of soaps. It is usually assumed that romance and the rituals of mating and marriage are what draw and hold women viewers. But although this is certainly a factor, I have always thought it was misleading to focus so heavily on these elements of soaps and to ignore what, to me, has always seemed so much more compelling—the sense of community. Men in soap operas—the good ones in their good phases, anyway—are wonderfully nurturing and caring. They become totally obsessed with the needs of the women in their lives and seem to devote every waking moment of work and leisure time to them. It is all too common, for example, to see a lawyer, doctor or cop stare soulfully into the eyes of a woman character in deep trouble and say, "I'm going to drop all my other cases and devote myself entirely to your case, because I care about you so much." And somehow, this becomes possible to accomplish without total destruction of the man's career or business.

In a storyline on the *The Guiding Light*, for example, a CEO of a major corporation (one of the stereotypical presences on all soaps) disappeared for weeks at a time from his job when his fiancé was being held by a psychopath who previously had raped her. Even before her abduction, when the poor girl was *merely* suffering the posttraumatic stress of the rape, her lover seemed to leave his office continuously at the merest hint that she was feeling down, in order to take her out for a special treat, or whisk her to his palatial penthouse where she could be pampered and coddled, and allowed to weep, talk about her ordeal or not, as the need arose, or simply sleep. Every woman who has ever complained that her male partner had no time for her because of work, or had no understanding of what she was going through after a traumatic experience, could only drool in envy.

Such are the common characteristics and behaviors of good men—and even the worst of them, if they become regulars, are periodically good—on soaps. But, as wonderful as they are, like their real-life counterparts, these men come and go. The sorrows and joys they bring are always fleeting. The marriage vows and family structures to which they commit themselves are always already disintegrating even as their Friday afternoon wedding vows are being said. Thus, crisis and trauma are always imperiling the sexual and family lives of even the most fortunately partnered women. At the very moment when things seem, at last, to be blissfully perfect in a marriage, every viewer knows that catastrophe looms. In fact, if any marriage goes untroubled for too long, it is a sure sign that the characters will soon be written out, shipped off to another town or country to return, perhaps years later, in different bodies and with new threads of chaos and tragedy ominously looming.

To avoid such annihilation, it is customary on soaps for even the best of longstanding characters to periodically undergo serious character lapses, if not outright transformations, in which they abandon or lose their wives and families, in order to free them up for new storylines. One of the very best of the many extraordinarily caring, compassionate, feminized men on soaps, has, in his long career on *The Guiding Light*, gone through many such periodic marital lapses. Indeed, there is hardly a longstanding, regular character on a soap who has not been through countless marriages and other romantic involvements, each of which, invariably, includes vows of undying love which are—as every fan knows—as easily forgotten as last year's hairstyle.

Marital and romantic upheaval and disaster, then, rather than family stability, are the norm in the lives of the most prominent and regular members of soap communities. But through all this family turmoil and crisis, the community itself always remains stable and solid. This is what really holds the women and children together. Every soap character—no matter how battered, how evil, how hopelessly fallen—can always rely on the emotional and material safety net of the soap community of extended family, social, and political relationships. No sooner has crisis struck than the character suddenly has more friends and attention than ever before. Suddenly, new career and social opportunities come from all quarters and once more her life is filled with adventure. Marriage, while always longed for—indeed, often schemed for—is in actuality far from the "happily ever after" event it symbolizes for soap characters. Actors—who do not know the fates of their characters very far in advance and therefore watch for telltale signs in their scripts that they are about to be written out of a show—grow nervous as their characters' weddings approach, for this is generally a sign of less visibility if not total annihilation.

Weddings, then, do not signal the kind of narrative closure one finds in romantic comedies or fairy tales. Nor do they even focus, primarily, on the bride and groom as the central figures. Rather, as in other public events on soaps, weddings offer an opportunity for the entire community to gather and celebrate as a group. It is traditional, on soap weddings for example, for the camera to pan to one character after another, as the vows are read, so that the particular dramas of each of their storylines can be highlighted. A character whose own marriage is in trouble, for example, will look appropriately anxious as the vows are said. And characters involved in extra-marital affairs will typically eye each other furtively as the lines about fidelity are repeated by the marrying couple. Even characters involved in shady business deals or political intrigue will be given a chance to remind viewers of their plights during the service in some, never very subtle, way. In this way, viewers thoughts are kept directly on the real action, the plotlines of those characters—and there are always many of them—who are engaged in the meaty issues that involve the community as a whole, as the marrying couple is swept gracefully out of sight and mind.

Thus, weddings, far from focusing on personal romantic closure and family stability, are a site of community unity and festivity, an anchor that reinforces the sense of unity and cohesion within the community itself. As such, they are also among the most anticipated of delights for viewers, not only because they allow for the largest number of cast members to be seen collectively, but because they present visions of luxury and pleasure which, again, mark the genre's resemblance to feminist utopian visions. Soaps characters all live in relative luxury, have an endless supply of always up-to-date furniture, clothing, and (it seems) hairdressers. For example, they have at their disposal gourmet cooking from places with names like "The Pampered Palate" that deliver at a moments notice. Nor are the poorer characters excluded from such treats. Sharing is endemic in Soapville, and, in fact, the first hint that a "bad" character is about to be converted may well be when a wealthy character invites her or him—out of compassion or an instinct that they are save-able—to share in some celebration or luxury.

And, as the "Eve" story line that so intrigued my daughter and me illustrates, soaps also offer the strongest portrayal of what we used to call "sisterhood"—female bonding and solidarity—of any genre on TV today. Women matter to each other on soaps in a way that rarely is the case elsewhere in the media, and not in some sugary, unbelievably cartoonish way. In a surprisingly realistic way, friendships between women are often, as in life, put to the test. They sometimes falter and, in many cases, bitterly end (temporarily) over moral disagreements or serious betrayals. But the love that women friends and colleagues share invariably moves them to resolve their differences, forgive each other, and retrieve the loss of closeness they had shared. Women are not perfect on soaps, but they are rarely as unredeemably evil as are many minor, male characters whose evil doings become so unforgivable they must be killed off.

In a recent storyline, for example, a woman increasingly bored with her longstanding marriage becomes involved with a sleazy but sexy sportscaster and almost—but not quite—has an affair with him before coming to her senses with the help of her best friend's sound advice. The advice comes too late for the marriage, however, and her husband leaves her. The friend then succumbs to the sportscaster's charms herself and sleeps with him, destroying her own marriage. For most friendships, this would be a real deal-breaker. But although both marriages gradually were saved; the heart of this storyline was in the break-up of such a long-standing friendship, the way in which each woman suffered the agonies of the loss, and how they came together, over many a tearful cup of coffee or tea, to repair their relationship. The repair of the marriages was much less emotional. There was no real talking out of what had gone wrong but rather a more contrived and predictable process by which the couples, over time, simply gravitated back together. To fans, in fact, it was clear that the writers had no plans to give either couple new front-burner love stories and that the resolution of their marital problems was actually a way of putting all four characters on the back burner for the time being, as other storylines and characters took center stage. But the depth of the seriousness with which the women worked though their problems and resumed their friendship was, although shorter lived, far more intense and moving.

Female bonding and sisterhood are not only, or most interestingly, played out in such one on one negotiations between friends. In fact, the most utopian aspect of the way in which sisterhood is portrayed on soaps often involves groups of women—many times women who were not necessarily close before, or who even disliked each other for various reasons—who find themselves in terrible situations engineered by unredeemably evil males who must, ultimately, be killed off. For example, three women on an episode in *As the World Turns* found themselves kidnapped and trapped in a bizarre clinic where they were being drugged into near helplessness. All three of these women had in one way or another antagonized each other in the past and were far from close. But finding themselves in a common predicament, they pulled together, the stronger helped the weaker to fight off the effect of the drugs, and eventually managed to escape. They are now the best of friends. In fact, all three had, when first introduced as new characters, been seen as placing more value on careers and men than female friendships. But living through a male-imposed ordeal had taught them what so many female characters on soaps already know: Women friends are, in the end, the ones you can really count on. Now, all three are long-running, major characters who regularly come to each other's rescue.

Soaps, then, are in many ways similar to the utopias envisioned in many feminist science novels—and not only because of the bonding and strength of women characters. Marge Piercy's (1985) Mattapoisett, the utopian community of *Woman on the Edge of Time*, in fact, offers a similar vision of community, abundance, pleasure, and community bonding across race, gender, ethnic, and other differences. Here, technology is fueled by collective decision making to produce the very best food and clothing for all, shared in communal dining and recreation areas or—as on soaps—alone if one chooses. Among the most delicious features, for example, of what a socialist-feminist imagination would do with technology in the service of pleasure and beauty—one which soaps mimic constantly—is Piercy's idea of disposable garments called "flimsies," which can be whipped up in instantly, cheaply, and to one's personal taste and measurement, for special occasions where formal attire or costumes are required. After wearing, the flimsies are easily disposed of and recycled.

A number of soap conventions resemble this kind of fantasized world of pleasure and beauty. Every soap periodically presents elaborate celebrations—masked balls, weddings, and so forth—at which everyone, rich and poor, seems to magically acquire the most elaborate, gorgeous evening wear immediately upon hearing of the occasion, even if it is scheduled for the next evening, as it often is. Here too, the costumes seem to magically disappear, never to be worn again, come the stroke of midnight. On soaps, in fact, the entire community seems to coordinate their attire in ways which allow for the whole event to take on a particularly collective, communal flavor. Such things do not normally appear in traditional male utopias, but Piercy's feminist world answers real women's dreams, as any proper, technologically advanced, post-scarcity utopia should.

In fact, the inclusion of complex interpersonal factors not usually allowed in legal and political procedures is one of the most politically interesting aspects of the form. For in creating characters who live and interact with each other, sometimes over decades, and who are thrust into so wide a variety of storylines and conflicts and crises, viewers are allowed to see characters as contradictory, complex and changeable. A good mother can be a terrible friend, or adulteress, or worse. A terrible tyrant in one sphere can be a doting godfather in another. A personally selfish, conniving woman can be a leading figure in a political or legal battle for a progressive cause. One often ruthlessly self-serving matriarch in *As the World Turns*, for example, dotes on the younger members of her dynasty and acts as a good and loyal friend to several other women characters, some decidedly beneath her socially. She is also often among the most welcoming and supportive characters to newcomers to the community, even as she ruthlessly schemes to rob and cheat her business and political opponents. Through complex narrative storylines, it is possible to portray a variety of women characters as being far from perfect, but truly admirable in many ways rarely seen in American media.

But even when women characters are at their worst, when they are, for example, telling off an enemy or business opponent in the most outspokenly harsh way, there is often something gratifying to many women viewers in these outbursts of anger and vitriol. In fact, the tough women in soap communities are often most likable to fans when they are least "lady-like" and "nice." There is something refreshing, I would argue, in hearing women lash out in ways most of us would never dream of allowing ourselves to do. What seems "strong" in male leaders is so often seen as "abrasive" in women. And while viewers know—or should know—that behaving professionally in this way is not a good idea, there is a vicarious pleasure for many of us in seeing our own socially repressed urges acted out on the small screen with positive rather than negative results. That's why so many "villainesses" are among fan favorites: They seem to speak for all of us silenced women, even when what they are saying is not always commendable.

But the complexity of soaps' structures and characters, and their open-endedness, serve more than a merely personal, psychological function. There is also a truly utopian vision of a feminized, radically democratic political process in which difference and subtlety are recognized and honored within a community structure. To give one example, in one storyline developed over months of endless intrigue and complication in *All My Children*, a woman accused her ex-lover—who was actually her husband's son—of acquaintance rape. As the community discussed the case, taking sides, reviewing in detail her past sins, and recalling bits of their own histories and those of other characters in an effort to come to terms with the moral nuances of this case, an ongoing "community meeting" of sorts took place around this publicly charged issue.

As the trial itself played out, things—quite realistically in this case—looked bad for the defendant. Her checkered past and recent adultery with the accused made it difficult to imagine a jury believing her. But then the defendant, having witnessed a gang rape that suddenly put his own act in a new perspective, confessed, entered counseling and volunteered, upon release from prison, to work in a rape crisis center. In this way, viewers were taken through the experience in real time, in all its subtly and nuance, and allowed to digest the emotional and political strands gradually, as one would indeed do in an ideal political setting in which all parties had adequate counsel and access to all the time and resources needed to locate and sift evidence, find and bring in witnesses, and deliberate. Soap operas, in this way, open a discursive space within which the characters and the audience form a kind of community. The experience is especially intense since the characters involved are so familiar to viewers and are "visited" virtually every day, for years on end.

The often bizarrely unconventional family and living arrangements that arise from the extended families and community relationships on soaps provide a similarly rich and complex representation of political structure and process. Again, Piercy's Mattapoisett is brought to mind in these utopian projections of a community that honors and accommodates the needs of all members for emotional and material support and security. Piercy's utopia articulates a private, family realm in which various choices of sexual and child-care arrangements are allowed, to suit the varied and often changing tastes and inclinations of citizens. Children in Piercy's world have three biological parents and do not necessarily live with any. They may choose households that suit them, just as those who remain childless may find ways to relate to the children of the community that does not involve custodial care or biological connection.

Similar things happen on soaps. For example, a typical custody decision might, as was the case on *The Guiding Light*, rule that two single mothers—one the birth mother, who was a stylist at a low-rent salon, and the other the adoptive mother, the CEO of a major corporation—share custody in a way that gave the child two homes and mothers linked by a common community of support.

But parenting isn't the only problem for which soap communities provide utopian solutions. It is also common, on soaps, for people to move in and out of relationships and households often. The end of a relationship does not involve the kind of trauma and agony that today sends so many desperate people searching far and wide—even into cyberspace—in search of "support groups." Not on soaps. Support groups come to you. They find you sitting alone somewhere, or being beaten by a boyfriend, and they invite you to live with them, or with some other character in need of just the service you can provide. Characters who are originally derelicts, ex-convicts or worse often wander into town and are immediately recognized for some wonderful character trait or talent and given a home and work.

Most theorists who have discussed utopia in popular or feminist works have described the engines of state as implicit. Richard Dyer (1985), in his analysis of Hollywood musicals, describes the ways in which popular commercial texts attempt—not always successfully—to work through and resolve the contradictions inherent in their efforts to suggest a utopian world within a system of representation very much tied to and dependent upon the existing order. For Dyer, the solution involves a substitution of emotion for detailed political mapping. "Entertainment does not . . . present models of utopian worlds, as in the classic utopias of Sir Thomas More, William Morris, et al.," he said. "Rather the utopianism is contained in the feelings it embodies" (p. 229). Nonetheless, there is something much closer to an actual social model in the soap representation of community than Dyer finds in Hollywood musicals, although the soap model contains the same contradictions and "gap[s] between what is and what could be" (p. 229) that Dyer rightly attributed to all commercial forms.

To see how this is done, it is useful to compare Piercy's Mattapoisett with the soap imaginary. Mattapoisett, as a socialist-feminist utopia, includes detailed, discursive blueprints for ownership and decision-making processes. The political and economic foundations of soap institutions, although elaborately laid out, are far more contradictory and implausible. The most important difference is in the portrayal of ownership and property issues. Where Mattapoisett's public hearings and trials, elections and economic negotiations, family and child-care polices all grow organically out of its radically democratic and collectivized ownership and decision-making structures, soap operas simply impose a retrograde, almost medieval—and insanely implausible—structure of ownership and power relations on their idyllic communities. In every soap, two or three corporate lords own virtually everything in the town and so provide all the employment and control all the media and other institutions. Nepotism and monopoly are givens in these realms.

Nonetheless, although these powerhouses are often the most "evil" of villains, things always work out in the interest of democracy, humanity, and justice because justice and virtue always magically triumph. The corporate, patriarchal tyrants, at the proper moment, invariably undergo an always temporary period of conversion to "goodness" that allows them, despite all their evil deeds and ways, to remain a part of the community. The date rape trial and resolution is typical. But such things happen regularly to even the most powerful male figures. The most evil of corporate despots, for example, will have moments of moral rehabilitation, only to revert to their wicked ways until, yet again, caught, chastised, and transformed.

Thus, "good" always emerges out of the "goodness" of human nature, a human nature that has no relation whatever to the social conditions in which it thrives. Race and gender and class never play a role in one's fate here—at least not for long. A "good" person—white or Black, male or female, well-born or orphaned—simply prospers through the goodness of his or her soul, as do the equally "good" power brokers and owners who provide material security and mete out perfect justice. If soaps are informed by a feminist set of values, then, it is a set of values based, in its root, on the most hopelessly essentialist assumptions, if not about gender difference, certainly about human nature. And even this essentialism is not consistent. Characters transform themselves from "good" to "bad" at the drop of a hat in accord with producers and sponsors, who have myriad considerations of their own in making these things happen.

It is by presenting so patently absurd a view of money and power that soaps manage to wholly elide the "Procter and Gamble" problem—the problem, that is, of how to present a world in which gender justice reigns without challenging the corporate structure that sponsors this fantasy world. Things happen on soaps in the same "magical" way—to use Raymond Williams' (1980) term—that they happen on commercials where, as Williams has shown,[5] happiness, justice, freedom and so on are seen—quite magically—to arise out of the consumption of commodities that, in fact, have not the slightest ability to provide them. Similarly, on soap operas, justice and freedom and goodness and bliss arise quite magically out of a system that, if realistically portrayed, would inevitably thwart, by its very foundational principles, the very happiness it is shown to promote. The date rape trial is again a perfect example. A legal system in which, somehow, characters are compelled to act on principle, even if their very lives, fortunes, or reputations are at stake, is a system very different from the one in which O.J. Simpson, for example, was tried and acquitted.[6] For in the real world, money, class, position, and the gender biases that inform all institutions are driving forces not only in legal proceedings, but also in the molding of a defendant's character and his decision-making processes.

Soaps are a bit like extended version of commercials, then, in which the "magical" thinking of sponsors is drawn out into long, equally implausible storylines. A social system in which an elitist ruling class runs every institution in its own interest somehow is presented as capable of meting out perfect justice and equity, even as commodities such as breakfast foods, fast food restaurants, shampoos, and cars are seen as capable of smoothing the fault lines of a capitalist, post-industrialist world and bringing family and romantic harmony and joy to their consumers. The relation between commercials and dramas, after all, is integral. Dr. Cliff Warner of *All My Children*—who also appeared in commercial saying, "I'm not a doctor, but I play one on television"—shamelessly sold aspirins to a TV audience that wished to believe the medical and pharmaceutical industries operate by the humane and ethical principles that drive the doctors and hospitals on the soaps.

The feminist-informed public world of soaps, then, is one that bears absolutely no relationship to economic and political reality. Nonetheless, a fairly elaborate set of laws, rituals and policies, unmoored from economic and political reality, govern the social world of soaps. The trials follow actual legal practice, to a point. The board meetings and nurses stations and police procedures, for all their clumsy gaffes and goofs in the interest of plotline, operate according to a logic and system that are relatively coherent. If it is difficult to recognize these images of public life as "political," it may be because the melodramatic conventions of soaps render their political vision so unrealistic. But it is, in fact, the very use of melodramatic conventions that allows soap operas to so easily incorporate and transform traditional male political, legal, and economic matters into an essentially feminine—and implicitly feminist—world-view. Again, the date rape trial serves as a perfect example. It followed understandable, recognizable procedures of testimony from witnesses and principals, arguments from defense and prosecution, and sentencing hearings and decisions. The way in which characters were allowed to testify, however, was often unbelievably absurd. Characters, for example, were allowed to simply rise up and demand to be heard because of the "urgency" of the testimony they were suddenly moved to share or the events they were suddenly driven by conscience to reveal. No real court of law would allow such irregularities. Similarly, hearsay, personal opinion about motives and character, and so on, were included with no objections if they were crucial to a feminist-informed understanding of the issues in the case. The rapists' confession, for example, would have demanded any number of hearings and rulings to be permitted, once he had pleaded innocent. In soaps, however, doing the right thing, from a feminine, humane, point of view, is all that is needed for testimony to be considered relevant, or even crucial.

I mentioned Carol Gilligan's (1982) moral vision as an implicit aspect of the soap imaginary. Similarly, Kathleen Jones (1988) applied feminist moral assumptions to traditional male theories of public sphere politics and suggests how they might lead to a radically transformed version of justice and political authority. "The standard analysis of authority in modern Western political theory begins with its definition as a set of rules governing political action, issued by those who are entitled to speak," she wrote. But these rules, she noted "generally have excluded females and values associated with the feminine" (p. 119). Moreover, she argues, the "dominant discourse on authority," in placing "strict limits on the publicly expressible, and limit[ing] critical reflection about the norms and values that structure 'private' life and which affect the melodies of public speech," further ensures that female values will be marginalized within a private realm. Thus, "compassion, and related emotions" are rendered "irrelevant to law and other policy matters," she explained[7] (pp. 130–131).

This is hardly the case on soaps. Compassion, especially, is always relevant. Because of this, all hearings and procedures arbitrate public matters in ways which implicitly, if implausibly, echo the political ideals of feminists. The 1960s model of consciousness-raising meetings and public speak-outs in which women linked private emotional suffering to public institutions and policies offers a useful comparison. In both, there is an effort to correct for the failings of the masculinist public sphere by recognizing the subjective and emotional realities of women's experience and demanding that they be included in official notions of justice and the common good. The custody hearing mentioned earlier, for example, was interrupted by the birth mother herself who, for love of the child, suddenly offered—without benefit of counsel—the compromise suggestion about shared mothering, which the female judge accepted as ideal based on a shared notion of what was best for the child rather than issues of property, money, or paternal rights. The key was the wrenching, heartbreaking sincerity of the two obviously deeply loving women. Nor was there ever any mention—and this would be unthinkable in the real world—of the financial arrangements between the two very differently propertied and positioned women; or any of the other social or material issues which, in real life, dominate custody hearings.

That soaps are excessively melodramatic and emotional—and therefore highly *un*realistic—is, from a feminist viewpoint, affirmative. In feminist theory, it is the exclusion of the values of the private, domestic sphere from issues of justice and equality that must be addressed and corrected. But, of course, in aggressively injecting such values into the portrayal of every sphere of life and flagrantly rejecting the conventions of esthetic realism valorized in our culture, soaps risk the laughter and derision of those who maintain the artistic and literary canons.

However, laughter and ridicule are very much a part of the viewing experience of fans. Viewers of course understand, and laugh about, most of the contradictions and "gaps" of the form, as any casual scanning of the cyberspace bulletin boards that cover soaps will reveal. This, indeed, is among the more sophisticated pleasures of viewing. Fans happily suspend disbelief for the pleasure of escaping into a fairy tale realm in which dreams and desires and fantasies—despite what we know is plausible—seem magically to be fulfilled. And among the most intensely discussed and adored topics of these chat groups is, as my conversation with my daughter illustrates, the portrayal of the women characters themselves—their relationships, their strengths, their moral fiber, their feistiness and savvy, their sins and redemptions and, most of all, their deep and abiding love for each other through the most difficult of conflicts and joyful of shared events.

NOTES

1. See, especially, Tania Modleski (1982) and Martha Nochimson (1992).
2. *Women, Class and the Feminist Imagination*, edited by Karen Hansen and Ilene Philipson (1990) collects some of the seminal, classic texts in which the politi-

cal nuances of the public/private split, as articulated by Second Wave social-ist-feminists, can be found.
3. See Thomas Schatz (1991), Christine Gledhill, (1987) and Fiske (1987). Francis Ford Coppola's *Godfather* series is a useful example of how these contradictions may be used self-consciously to critique the social structure which enforces them.
4. This is a feature of daytime soaps, it should be added, which strongly differentiates them from their nighttime counterparts. Ien Ang (1985), in her discussion of *Dallas*, for example, points out that it is family that serves as a haven from the heartless, outside world of business and politics which is seen as "a hotbed of activity threatening to the family" (p. 71). This is radically different from the daytime strategy in which the line between the spheres blurs.
5. I am not suggesting here that the Simpson verdict was incorrect. I am only commenting on the behavior of Simpson himself, as a man already known to be violently misogynist, whether or not he committed the particular crime of which he was accused.
6. The tricky relationships among the various elements of soap textuality and viewership are developed in the Paper Tiger Television segment I did entitled Elayne Rapping Reads Soap Operas. The producer, Dee Dee Halleck, intercut my analysis of the form with ironically juxtaposed story clips, Procter and Gamble commercial clips, and interviews with residents of Staten Island— where the P&G plant is located—about the health problems they have experienced because of the toxic pollution caused by the guys who make Ivory soap "99 and 44/100% pure."
7. Feminist legal theorists have written extensively and with particular relevance on this point. See, especially, Martha Fineman and Nancy Thomadsen (1991) and Martha Fineman and Martha McCluskey (1996).

REFERENCES

Ang, I. (1985).*Watching Dallas: Soap opera and the melodramatic imagination*. New York: Methuen.
Bammer, A. (1991). *Partial visions: Feminism and utopianism in the 1970s*. New York: Routledge.
Bartkowski, F. (1989). *Feminist utopias*. Lincoln: University of Nebraska Press.
de Beauvoir, S. (1961). *The second sex*. New York: Bantam Books.
Dyer, R. (1985). Entertainment and utopia. In B. Nichols (Ed.), *Movies and methods* (Vol. 2, pp. 200–232). Berkeley: University of California Press.
Ehrenreich, B., & English, D. (1978). *For her own good: 150 years of the experts' advice to women*. New York: Anchor.
Fineman, M., & McCluskey, M. (1996). *Feminism, media and the law*. Oxford: Oxford University Press.
Fineman, M., & Thomadsen, N. (1991). *At the boundaries of law: Feminism and legal theory*. New York: Routledge.
Fiske, J. (1987). *Television culture*. New York: Methuen.

Foucault, M. (1965). *Madness and civilization.* New York: Random House.

Gilligan, C. (1982). *In another voice: Psychological theory and women's development.* Cambridge, MA: Harvard University Press.

Gledhill, C. (1987). *Home is where the heart is: Studies in melodrama and the womens' film.* London: BFI.

Hansen, K., & Philipson, I. (1990).*Women, class and the feminist imagination.* Philadelphia: Temple University Press.

Jameson, F. (1975). World reduction in LeGuin: The emergence of utopian narrative. *Science Fiction Studies, 2*(3), 221-230.

Jameson, F. (1990). Reification and utopia in mass culture. In *Signatures of the visible* (pp. 9-34). New York & London: Routledge.

Jones, K. (1988). On authority: Or, why women are not entitled to speak. In I. Diamond & L. Quinby (Eds.), *Feminism and Foucault: Reflections on resistance* (pp. 119-134). Boston: Northeastern University Press.

Marcuse, H. (1968). *Negotiations.* Boston: Beacon Press.

Modleski, T. (1982). *Loving with a vengeance: Mass-produced fantasies for women.* New York: Methuen.

Nochimson, M. (1992). *No end to her: Soap opera and the female subject.* Berkeley: University of California Press.

Piercy, M. (1985). *Women on the edge of time.* New York: Fawcett Books.

Schatz, T. (1991). *Hollywood genres: Formulas, filmmaking and the studio system.* Philadelphia: Temple University Press.

Spence, L. (1995). "They killed off Marlena. But She's on Another Show Now": Fantasy, reality, and pleasure in watching daytime soap operas. In R. Allen (Ed.), *To be continued . . . : Soap operas around the world* (pp. 182-198). New York: Routledge.

Williams, R. (1973). *Key words: A vocabulary of culture and society.* Oxford: Oxford University Press.

Williams, R. (1980). Advertising: The magic system. In *Problems in materialism and culture* (pp. 170-195). London: Verso.

14

The Dialectical Relationship of Women and Media

Carolyn M. Byerly

The white male hierarchy has to be told—in no uncertain terms—
that their gender and race bias is destroying the institution they
love. That they fail to promote and retain women and do not include
women in their news columns and ignore issues of concern to
women and that is reflected in low readership among women. That
black and Latino Americans, as well as other people of color, know
full well how they treat minority employees and they therefore have
little to no confidence in the accuracy of the news published. And, if
they cannot reach women and minority audiences, they will eventually go out of business.

—Rita Henley Jensen (founder and publisher
Women's eNews)

Feminist media analysis throughout the years has been conducted largely within what might be called the paradigm of the misogynist media.
Since the earliest baseline studies that appeared in *Hearth and Home*

(Tuchman, Daniels, & Benet et al., 1978), researchers have focused on the specific ways that messages and images excluded, marginalized, misrepresented, or exploited women, and on patterns that characterized women's professional limitations within the industries. All of these problems exist, as vast amounts of documentation shows. Moreover, they have persisted over time, showing a remarkable endurance despite feminist challenges on a number of fronts and in virtually all countries. This volume is replete with examples of recent research that demonstrates the persistence of the misogynist media.

This chapter does not take issue with these facts but rather tries to place them within a larger analytical framework. The goal in the discussion is to consider women's various responses to the misogynist media—responses that represent feminist media struggle in a historical process, taking place over several decades and in multiple nations—as well as the backlash that such activism has prompted. I also take stock of some of the gains that such activism has brought, focusing particularly on the news media and public discourse.

Other scholars have referred to feminist struggle in media relations and have observed its changing nature over time (Beasley & Gibbons, 2003). That struggle has generally sought to challenge the ideology of patriarchy operating in media policies and routines, to gain access for women (and women's ideas), and to make media industries more egalitarian in the treatment of women professionals and women as subject matter. Feminist struggle, seen through a number of different forms of women's media activism, has also sometimes circumvented the dominant mainstream media (where misogyny functions) by establishing women-owned media enterprises. In the course of the discussion, I define the gendered dialectical process that has grown out of these activities and explore the backlash that I believe has been part of that process. The discussion is weighted toward developments within my own nation, the United States, but also makes comparisons to and draws examples from other nations to illustrate universal aspects of the women-and-media relationship. Space limitations preclude a thorough analysis of feminist struggle across media forms; therefore, I focus mainly on news. The discussion draws from a range of recent research, including my own with British feminist scholar Karen Ross (Byerly & Ross, 2006), which investigated women's cross-cultural media activism.

A GENDERED DIALECTICAL PROCESS

A dialectical process is characterized by a long-term struggle in which progress and resistance to progress occur simultaneously and over time.

Backlash is a predictable part of resistance—in this instance, in relation to women's demands for changes in media systems both at the structural and content levels. The women-and-media relationship may be situated within a modern historical timeframe that has occupied the decades since the early 1970s, when global feminism emerged by way of the UN's Decade for Women (1976–1985) and other international events that brought together proponents of a shared vision for women's advancements.[1] Because feminist critiques of the media and many of their goals for change have been shared from nation to nation, it is important for researchers to assume a global perspective. Feminist media activism has been part of a larger struggle for women's rights and advancement.

SCOPE OF THE MISOGYNIST MEDIA

Both the global nature of media misogyny and its endurance may be seen in the results of all three rounds of the Global Media Monitoring Project (GMMP), which synchronized the monitoring of major electronic and print news media on 1 day across more than 70 countries in 1995, 2000, and 2005 to explore patterns of gender representation in news. In the first study, it was discovered that globally, 19% of individuals featured in news stories were women, with the most popular roles they occupied being victims, mothers, and wives (Media Watch, 1995). The second GMMP study, with approximately the same number of countries and more than 50,000 separate news items, found almost identical results, although the proportion of women featured in news stories actually decreased by 1% (Gallagher, 2001). The 2005 monitoring revealed that women are still grossly underrepresented in world news—they were only 21% of news subjects, and most often as celebrities or royalty (Gallagher 2006, p. 17). Once again, the "woman-as-victim" image was the most popular; women were more than twice as likely as males to be portrayed as victims. Additionally, women reporters cover only 32% of the serious, "hard" news stories, according to the 2005 round of the GMMP. In all three studies, radio, TV, and the press were monitored nationally, regionally, and locally, showing some slight signs of hope within a few nations, particularly the United States, where, in 2005, women accounted for about 28% of the subjects in stories about economics and business, and about 38% of the stories on science and health. In other ways, however, the GMMP conveys an eerie sameness in the news treatment of women's experience and social contributions either in the United States or elsewhere, despite changing times. Even in the case of the United States, the slight improvements seem unbelievably small in a nation that has had a robust feminist movement for more than three decades.

The project also revealed underrepresentation of women journalists across the world; in the United States, only 34% of TV reporters and 37% of newspaper reporters were women in the media monitored. Ramona R. Rush (2004), who first investigated women in journalism and mass communication within the U.S. context in the 1970s, referred to women's constant falling behind in their professional media pursuits as a *flooring effect* (something later called the *glass ceiling effect*). Rush's recent work updating her original research has found the problem still in place, with women statistically residing at between 25% and 33% of the decision-making positions in media, both within the United States and generally across the world.

International evidence of the misogynist media phenomenon is also seen in global culture. The film industry, for example, has strived for an increasingly multicultural audience and sought to elevate the prominence of women actors. For example, both Radhika Parameswaran (2002) and Ellen Riordan (2004) critiqued the visually stunning martial arts film *Crouching Tiger, Hidden Dragon* for its hegemonic packaging of ethnic culture for profit and its subversion of strong woman characters by familiar stereotypes of male dependency and feminine prowess. Parameswaran (2002) also views Malaysian actress Michelle Yeoh, star of the film, as an orientalist construct—displaying fearless, athletic grace as a warrior woman while at the same time "subtly cocooned by the vestiges of patriarchal [Western] femininity" (p. 296).

FEMINIST INTERVENTION

Feminism is by nature interventionist, seeking to interrupt social practices that lead to women's secondary status and to replace them with new practices that better ensure women's full participation. In relation to media, the goals of feminist intervention were first spelled out at the international level in 1975 in the World Plan of Action, adopted by delegates at the first UN Decade for Women conference, held in Mexico City. Among other things, the plan called on the world's news media to remove prejudices and stereotypes and to promote women's full integration into their societies (Byerly, 1995). Feminists next succeeded in getting UN agencies to fund a range of activities that included research on the media's treatment of women, as well as programs to increase media content from a feminist perspective. The Women's Feature Service Project, for example, included five programs (administered within existing regional news agencies) in developing nations that had the mission of reporting news about women for circulation to both specialized and mainstream news media, government offices, and nongovernmental organizations (Byerly, 1995). During the decades of the 1970s and 1980s, women around the world, both in developed and developing nations, established their own newsletters, newspapers, magazines, book publishing houses, film and video production companies, and other media.

Delegates to the Fourth UN Conference on Women, held in Beijing in September 1995, reaffirmed women's right to communicate through the media. In their summary document, Platform for Action, "Section J: Women and the Media," the delegates asserted that the role women play in the media and the media's representation of women are keys to implementing all other proposals in the document (cited in "Empowering women," 1996).

These events coincided with feminist activities in political, educational, and other areas of society, which the news media covered with greater frequency after the early 1970s. Therefore, there is value in assessing the ways in which feminism as a political and cultural force has begun to embed ideas, terminology and experiences of women in the news media and, by effect, public discourse.

FEMINISM'S AGENDA-SETTING EFFECT

The term *agenda setting* has been used since the early 1970s by mainstream mass media and public opinion researchers to identify the media's ability to define public issues, generate public discourse about those issues, and influence public policy (McCombs & Shaw, 1972; McQuail, 1983). Researchers have given much less attention to the possibility of a reverse phenomenon—the power of social change groups to set news agendas, including which issues should be covered and how they should be framed. For at least a century, social movements that began outside of the mainstream, like feminism, have found varied ways of getting news coverage to increase visibility for their issues and work—from their early stages, when building legitimacy and membership, to the later stages, when they were more concerned with maintaining momentum (Kielbowicz & Scherer, 1986). We can discern the power of social movements to place issues within routine news by examining when, why, and how many of those movements' issues surfaced as news stories.

Feminism in the United States, in its developmental stages in the 1960s, was largely overlooked by the news media, in part because its leaders' emphasis was on hard-to-cover events like grassroots organizing, identifying issues, and setting their own agenda for action

(Tuchman, 1978). The movement became more newsworthy when it succeeded in bringing attention to specific issues, tied them to events (like
lobbying legislation), and when it laid out a media strategy for coverage.
The New York Times, the nation's top agenda-setting newspaper, had
been primed to follow feminists' efforts to legalize abortion in the face of
organized opposition in New York state as early as 1965. Thirty-eight
abortion-related stories appeared that year, along with another five on
equal rights for women. In 1966, the year that the National Organization
for Women (NOW) was established, 37 stories were listed under the
entry "Women-U.S." Within 5 years, 155 stories were listed—more than
a 400% increase. That figure nearly doubled in another year, with 270
stories. Additionally, by 1972, the *Times Index* had added the word *feminist* to its index categories, thereby recognizing that movement as a continuing and significant news category.

In a different national context, women in India mobilized public
support and media attention in connection with a series of women-led
political campaigns in the 1970s. First was the Chipko movement to
protest deforestation and environmental degradation, then the rape of
women by police while in custody. Examples of the latter are seen in the
Mathura rape case in 1978, and the Maya Tyagi rape case in 1980, both
custodial rape cases, which led to nationwide protests by women, cap-
turing public attention (Sen, 2004). As women mobilized around rape,
forming groups like the Bombay Forum Against Rape, other feminist
action groups emerged to spearhead reform of rape laws and to address
issues such as the sexualization of women in advertising and female feti-
cide (Sen, 2004).

In their study of feminism's agenda-setting effect, U.S. researchers
Cancian and Ross (1981) found that news coverage of women between
1900 and 1977 had been highest when the U.S. feminist movement had
been strong and voiced specific goals rather than general concerns.
News content, they said, also was most likely to have a feminist-orienta-
tion, focusing on women's changing roles and new demands, during the
movement's strong periods. By contrast, the news focused on women's
traditional roles of mother and caretaker when the movement waned.

FRAMING FEMINISM

Tuchman (1978) and Gitlin (1981) were among the earliest news sociologists to show that news stories are structured—or framed—in ways that
convey value-laden messages about issues central to news events.
Framing analysis allows the researcher to locate these values (and their

associated meanings) in stories by identifying which facts are included or omitted, which sources are used, and how information is arranged to provide a narrative structure. Such analysis reveals the extent to which news stories adopt, negotiate, or reject philosophies and feminist meanings[2] about women that the movement has sought to institutionalize. For example, Butler and Paisley's (1978) important early study of mainstream popular magazines considered the subtle ways that news reports of the ill-fated Equal Rights Amendment (ERA) had framed stories by emphasizing one of two positions: (a) that the ERA *would strengthen* women's legal protections; or (b) that the ERA *would not weaken* existing protections for women. The second emphasis, the authors believed, gave readers the assurance that the ERA would leave intact traditional arrangements between men and women. Butler and Paisley concluded that articles about the ERA regarding economic and legal issues tended to be framed using the first position by showing that the ERA would strengthen women's protections, whereas ERA stories on marriage and family issues used the second position.

Rapping's (1994) assessment of the news coverage of women is that the news media are neither monolithic nor static, but widely variable in their ability to incorporate oppositional perspectives of feminism. Rapping adopts views not unlike those of Entman (1993), whose work using framing analysis emphasized the significant power of reporters to "promote a particular problem, definition, causal interpretation, moral evaluation, and/or treatment recommendation" (p. 52).

News stories about violence against women, rape, incest, sexual harassment, battering, and so forth, can be considered to have a feminist frame when they place feminist language and analyses about women's victimization central to the story, and when victims are allowed to speak about their experiences in their own words. Feminists placed anti-violence issues and events at the top of their political agendas in the 1970s after women began to reveal they had been raped or battered. Informed news coverage was essential to a new social analysis of these crimes from women's perspective if new, more enlightened public policy was to be adopted. Rape law reform, the establishment of women's shelters and rape crisis centers, and volumes of new academic research all have benefited from advancements in news reporting (Byerly, 1994). Through the years, feminists working in rape crisis centers and battered women's shelters have become increasingly adept at bringing news attention to their antiviolence campaigns, and at educating reporters working for both local and national news media to understand the causes of violence, its effects on victims, and the importance of women being able to tell their stories publicly. The prominent, agenda-setting *Washington Post* regularly carries useful, well-informed stories about violence against women, such as one in Spring 2006 in which Prince George's County Councilwoman Camille Exum expressed alarm in the dramatic rise in both rape and battering within her jurisdiction. The article, in which she was quoted calling for better police and prosecutorial action, included statistics on these crimes within both her own county and adjacent Washington, DC, for a 2-year period, as well as possible reasons for increases (Raghavan, 2006).

Such reporting has helped to expand both the amount of news about violence against women, as well as the likelihood that news frames would reflect a feminist philosophy. Benedict's (1992) historical analysis of how the media have covered sex crimes found that before the civil rights and feminist movements, the U.S. media typically reported on cases in which Black assailants allegedly violated White women. However, "after 1971, rape stories not only discussed racial prejudice but, for the first time, examined prejudice against victims, too" (p. 42).

Statistical analysis of *The New York Times* shows that coverage of sexual assault issues increased more than 250% between 1972 and 1974. Rape speak-outs, debates over rape reform legislation in the New York Assembly, and the publication of Brownmiller's (1975) *Against Our Will,* the first historical examination of rape from the victim's perspective, all were covered at length by the newspaper. Such expanded coverage was explained in research by Barker-Plummer (1995), who found that the NOW, the leading U.S. feminist lobby group, had developed a sophisticated public relations program in the early 1970s to increase news coverage of its state-by-state legislative program, which focused on rape law reform, abortion rights, and other women's issues. NOW developed press kits and located sympathetic reporters, among other things.

Such feminist action was particularly effective in helping to shift public perceptions of crimes of violence against women. For example, Byerly (1994) noted the surge in public support for a marital rape bill to be voted on by the Washington state legislature in 1982, after a savvy female reporter from a major Seattle television station included in her evening newscast footage of a veteran state senator standing on the Senate floor asking, "Well, if you can't rape your own wife, who can you rape?" (p. 60). This TV broadcast emphasized the reasonableness of lifting the marital rape exclusion from state law, and conversely, the unreasonableness of the mostly male legislators' opposition to it. Media visibility for the marital rape issue increased again through radio and television interviews in the Seattle area with sociologist Diana E. H. Russell, who had just published her ground-breaking study, *Rape in Marriage* (1982). Russell had been brought to Washington state by feminists to testify on the proposed marital rape legislation and to give public lectures on her research. The outrageousness of the bill's opponents contrasted sharply with the evidence offered by Russell and other feminist leaders, and reporters actively followed the debates for several weeks before the bill's passage.

A major indication of feminism's enduring impact on news reporting of sexual violence can be seen in today's newsroom policies, most of which protect the identity of victims. Additionally, many newsrooms have adopted written policies for sensitively handling sex crime stories. Both general assignment and sports journalists have been increasingly likely in the last few years to report on sexual assaults and battering by athletes. The 1995 O.J. Simpson case in which the former pro-football player was charged with the murder of his ex-wife Nicole and her friend Ron Goldman, inspired many of these. Stories appeared in major agenda-setting newspapers, such as *The Washington Post, Los Angeles Times,* and the *Nashville Tennessean,* exploring football players' off-the-field violence against women and the National Football League's (NFL's) program in violence prevention and counseling with athletes. Bill Brubaker's (1995a, 1995b, 1995c) three stories in *The Washington Post* presented a feminist frame by foregrounding the players' responsibility for the violence and the harm to victims. Extensive interviews with victims, their advocates and psychologists, profiles of abusive men, and data on the arrest and conviction rates of NFL players helped to develop the series, which got front page and inside front-section placement.

Given the dialectical nature of social movements' impact on news, such advancements are neither uniform nor complete. Some news coverage still sustains the frame of victim-blaming, thereby rejecting feminism's goals. This resistance aspect of the women-and-media dialectical relationship spills over into entertainment media where sexual and other violence against women have become a staple. One example is seen in the popular U.S. television program on the NBC network *Law and Order: Special Victims' Unit (SVU),* which focuses specifically on sexually violent crimes against women and children. *SVU* situates its action within the kind of investigative police units that U.S. feminists working in rape crisis centers pushed for beginning in the early 1980s, but the resemblance stops there. Rarely in its 9-year run has the program even mentioned (let alone included) a rape advocate or a clear feminist voice, both of which are associated with the work of real SVUs. Additionally, victims are often sexualized and depicted as having enticed their assailants in some way. The central character of Detective Olivia Benson (portrayed by Mariska Hargitay), the child of a brutal rape by an unknown assailant, is consistently sexualized with low-cut sweaters and tight pants, as well as undermined by self-doubts, unresolved emotional distress, and even victimization (e.g., stalked by a suspect in one episode). Although the program makes abundant use of appropriate psychological terms and dynamics (especially in regard to perpetrators), it avoids an analysis of violence against women as the gendered crimes they are, and the program virtually never gives the crimes a feminist context that constructs these crimes as public issues.

Similarly, the popular prime-time A&E cable productions of *American Justice* and *Cold Case Files*, both narrated by award-winning journalist Bill Kurtis, investigate real homicide cases, which typically involve violence within families or between acquaintances. These cases, which follow a factual chronological format, highlight the use of forensic science in solving crimes that typically involved a man's brutal killing of one or more women. The programs are appealing because of their authenticity, intrigue, clear good guy–bad guy delineations, and the culmination in moral and legal justice. Many cases feature well-known criminals—for example, Ted Bundy, Kenneth Bianchi (the "Hillside Strangler"), and Gary Ridgeway (the "Green River Killer"). However, gender politics—in many ways the most obvious and unifying thread running through these programs—is never problematized beyond the occasional court testimony that acknowledges that the defendant hated women or had a history of assaulting women. Neither program places individual crimes in a larger context of women's victimization, nor mentions the central role of feminist advocates in supporting victims, mobilizing pressure on police to investigate cases, or conducting community education.[3]

INSIDE FEMINIST MEDIA STRUGGLES

Gaining additional insight into what appears to be women's slow slog to overcome the problem of media sexism requires us to enter the struggle that feminists have engaged these last few decades. In Byerly and Ross (2006) we sought to learn more about the dialectical process that women individually and collectively, over time and across nations, had engaged in for the purpose of giving women a bigger voice and increasing their public influence through the media. We conceptualized women's agency through media activism from the 1970s to the present examining various forms of that activism across 20 nations through the first-person experiences of 90 women. Our study was situated in a complex conceptual and theoretical framework that culminated in the posing of a new model, the Model of Women's Media Action. The model recognized women's intrinsic right to communicate and identified the media as a primary mechanism for women to achieve that and participate in the modern-day public sphere—that imagined site central to Habermas' (1987) theory of communicative action where citizens debate their common interests free of economic and governmental interference and develop agendas for social action. Ross and I considered the ways in which women had used media of various kinds to form a feminist public sphere that overlapped with the dominant (masculine) public sphere, as well as other multiple spheres formed by marginalized groups.

Feminists have had varying responses to the public sphere discourse, which has proliferated in critical scholarship since the 1980s. McLaughlin (1993), for example, agreed that the emancipatory potential of the public sphere is attractive to feminists, whereas Fraser (1993) showed specifically how feminism emerged publicly via the circulation of new feminist terminology. She said that "feminist women invented new terms for describing social reality, including 'sexism', 'the double shift', 'sexual harassment', and 'marital, date and acquaintance rape', thereby reducing, although not eliminating, the extent of our disadvantage in official public spheres" (p. 123). Fraser thus traces the route of feminist language from the private sphere (of personal experience) to a feminist-created women's public sphere, and then on into the dominant sphere and presumably also other counter public spheres (i.e., communicative forums created by those traditionally on the social margins, such as racial and sexual minorities, the elderly, and anti-war advocates). Both mass and alternative media provided the means for circulating new terminology (and the ideas it embodies) both within and among the respective public spheres.

Participants in our (Byerly & Ross, 2006) cross-cultural study took various approaches—which we called paths—in their media activism. Those following the "first path" learned to "do" some form of media in order to reach mainstream audiences with feminist ideas. For example, in Colombia, Angela Cuevas de Dolmetsch[4] (personal communication, November 12, 2003), an attorney and a member of Consensus of Women of the Peace Boat, decided to host a weekly women's affairs television and radio program, beginning in the mid-1990s, called "Looking at the World Through Women's Eyes" to help break the silence about women's reality and to help women enter public life. Her ultimate goal has been to bring women formally into negotiations between the government and guerrillas to help end the two-decade-old Colombian civil war. Those following the "second path" have included media professionals who, in the course of their careers, sought ways to expand women-related content or to reform the industry's policies to improve women's professional status. Stacey Cone (personal communication, November 14, 2003), a former producer for CNN, the all-news cable TV network based in Atlanta, Georgia, said that by the late 1980s, she had become "quietly pro-active," pushing for more coverage of women's and minorities' issues and volunteering for projects that focused on the treatment of women, such as a five-part series on women who go to prison for killing their abusive partners.

Those who followed the "third path" of women's media activism have operated as advocates for media change, often accomplished through an established nonprofit organization that pressures the media to improve treatment of women in one or more ways. The outside advocate's path often entails research and analysis about women and media, including publication of reports or articles, or it may mobilize a constituency to write letters or take some other action. For example, Hilary Nicholson (personal communication, April 1, 2004) and a small group of other women who wanted to conduct public education around gender and media issues, including the depiction of violence against women in the media, founded Women's Media Watch (WMW)-Jamaica in 1987. Over the years, Nicholson said, WMW has held symposia on gender and media; offered hundreds of workshops on how to conduct what she called "gender-sensitive media analysis" for community groups, youth clubs, teachers, trainee journalists at the Caribbean Institute for Media and Communications, and media professionals; and conducted media monitoring that has led to published reports.

Women media activists who follow the "fourth path" have established their own media in order to assure the maximum control over message production and distribution. The quote that opens this chapter by Women's eNews founder Rita Henley Jensen suggests why some women may want to establish their own media enterprises (personal communication, August 30, 2003). Women's eNews is a nonprofit Internet-based news service in New York City, which was launched in June 2000 under sponsorship of the National Organization of Woman but went independent 1 year later. The service shifted its focus from national to international reporting after Jensen realized that "[women's] international news was so compelling." Although mainstream news has made some strides—for example, adopting more gender-neutral language, covering violence against women, and giving space to the occasional female newsmaker—Jensen said she believes newsrooms are still hostile to women's success, ideas, and concerns. A veteran journalist who worked in mainstream print journalism for many years before founding Women's eNews, Jensen believes that women need their own reliable sources of news and that "we have to measure our success by our own performance" (Jenson, personal communication, August 30, 2003).

REPORTER CONSCIOUSNESS

Veteran feminist journalists who look back on their years in newsrooms arrive at varied assessments. Former *Los Angeles Times* columnist Kay Mills (1988) theorized that the feminist movement has had a major impact on the thinking of today's reporters and editors, and, in turn, on the way that news is defined, selected, written, and edited. Mills is joined by others who struggled in a male-dominated profession during the 1960s and 1970s as feminism arose around them, challenging them to respond.

Sanders and Rock (1988), for example, described at length how they and other women in broadcasting convinced their male supervisors in the late 1960s to let them put a human face on feminism, from the movement's perspective. Dorothy Gilliam, an African-American journalist who found employment in mainstream newspapers in the 1960s, believes she was able to get many of her stories because she could empathize with and speak for the poor rural and inner-city Black people she was sent out to interview (cited in Mills, 1988). After becoming a columnist, Gilliam devoted herself to issues of race and gender.

Many female feminist reporters have brought their male colleagues along with them to feminism. As a result, many women and men journalists today write insightfully about a range of human concerns, including war, poverty, violence, and other issues, in ways that reflect what they have learned and adopted from feminism. One example is the Pulitzer-winning *Dallas Morning News* series in 1993 on violence against women in nations around the world, in which both female and male journalists brought solid research and substantial knowledge to bear in stories that covered forms of violence from nation to nation, reflecting cultural and religious factors, changes in laws and behavioral standards in recent years, and recent global feminist efforts to make violence against women a human rights issue. All stories asked the questions that feminism raised with regard to the effect of violence on women's overall status, and in all stories women's voices and feminist analysis shaped the dominant narrative.

Critical communication scholars, both feminist and otherwise, have long argued the inevitability of ideology and subjectivity in newsmaking. However, on the whole, the critical literature is limited concerning research about how journalistic consciousness is formed and acted on in the newsmaking enterprise. Hall's (1980) early work theorized that "frameworks of knowledge" enter into media professionals' formulation of story content. Tuchman (1978) and Fishman (1990) showed how bureaucratic routines help to define what will become news and how news issues will be imbued with dominant values through framing devices used to create a smooth, coherent narrative. Herman and Chomsky (1988) focused on structural and ideological factors that filter information about news events and issues, privileging the interests and agendas of the powerful over those of others. These last two authors' propaganda model provides a framework for understanding structural relations in the media, but feminists have yet to extend it in ways that would bring gender into the filtering process. Most stop short of a deeper questioning of what motivates journalists to perpetuate dominant (main-stream) values and ideas in their stories, or, conversely, what motivates them to adopt new ideas that challenge and oppose dominant values.

Feminist political economy offers the best possibility for placing gender into an analysis of how consciousness operates in the women-and-media relationship. After all, gender relations in the media emerge out of macro-level economic conditions that see powerful, wealthy men at a distinct advantage over women (and others with less status). Men control all social institutions, including the media, as abundant evidence shows, and this hierarchy filters down into both meso and micro levels where production and content, respectively, are negotiated. Meehan and Riordan's (2002) useful text *Sex and Money: Feminism and Political Economy in the Media* contains a collection of studies that show how gen-der politics enter into the day-to-day world of media industries, and how feminism has served as a force for change over time. That force has struggled against entrenched patriarchy in a range of ways.

SITUATING BACKLASH

As we have seen, the rise of feminism as a major political, social, and cultural force within and across nations in the 1970s brought incredibly important critiques of media sexism as well as challenges to that sexism. Although feminists have usually understood that the advancement of women is intertwined with other kinds of advancements—for example, the gaining of rights for other socially marginalized people and various kinds of local and national development—they have also been faced with the reality that their work was meant to shift the balance of social power from male domination to gender egalitarianism (and democracy). Powerful men (and the women working in alliance with them to main-tain the patriarchal order) have not always taken easily to such upheavals in economic, governmental, legal, educational, religious, familial, and other institutions, including media. Thus, the 1980s and 1990s proved to be decades when the proponents of patriarchy flexed their muscles in many places around the world, forming a powerful backlash to the rights that women had begun to achieve.

Former *Wall Street Journal* investigative reporter Susan Faludi (1991) documented these events in her book *Backlash: The Undeclared War Against American Women*, which examined the backlash phenomenon within a particular national context. Faludi showed how the conserva-tive and powerful religious right, firmly in charge of U.S. government, business, university, and much of the religious establishment by the early 1980s, purported that feminism had produced new problems for women, including "the man shortage," "the biological clock," and the "mommy track," among others. These alleged results of feminism, advanced and affirmed by prestigious university studies and reported by increasingly conservative news media, supposedly threatened the personal happiness and careers that many women had chosen instead of (or, in some cases, in addition to) traditional home and motherhood. Faludi also criticized the notion of "postfeminism," which embodies the belief that the women's liberation movement is over.

Faludi's book, which built on her earlier published articles, won her a Pulitzer Prize for explanatory journalism in 1991, lending mainstream credibility to her backlash theory and giving her a high profile in the very media that she had criticized. Faludi contended that the backlash against feminism and the gains made by women could not have occurred without the news and entertainment media's leadership.[4] She used extensive government data, anecdotal and other evidence to build her case against the news and entertainment media. Although the backlash was not orchestrated from a central place, she said, it had a central mission, and it engaged the media in what Faludi called a "relentless whittling-down process—much of it amounting to outright propaganda—that served to stir women's private anxieties and break their political wills" (p. xvii). The media, she said, gave credence to the "pro-family" diatribes of fundamentalist preachers with sympathetic and even progressive-sounding rhetoric. In the process, the media popularized the backlash beyond the New Right's wildest dreams.

Faludi's case against the U.S. media found considerable currency among feminist communication scholars, many of whom had encountered obstacles to feminist ideas and research in their own academic departments and institutions. Although I acknowledge the existence of backlash, I have always found Faludi's critique to be lacking in at least three ways. First, it failed to recognize that the backlash to feminism occurring within the United States was also occurring in other parts of the world—that it was a global phenomenon. Second, her critique lacked an understanding of history and the dialectical process that shapes history. Women's struggle for advancement—with the right to communicate through media being only one aspect—must be understood as a process characterized by gains and losses that often occur in overlapping patterns, as well as by resistance to change by those in power (in this case, as noted earlier, by the guardians of patriarchy). Third, Faludi misses the deeper structural implications of the backlash, namely that it was central to an emerging neoliberal world order that was marked not only by the (re)subjugation of women, but also by the weakening of labor unions, the concentration of ownership in telecommunications, banking, and other industries, the eradication of civil liberties, and the suppression of dissent (Byerly, 2004). Because the media help generally to spread neoliberal values (including anti-feminism), fuller understanding of the women-and-media relationship will require feminist scholars to reveal how women fit into all aspects of the globalization phenomenon, including media (Byerly, 2004).

CONCLUSION

Social change often occurs in fits and starts, with periods of backsliding and sudden lurches forward. Women's struggle to advance socially, economically, and politically has indeed followed this course for more than 150 years. For this reason, feminist social transformation has all the hallmarks of what Mitchell (1992) called the longest revolution. Feminist scholars who want to reveal the movement's real impact on media structures and messages must look at a larger window of time than a few short years to make their analyses, and we must seek signs of feminism's embeddedness within all aspects of the media. Thirty years (the length of time of our modern feminist movement) is not very long in the scheme of things. Put into its proper historical perspective, women's agency through media activism, women's advances (however uneven and unfinished) in both employment and content, and the inevitable nemesis of backlash that threatens always to undermine small and large gains alike must eventually be understood as parts of the longer, ongoing struggle in gender relations and its companion phenomenon, the struggle of all marginalized people for self-determination. The central facet of this process, of course, is mediated communication, the means by which ideas and counter ideas are expressed and debated, and from which human responses flow. Women's best hope for advancement everywhere is in trying to gain greater access to existing commercial and noncommercial media, and, when possible, to establish their own independent media systems to provide mechanisms for woman-made messages and images.

NOTES

1. Feminist media activism has roots dating to the 19th century, when women in the U.S., Britain and other nations mobilized to obtain suffrage and other women's rights. In the process, many set up their own magazines and news-

papers. However, feminist media activism has been better organized, more diverse in its collection of goals and activities, and more effective in marking changes in the modern era. Thus, I situate this examination in the present timeframe.

2. Feminist meanings would include an understanding of women's equality, their right to jobs and other social access, and a recognition of their abilities, competence, and achievement, among other things. Such meanings might also include analyses of patriarchy and masculine hegemony.

3. Such activity by feminists has been key in a number of unsolved cases, including the Green River murders in the Seattle area, which occurred between 1982 and the early 1990s. Women's groups kept pressure on police agencies in those years and held public vigils and other demonstrations to keep public attention alive. Using DNA evidence, police finally arrested Gary Ridgeway (who had long been a person of interest) in 2001 and subsequently obtained his confession to the murder of 48 women (Green River killer avoids death in plea deal: http://www.cnn.com/2003/LAW/11/05/ green.river.killings)

4. Personal communication from Angela Cuevas de Dolmetsch, Nov. 12, 2003.

REFERENCES

Barker-Plummer, B. (1995). News as a political resource: Media strategies and political identity in the U.S. women's movement, 1966-1975. *Critical Studies in Mass Communication, 12*(3), 306-324.

Beasley, M. H., & Gibbons, S. J. (2003). *Taking their place: A documentary history of women and journalism* (2nd ed.). State College, PA: Strata Publishing.

Benedict, H. (1992). *Virgin or vamp: How the press covers sex crimes.* New York: Oxford University Press.

Brownmiller, S. (1975). *Against our will: Men, women and rape.* New York: Simon & Schuster.

Brubaker, B. (1995a). NCAA intensifying educational effort. *The Washington Post,* p. A25

Brubaker, B. (1995b). NFL teams support Perry despite past. *The Washington Post,* p. A24.

Brubaker, B.(1995c). Violence follows some in football off field. *The Washington Post,* pp. AI, A24.

Butler, M., & Paisley, W. (1978). Magazine coverage of women's rights. *Journal of Communication, 28*(1), 183-186.

Byerly, C. M. (1994, Spring). An agenda for teaching news coverage of rape. *Journalism Educator, 49*(1), 59-69.

Byerly, C.M. (1995). News, consciousness and social participation: The role of women's feature service in world news. In A. Valdivia (Ed.), *Feminism, multiculturalism and the media: Global diversities* (pp. 105-122). Thousand Oaks, CA: Sage.

Byerly, C.M., & Warren, C A. (1996, March). At the margins of center: Organized protest in the newsroom. *Critical Studies in Mass Communication, 13*(1), 1-23.

Byerly, C.M. (2004). Women and the concentration of media ownership. In R. R. Rush, C. E. Oukrup, & P. J. Creedon (Eds.), *Seeking equity for women in journalism and mass communication: A 30-year update* (pp. 245-262). Mahwah, NJ: Erlbaum.

Byerly, C. M., & Ross, K. (2006). *Women and media: A critical introduction.* New Malden, MA: Blackwell.

Cancian, F. M., & Ross, B. L. (1981). Mass media and the women's movement: 1900-1977. *The Journal of Applied Behavioral Science, 17*(1), 9-26.

Ceulemans, M., & Fauconnier, G. (1979). *Mass media: The image, role and social conditions of women.* Paris: UNESCO.

Cuklanz, L. (1992, August). *Media coverage of the Webb-Dotson rape recanting case.* Paper presented at the Association for Education in Journalism and Mass Communication, Montreal, Canada.

Empowering Women in the Media: A Call to Action (Report). (1996, July). Washington DC: International Women's Media Foundation.

Entman, R. M. (1993). Framing: Toward clarification of a fractured paradigm. *Journal of Communication, 43*(4), 51-58.

Faludi, S. (1991). *Backlash: The undeclared war against American women.* New York: Crown.

Fishman, M. (1990). *Manufacturing the news.* Austin: University of Texas Press.

Fraser, N. (1993). Rethinking public sphere: A contribution to the critique of actually existing democracy. In C. Calhoun (Ed.), *Habermas and the public sphere* (pp. 109-142). Cambridge, MA: MIT Press.

Gallagher, M. (2001). *Gender setting: New agendas for media monitoring and advocacy.* London: Zed Books and London: WACC.

Gallagher, M. (2006). *Who makes the news?* (Report of the Global Media Monitoring Project). London: WACC.

Gitlin, T. (1981). *The whole world is watching: Mass media in the making and unmaking of the new left.* Berkeley: University of California Press.

Green River killer avoids death in plea deal. (2003, Nov. 6). *CNN*-online. Retrieved Jan. 15, 2005.

Habermas, J. (1987). *The theory of communicative action, volume 1: Reason and the rationalization of society* (T. McCarthy, Trans.). Malden MA: Beacon Press.

Hall, S. (1980). Encoding/decoding. In S. Hall, D. Hobson, A. Lowe, & P. Willis (Eds.), *Culture, media, language.* London: Hutchinson.

Herman, E. S., & Chomsky, N. (1988). *Manufacturing consent: The political economy of the mass media.* New York: Pantheon Books.

Kielbowicz, R. B., & Scherer, C. (1986). The role of the press in the dynamics of social movements. *Research in Social Movements, Conflicts and Change, 9,* 71-96.

McCombs, M., & Shaw, D. (1972). The agenda-setting function of mass media. *Public Opinion Quarterly, 36,* 176-187.

McLaughlin, L. (1993). Feminism, the public sphere, media and democracy. *Media, Culture and Society, 15,* 599-620.

McQuail, D. (1983). *Mass communication theory: An introduction.* Beverly Hills: Sage.

Media Watch. (1995). *Women's participation in the news: Global media monitoring project.* Toronto: Media Watch.

Meehan, E., & Riordan, E. (Eds.). (2002). *Sex & money: Feminism and political economy in the media*. Minneapolis: University of Minnesota Press.

Miller, K. (2002). *Communication theories: Perspectives, processes, and contexts*. Boston: McGraw-Hill.

Mills, K. (1988). *A place in the news*. New York: Dodd, Mead.

Mitchell, J. (1992). Women: The longest revolution. In K.V. Hansen & I. J. Philipson (Eds.), *Women, class and the feminist imagination* (pp. 43-73). Philadelphia: Temple University Press.

Parameswaran, R. (2002). Local culture in global media: Excavating colonial and material discourses in *National Geographic*. *Communication Theory, 12*(3), 287-314.

Rapping, E. (1994). *Mediations: Forays into the culture and gender wars*. Boston: South End Press.

Raghavan, S. (2006, April 12). Step up fight against rape, county official urges. *The Washington Post*, p. B4.

Riordan, E. (2004). The woman warrior: A feminist political economic analysis of *Crouching Tiger, Hidden Dragon*. In K. Ross & C. M. Byerly (Eds.), *Women and media: International perspectives* (pp. 81–104). Malden, MA: Blackwell.

Rush, R. R. (2004). Three decades of women and mass communications research: The ratio of recurrent and reinforced residuum revisited. In R. R. Rush, C. E. Oukrup, & P. J. Creedon (Eds.), *Seeking equity for women in journalism and mass communication: A 30-year update* (pp. 263-274). Mahwah, NJ: Erlbaum.

Russell, D. E. H. (1975). *The politics of rape*. New York: Stein & Day.

Russell, D. E. H. (1982). *Rape in marriage*. Bloomington: Indiana University Press.

Sanders, M., & Rock, M. (1988). *Waiting for prime time: The women of television news*. New York: Harper & Row.

Sen, I. (2004). Women's politics in India. In M. Chaudhuri (Ed.), *Feminism in India* (pp. 187–210). New Delhi: Kali for Women & Women Unlimited.

Tuchman, G. (1978). *Making news: A study in the construction of reality*. New York: The Free Press.

Tuchman, G., Daniels, A., & Benet, S. (1978.) *Hearth and home: Images of women in mass media*. New York: Oxford University Press.

Window dressing on the set: Women and minorities on television. (1977). Washington DC: U.S. Civil Rights Commission.

About the Contributors

S. Elizabeth Bird is professor and chair in the Department of Anthropology at the University of South Florida in Tampa. She studies the role of the media and popular culture in everyday life, and has taught classes in media studies, popular culture, and folklore. She is the author of *For Enquiring Minds: A Cultural Study of Supermarket Tabloids* (University of Tennessee Press, 1992) and editor of *Dressing in Feathers: The Construction of the Indian in American Popular Culture* (Westview Press, 1996). Her book *The Audience in Everyday Life: Living in a Media World* (Routledge, 2003) won the International Communication Association's Outstanding Book Award for 2004. She has published more than 50 academic articles and chapters, and written for newspapers and magazines.

Carolyn M. Byerly is an associate professor in the School of Communications at Howard University in Washington, DC, where she teaches seminars in media theory, research methods, political communication, and other mass communication issues. She studies the media with respect to gender, race, ethnicity, and sexual orientation. At present, she is examining patterns in and barriers to women and minority ownership of media. She is the co-author of *Women and Media: A Critical Introduction* (Blackwell, 2006), and co-editor of *Women and Media: International Perspectives* (Blackwell, 2004). Her articles and book chapters have appeared in *Critical Studies in Mass Communication, Feminist Media*

Studies, Journalism and Mass Communication Educator, Journal of Mass Media Ethics, and many edited volumes. She completed her PhD and MA in mass communication at the University of Washington, Seattle.

Jane Caputi is a professor of Women's Studies at Florida Atlantic University in Boca Raton. She is the author of *The Age of Sex Crime* (Bowling Green State University Popular Press, 1987), *Gossips, Gorgons and Crones: The Fates of the Earth* (Bear & Co. 1993), and *Goddesses and Monsters: Women, Myth, Power and Popular Culture* (Popular Press, 2004). She also collaborated on *Websters' First New Intergalactic Wickedary of the English Language* (Beacon Press, 1987) with Mary Daly. Most recently, she completed an educational documentary, *The Pornography of Everyday Life*, distributed by Berkeley Media, www.berkeleymedia.com.

Brittney Cooper is a PhD candidate in American Studies at Emory University in Atlanta. Her dissertation focuses on public and private constructions of subjectivity among historically prominent local and national Black female leaders at the discursive and social intersections of race, class, gender and nation. She also is interested in the convergences between generational Black feminist concerns and popular representations of Black women within U.S. popular culture.

Rebecca C. Hains is an assistant professor of Communications at Salem State College in Massachusetts. Her research focuses on girls, media, and popular culture. She has published several articles and chapters analyzing girl power cartoons, such as *The Powerpuff Girls, Kim Possible,* and *My Life as a Teenage Robot,* from a feminist cultural studies perspective.

Jill Birnie Henke was an associate professor of Communication and Theatre at Millersville University in Pennsylvania, where she taught for 20 years. Her research interests include media portrayals of women, political communication, and environmental communication. She now teaches at Hope College in Holland, Michigan.

Susana Kaiser is an associate professor at the University of San Francisco, where she teaches Media Studies and Latin American Studies. Her research focuses on communication, cultural/political memory, and human rights. She has studied the communication strategies developed by the mothers and the children of the *desaparecidos* in Argentina, her country of origin, and the construction of memories of political violence. Her book *Postmemories of Terror: A New Generation Copes with the Legacy* *of the "Dirty War"* (Palgrave Macmillan, 2005) explores young Argentineans' memories of the military dictatorship that lasted from 1976 to 1983.

Rebecca Kern is a PhD candidate in Mass Media and Communication at Temple University in Philadelphia. Her research interests include television studies, cultural studies, rhetoric and discourse, and qualitative methodologies, primarily in relation to gender and sexuality. Her dissertation examines the audience reception and interaction of viewers of *The L Word*, as well as the political economy and media coverage surrounding the show.

Debra Merskin is an associate professor and head of the Communication Studies sequence in the School of Journalism and Communication at the University of Oregon in Eugene. Her research on race, gender, and media appears in journals such as *The Howard Journal of Communication, Sex Roles, Feminist Media Studies, Peace Review,* and *Mass Communication & Society.* She has contributed chapters to anthologies on media and politics in the Iraq war, sex in consumer culture and marketing, and girls and the internet. She is currently writing a book on race, gender, and mass media portrayals.

Marian Meyers is an associate professor of Communication at Georgia State University in Atlanta. Her research interests are the representation of women in popular culture and the intersectionality of gender, race, class, and sexual orientation in the media, as well as news coverage of women and violence against women. Her current work involves an examination of gender, race, and class inequities in higher education. She is the author of *News Coverage of Violence Against Women: Engendering Blame* (Sage, 1996) and editor of *Mediated Women: Representations in Popular Culture* (Hampton Press, 1999).

Karen Pitcher is an assistant professor of Communication at Eckerd College in St. Petersburg, Florida, where she teaches courses in media studies, communication theory, and cultural studies. Her research lies at the intersections of media and society, with particular interests in mobile technologies and critical feminist perspectives on gender and sexuality in popular culture.

Anjali Ram is an associate professor of Communication at Roger Williams University in Bristol, Rhode Island. Her research examines gendered identity in the context of popular culture, migrant identity and globalization. Her publications have appeared in journals such as *Women's Studies in Communication, Human Development, Culture and Psychology,* and in edited anthologies.

Elayne Rapping is a professor of American Studies at the University of Buffalo/State University of New York and the author of numerous books and articles dealing with the media and popular culture, including the books *MEDIA-TIONS: Forays into the Culture and Gender Wars, Law and Justice as Seen on TV,* and *The Movie of the Week: Private Stories/Public Events.* She teaches courses on television and society, modern cinema, the culture of celebrity, popular music, gender and media, and gender and Hollywood genres.

Rosa E. Soto is an assistant professor of American & Latino Literature in the Department of English & Latino and Latin American Studies at William Paterson University in Wayne, New Jersey. A Puerto Rican scholar born in Miami, Florida, she earned her PhD in English literature (with a specialty in gender and sexualities) at the University of Florida. At WPU, she teaches courses in Latino literature, American literature/studies, and cultural studies.

Kimberly Wallace-Sanders is an associate professor of American Studies in the Institutes of Liberal Arts and Women's Studies at Emory University in Atlanta. Formally the associate director of the Spelman College Women's Research and Resource Center, she is the co-founder of the Comparative Women's Studies program at Spelman College with Beverly Guy-Sheftall. At Emory, she teaches courses on cultural representations of the female body, representations of race and gender in American culture, 19th century African American popular culture, and African American material culture. Her research has appeared in the journals *American Quarterly, Initiatives,* and *SAGE: A Scholarly Black Woman's Journal,* as well as in various edited volumes. Her anthology *Skin Deep, Spirit Strong: Critical Essays on the Black Female Body in American Culture* (University of Michigan Press, 2002) was nominated for the 2003 NAACP Image Award for Literature. Her most recent book is *Mammy: A Century of Race, Gender and Southern Memory* (University of Michigan Press, 2007).

Author Index

Subject Index

CPSIA information can be obtained
at www.ICGtesting.com
Printed in the USA
FSOW01n2136031216
27927FS